PRAISE FOR THE AUTHOR AND HIS BOOKS

"Florid cinematic detail."   —*The New York Times*

"Masterfully researched."   —*The New York Journal of Books*

"Lachman's research and crisp, clear writing keep the reader eager to learn more."   —*The Buffalo News*

"Brilliant."   —*New York Post*

"Fascinating and well researched . . . A skilled storyteller."
                    —*Publishers Weekly*

"Important and engaging . . . Absorbing [and] well researched."

—Jean H. Baker, author of
Mary Todd Lincoln: A Biography

"Spellbinding."
—Frank J. Williams, founding chairman, The Lincoln
Forum; chief justice, Rhode Island Supreme Court

"Lachman tells a fine tale with considerable research."
                    —*The American Chronicle*

FOOTSTEPS
IN THE SNOW

....

CHARLES LACHMAN

BERKLEY BOOKS, NEW YORK

364.1523
LAC

THE BERKLEY PUBLISHING GROUP
Published by the Penguin Group
Penguin Group (USA) LLC
375 Hudson Street, New York, New York 10014

USA • Canada • UK • Ireland • Australia • New Zealand • India • South Africa • China

penguin.com

A Penguin Random House Company

FOOTSTEPS IN THE SNOW

A Berkley Book / published by arrangement with the author

For information, address: The Berkley Publishing Group,
a division of Penguin Group (USA) LLC,
375 Hudson Street, New York, New York 10014.

ISBN: 978-0-425-27288-6

PUBLISHING HISTORY
Berkley premium edition / November 2014

PRINTED IN THE UNITED STATES OF AMERICA

10 9 8 7 6 5 4 3 2

Cover photos: *Footprints* © by Daizuoxin/Shutterstock
and *Mittens* © by Emka74/Shutterstock.
Cover design by Jane Hammer.
Interior text design by Kelly Lipovich.

DEC 2 2 2014

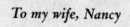

To my wife, Nancy

Acknowledgments

This book could not have been written without the full cooperation of the Ridulph and Tessier families. I am deeply indebted to Chuck Ridulph and Pat Ridulph Quinn. The Tessiers have also been extraordinarily generous and open with me. They all have my sincere thanks, especially Jeanne, Janet, Bob, and Mary.

Jack McCullough has my appreciation for agreeing to cooperate with the research of this book, as do his wife, Sue McCullough; his stepdaughter Janey O'Conner; and her husband, Casey Porter, who all continue to champion his innocence.

Doris Cross is a wonderful editor and made indispensable contributions to the manuscript.

Thanks also to Seattle detectives Michael "Mike" Ciesynski and Cloyd Steiger and Sycamore detectives Dan Hoffman and Tiffany Ziegler. Dave Zulawski gave me fascinating insight into the tradecraft of police interrogations. Joseph Giacalone, a retired NYPD detective sergeant, offered his unique perspective on cold-case investigations.

Many people in Illinois and Washington State and elsewhere have been supportive throughout this long process, including Kathy Sigman Chapman, Mike Chapman, Jan Edwards, and Michelle Weinman. The two living ex-wives of Jack Mc-Cullough didn't want to be identified by name in this book, but they have my gratitude.

Kay Ridulph's son Lawrence "Larry" Hickey Jr. was kind enough to permit me to use excerpts from his late mother's diaries.

Several journalists have tackled the Maria Ridulph case, and I would like to recognize the outstanding work of Greg Fisher, Judy Rybak, and Erin Moriarty of *48 Hours*; CNN's Ann O'Neill; and the staff of the *Daily Chronicle* in Sycamore and its editor, Eric Olson.

TV producer and author Charlie Carillo gave me excellent suggestions. James Cunsolo and Jarrod Cushing helped design the book's internal graphics.

My literary agent, Paul Fedorko, believed in this project from the first night we met to discuss it and never gave up. He is an exceptional agent and advisor. Carole Cooper, of N. S. Bienstock talent agency, has been another important advocate in my television and writing career. I am indebted to Tom Colgan, executive editor at The Berkley Publishing Group, for acquiring *Footsteps in the Snow*.

Let me end by acknowledging the encouragement and love of my wife, Nancy Glass, who read *Footsteps* in manuscript form and contributed in meaningful ways to the final product, and to our children, Max, Pamela, and Sloane. May all their dreams come true.

BOOK I

I

· · · · · · · · ·

SYCAMORE, ILLINOIS

Evening, December 3, 1957

It was an ordinary night in a small town very few Americans outside its boundaries even knew existed.

It was snowing, just a dusting, and Maria Ridulph, seven years old, was eager to experience the first snowfall of the winter. She had just eaten dinner, and her mother, Frances Ridulph, had given her permission to play outside. Maria ran to the phone and called her best friend from five houses away, Kathy Sigman.

"I can go out! Can you?"

Kathy said she'd be right there.

Maria wanted to wear her new winter coat, but Frances told her no, put on the old one. It was a tan three-quarter-length wool overcoat. One button was missing, and the point of the collar on the right side had been chewed down.

Maria hated the coat because it was a shabby hand-me-down from her brother, Chuck, who was eleven.

Maria and Kathy met at the corner of Archie Place and Center Cross Street and started a game of Duck the Cars, a pastime of their own invention. Whenever a car drove by, they had to duck behind a towering elm tree, and if the headlights hit one of the girls, she'd lose.

At 6 P.M., Frances had to drive her fifteen-year-old daughter, Kay, for a music lesson, and as she backed out of the driveway, she saw Maria on the corner with little Kathy. Frances gave Maria a quick wave, and, ten minutes later, having dropped Kay off, when she got back, she saw that Maria and Kathy were still on the corner jumping up and down.

Inside 616 Archie Place, a modest wood-framed bungalow, Mike Ridulph, the man of the house, was watching a TV western, *Cheyenne*. He was looking forward to a big night on television—Tallulah Bankhead was going to be the guest star on the Lucille Ball show. Pat, the studious eldest Ridulph daughter, was doing homework in the dining room. Chuck, the athlete of the family, was in the den with his best buddy, Randy Strombom, who lived next door. They were going through their baseball-card collections while listening to Elvis Presley on the hi-fi. Frances went to her bedroom and settled down with the evening newspaper, the *Sycamore True Republican*.

Great events were taking place in the world. Sputnik had been launched by the Soviet Union, and the space race was on. These were momentous times. But in Sycamore, the news was strictly small-town America. Three local boys had been inducted into the armed forces; *Operation Madball*, starring Ernie Kovacs and Jack Lemmon, was playing downtown; lettuce was ten cents a head at the Piggly Wiggly.

Just an ordinary night.

The street was dark and empty; then, out of nowhere, a man they didn't know appeared.

"Hello, little girls," he said, stooping down so his eyes met theirs. "Are you having fun?"

He took off his hat, and the girls saw that he had blond hair in a DA cut, that is, combed back along the sides of the head and parted at the nape of the neck so it looked like a duck's ass. "Would you like a piggyback ride?" he asked, crouching, waiting for one of them to say yes.

The girls looked at each other. Maria's parents had taught her to be wary of strangers; just the same, she climbed onto the man's back. When he rose to his full height, her legs dangling over his chest, he took off in a trot up Center Cross Street, carrying her for some forty feet as snow swirled around them. Kathy stayed there on the corner in the cold under the streetlamp, watching, a little envious that Maria was having all the fun. When they came back, the man bent down, and Maria climbed off his back. She was grinning.

"My name is Johnny," he said. "I'm twenty-four years old, and I'm not married."

He asked their names and they told him. He seemed so nice.

"I'd give you another piggyback ride," Johnny said to Maria, "if you had a dolly."

Maria said she had lots of dolls, and she'd be right back with her favorite one.

Kathy found herself standing there alone with Johnny, watching Maria race to her house.

"Kathy, I like you," he said.

Not knowing what else to say, she said, "I like you, too."

Johnny put his hand on her arm and asked her whether she'd like to go for a walk around the block with him, then, "What would you like, a bus ride or train ride?"

"I don't want any ride," she told him.

For Maria, it was a short dash to 616 Archie Place. She flew into the house, her face flushed from the excitement and night air, found her mother in the bedroom, and asked her if she could take her favorite doll outside. Frances told her to take the cheap rubber one instead because it was still snowing. Frances recalled later that her daughter's eyes were "beaming," and she was giddy with excitement.

Maria headed straight for Maria's Corner, where she kept her doll collection. Her father heard her rummaging around until she grabbed an inexpensive six-inch rubber baby. It was dressed in a red-and-white skirt that had tiny pockets at the hem, with a neatly folded peewee handkerchief inside one of them. Then Mike heard his daughter streak out the front door. His eyes never left the TV.

After a minute or two, Maria, clutching the doll, got back to where Johnny and Kathy were waiting for her. She showed it to Johnny, who expressed his delight with it.

What a pretty dress, he told her, what a pretty doll. As promised, he let her climb onto his back again for her second ride, this time with her doll.

When they got back it was supposed to be Kathy's turn, but she told Johnny that her fingers were getting numb from the cold, and she needed to run home and put on her mittens. She asked him the time. Johnny said it was seven o'clock, and off she went. A few minutes later, she expected to see Johnny and Maria waiting for her. She was looking forward to the nice man's piggyback ride, but the corner where she'd left them was deserted. Where were they?

She went to the Ridulph house and knocked on the side door. Maria's brother Chuck opened it, and Kathy asked him if Maria was there.

No, Chuck told her. "She must be hiding from you," he said.

Kathy left to look for Maria again. She went up and down Archie Place, calling out, "Mah-reeee-ah! Mah-reeee-ah!"

Five minutes later she was back at the Ridulphs' door. "I can't find Maria," she told Chuck.

Chuck found his mother in the bedroom and told her what was going on. Then Frances told her husband, Mike, and he grabbed a police whistle that he sometimes used to summon the children. Mike and Frances went outside looking for their youngest daughter. They walked to the corner and called out Maria's name. They searched the backyard. Mike blew his whistle.

Chuck grabbed a flashlight and went looking too, with

his friend Randy. They walked down Archie Place and circled the block calling out Maria's name. They stopped at a house on DeKalb Avenue where a friend of Maria's lived, just in case she had gone there, but she hadn't. A squad car drove by, and Chuck wondered whether he should hail it down, but he decided that he and Randy should just keep looking.

With mounting panic, Frances returned home and called Kathy Sigman's mother, Edna. Only then did Frances hear a disturbing story about a stranger who had come out of nowhere to play with the girls. She ran out, hopped in her car, and found Mike, still searching the neighborhood. She told him what she'd just heard from Edna Sigman and said she wanted to call the police, but Mike told her absolutely not. Maria had probably strayed, and they'd find her any minute. It would be "embarrassing" and cause a "commotion" if they called the cops.

The Ridulphs drove to a dead-end street, Roosevelt Court, where Maria sometimes played. Mike got out of his car and blew his police whistle again. A light coming from a house drew his attention. Maybe Maria had come here. Peeking into the living room, all he saw were two elderly ladies watching TV, and he backed off.

When Mike and Frances got back to Archie Place, Frances called Mrs. Sigman one more time. The story was coming out in bits and pieces. Now, little Kathy was saying that the stranger who played with the girls had given Maria a piggyback ride. The full impact of what had happened finally registered, with all its strands of worrisome detail.

Dear God, Frances was thinking, *what happened to my daughter?* Frances hung up. Whether her husband approved or not, she was going to tell the police. She charged out the house and drove off.

It was 7:25 P.M.

Kay Ridulph had walked home from her music lesson and found a neighborhood in chaos. She couldn't believe what she was hearing. Her little sister Maria was missing. She grabbed her brother, Chuck, and together they marched to the Sigmans' house to speak directly to Kathy. The little girl told them about Johnny and the piggyback ride. She described him as a white man, about twenty-four. She said he told them he wasn't married, and one other interesting thing: that Johnny talked "like we used to."

From this, Kay gathered that the kidnapper must be a "hillbilly."

Kay turned to Mrs. Sigman, "Did you tell my mother all this?"

Mrs. Sigman assured her that she had.

Kay hurried back to 616 Archie Place and found her father alone in the house. The time had come to notify the police—Kay insisted—and now even Mike had to agree. He jumped into the family's second car and drove to the Sycamore police department to report a missing child. He didn't need to.

Frances was already there.

2

·········

THE SEARCH

A clarion call had shot through the neighborhood, and it seemed like every man and woman who lived on Archie Place was out searching for Maria.

Maria had bright brown eyes and wore her long brown hair in bangs. She stood forty-four inches tall and weighed fifty-three pounds. She'd been wearing black corduroy slacks and a black-and-white checked blouse. Her hand-knit rust-colored mittens had red borders at the top. Her white saddle shoes were trimmed in black and had side zippers with leather tassels. Her socks were brown and fit somewhat loosely. She was in the second grade.

Stanley Wells was a contractor who lived across the street from the Ridulphs. He had been home all night sick with the flu. He'd heard a child's "fading" scream sometime after dinner.

"I'd wish I'd gotten up," he was now saying.

Another neighbor, Mrs. Thomas Cliffe, had been watching TV and hadn't heard a thing. Her husband, who had been in the basement doing the laundry, also said he'd heard nothing out of the ordinary.

Tom Braddy had delivered oil to the Cliffe house earlier in the evening. He was home, about three blocks away, when his phone rang. It was Mrs. Cliffe.

"Did you see any stranger with the Ridulph girl when you were here making the oil delivery? Kathy said some man was with them."

Braddy said he had definitely seen Maria and Kathy under the streetlight at Archie and Center Cross Street. He had heard them "squealing," he said, as they chased each other around the tree. But he hadn't seen any stranger walking around. He returned to Archie Place with his son, Dale, and joined the search.

The 4-H Club was the hub of social activity for Sycamore's preteens. On the night of December 3, twelve-year-old Katheran Tessier stood up with the other 4-H girls and recited the club pledge:

I pledge my head to clearer thinking,
my heart to greater loyalty,
my hands to larger service,
my health to better living,
for my club, my community, my country and my world.

Katheran was there until 7:00 P.M., when her father, World War II veteran Ralph Tessier, who worked at Hagen's Ace Hardware store, arrived to take her home.

The Tessier family lived at 227 Center Cross Street. They were neighbors of the Ridulphs. Katheran was the eldest Tessier daughter.

Coming down DeKalb Avenue, Katheran was struck by the presence of so many DeKalb County sheriffs' vehicles and Sycamore police cars with lights flashing and sirens howling. When her father made a left turn on Center Cross Street, she could not believe the scale of law-enforcement activity.

"What happened? Why are all these police cars here?"

Ralph didn't really have an answer. The neighborhood had been tranquil when he'd left to pick her up, he told her. Now there was pandemonium.

When they got home, Katheran could tell that her mother was extremely upset. The little Ridulph girl was missing, Eileen said, but before Katheran could get the full story, some neighbors turned up, wanting Ralph Tessier to open his hardware store. They said they needed every available flashlight, lantern, and flare he had in stock.

Ralph and Eileen put on their coats. The womenfolk of Sycamore were gathering at the armory to make coffee and sandwiches for the men who were out searching for Maria, and Eileen was expected to do her part. Before they left for the armory, Ralph took a two-by-four and jammed it against the back door to make sure no one could break in. Then he told Katheran and her ten-year-old sister, Jeanne, to lock the front door behind them when they left and make sure they stayed up to let him and their mother back in. Sycamore was so safe that it was the first time the Tessiers had ever used the lock. They couldn't even remember where they'd put the key.

Panic spread like contagion.

Over at the hobby shop on State Street, with Christmas only three weeks away, two high school students were putting up holiday ornaments in the store window. Jan Edwards, a pretty junior who attended Sycamore High School, had promised her brother, Derryl, she'd decorate the family store that evening and had asked her friend Cheryl Wiley to come over and lend a hand. Cheryl, a Sycamore High sophomore who in the summer months worked in the fields detasseling corn, was happy to help out. The Edwards' hobby shop sold marbles and model airplanes and model cars, and it was in a prime location, right next to Sycamore's only movie house, the State Theater.

Cheryl and Jan figured they had three hours of work ahead of them and had arranged to have Jan's boyfriend, John Tessier, pick them up and drive Cheryl home in time for her 10:00 P.M. curfew.

The girls were working on the window when, suddenly, police cars were driving up State Street, sirens blaring and searchlights flashing, broadcasting a terrifying announcement: a child was missing, and everyone was needed to search for her. A moment later, the phone rang. It was Cheryl's father, frantic, calling to say that a girl from Sycamore had been abducted. He wanted Cheryl to lock the doors of the hobby shop now; he'd be right there to pick her up. In minutes, his car pulled up as Jan was closing the shop, and she and Cheryl climbed in. They dropped Jan off at her house on Somonauk Street, then drove home. Wiley told Cheryl that under no circumstances was she to leave the house.

Next to the State Theater was the Pantry, an old-fashioned family-style restaurant run by Ed Berg and his mother-in-law, who everyone called Gram. Gram made all the pies—apple, cherry, peach, and blueberry her specialties. On the evening of December 3, Nancy Jackson, the only waitress left in the Pantry, was cleaning up and preparing to close. She was anxious to get home. It was the eve of her seventeenth birthday, and she knew her mom would be in the kitchen baking a marble cake with chocolate icing.

Nancy, a pretty girl with glasses, which she had worn since kindergarten, was wearing a white waitress's uniform and apron, saddle shoes, and ankle-length bobby socks. Her long hair was tied in a ponytail. She didn't have much makeup on, just a touch of drugstore lipstick called Sweet Talk, a soft pink shade. Suddenly, she was startled by the police sirens and bright lights that had descended on State Street. A crowd was gathering, and the sirens kept screaming. Then someone came in and told her that a little girl was missing. Her name was Maria Ridulph.

Nancy knew Maria's sister Pat, and on school mornings, she had occasionally given her a lift in her 1947 coupe.

Sometimes, she'd see little Maria playing with dolls and thought she was adorable. Now Maria was missing. It was hard to grasp: these things just didn't happen in Sycamore. Child abduction was a big-city crime, in places like Chicago, sixty-five miles away—but not in Sycamore. Nancy locked up, went out into the freezing night, got in her car, and drove home as quickly as she could.

Tom Braddy, his son Dale, and Kathy Sigman's father, Bud, were walking south on Center Cross Street when they discovered a trail of footsteps in the snow, leading in a southwesterly direction, in the field behind the Ridulphs' house. It hinted at something terrible. In the dusting of snow that covered Sycamore, they found the footsteps of a man, and to the right of them, a second set of footsteps: those of a child. Braddy planted his foot next to the adult's footstep and compared. It looked like a size 9, maybe a 10. The footsteps went up about a hundred yards, then the adult's pivoted sharply to the right. It reminded Braddy of somebody making a sudden move. The footsteps led straight to the Johnsons' barn. The kidnapper must be hiding behind the barn, the men thought.

"Go around and we'll have him," Braddy told Dale and Bud Sigman.

There was nobody there.

Then Braddy noticed a fresh set of tire tracks. They were regular tread, not snow tires. Somebody had pulled out in the last hour or so and driven north on to Route 64.

Even these amateur sleuths could figure out the chain of events: Johnny had taken Maria on a piggyback ride, and when they got to the barn where his car was parked, he had put her down, walked with her to the car, put her in it, and driven away.

3

....

"A GIRL IS MISSING!"

A citizens' army bundled up against the subzero temperature fanned out across the town, the men adrenaline-charged by rage. Determination was etched on their faces—to find Maria and to hunt down her abductor. Shock gripped the entire community but also a measure of shame that this could have happened here.

Police reinterviewed Kathy Sigman. Under tremendous pressure to recall everything, she was able to come up with some important new details. Johnny, she said, was about twenty to twenty-four years old, maybe as old as thirty-five, and stood about five feet eight and weighed 180 pounds. She said she had never seen him before. Strangely, given the weather, he wasn't wearing a coat, just a heavy crewneck sweater knitted with green, blue, and yellow wool. He absolutely had blond hair, Kathy said. She was sure because he'd taken off his cap, which was gray. He spoke in a "thin high voice," and he had "long teeth" and possibly a tooth missing on the upper row. He had on blue jeans, with a narrow belt and a shiny buckle. He was clean-shaven and didn't look seedy.

Children generally make terrible witnesses in criminal cases. In police work, it's a fundamental reality. But in Kathy Sigman, the police believed they had an exception to the rule.

The Ridulphs assured the police that there was no way Maria was a runaway. Mike Ridulph's response was unequivocal: "She has never run away from home before, and she wouldn't now. Someone must have taken her." On this point, his wife, Frances, agreed. Stating the obvious, Sycamore police chief William Hindenburg declared, "It definitely looks like a kidnapping."

As Hindenburg's department consisted of only eight officers and seven reserve personnel, and the sheriff's office of four deputies, he notified the state police that a child from Sycamore was missing. Roadblocks were set up around Sycamore. A bloodhound named Duke was brought in and given the scent of Maria's clothes. He sniffed along the path of the footsteps in the snow but was unable to pick up the trail. Chief Hindenburg told the state police that the Sycamore cops had not been called until seventy minutes after Maria's disappearance. "Seventy minutes could have meant seventy miles," Hindenburg said. In other words, by now, Maria could well be beyond the DeKalb County borders.

Just as television viewers were settling in to watch the

popular quiz show *The $64,000 Question* on CBS, a police car equipped with a public-address system got the word out to the rest of Sycamore.

"Attention! Attention! A girl is missing!" went the announcement.

Home owners were told to step outside and inspect their properties. Porch lights all over the city were switched on, and as snow cascaded down, people in pajamas put on winter coats and combed through their garages, backyards, and, just in case, cesspools. Home owners who failed to do their civic duty had their addresses jotted down and reported to the police chief. Many years later, a man who had been a youngster in 1957 could still recall how a company of volunteers had come to his house and told his father, "We're searching your house." It was not a polite, neighborly appeal. Some of the men looked as if they had been drinking, and in a town where just about every adult male was a hunter, it was not surprising that they all carried sidearms or rifles. The man who related the story pronounced the night of December 3, 1957, the scariest of his life.

By 9:00 P.M., the entire city had been mobilized.

At 10:30 P.M., Pat and Kay Ridulph made a remarkable discovery. The sisters were roaming the neighborhood with Randy Strombom's mother when they found Maria's rubber doll in the snow on the southern edge of Mrs. Cliffe's property. Pat and Kay looked at each other and burst into tears. What made their find so remarkable was that the land, indeed that very spot, had been thoroughly scoured earlier in the evening by a DeKalb County deputy sheriff and three Sycamore city police officers, all of whom were carrying powerful flashlights. One cop who had actually stood on a rock right next to where Pat and Kay and Mrs. Strombom later came upon the doll swore it had not been there when he'd searched the spot.

The assistant state's attorney, James Boyle, was at the scene when the doll was discovered. He was perplexed.

"Every inch of the grounds of the Ridulph home and the other homes on that block had been searched," Boyle said. "They found nothing. Yet, one hour later, lying in plain view a few feet from the door of a garage of the house two doors east—there they found Maria's doll with its red-and-white dress." Someone must have put the doll there.

Kay Ridulph stayed out until 3:30 in the morning searching the neighborhood for her missing sister. When she got home, she went to her room, but before she turned out the lights she recorded her thoughts in her diary. "It didn't really hit me until they found her doll at the garage. I'm sure she'll return alive." It was 4:00 A.M. when Kay finally fell asleep. Her father spent the night with the other searchers until, at 5:00 A.M., they all went home, utterly exhausted. Human endurance, said Chief Hindenburg, "could stand no more."

On Wednesday, December 4, when daylight came, a fresh crop of volunteers resumed the search. Kay woke up at seven, after just three hours of sleep, and turned on the radio. Maria's kidnapping was the lead story on every station. Hearing her sister's name on the news made her physically ill. Her boyfriend, Lawrence "Larry" Hickey, came over to comfort her. Reporters from the Chicago newspapers and TV stations descended on Sycamore to interview Frances.

Frances Ridulph was forty-four years old, a petite and intelligent brunette who wore glasses and had a keen head for business. She had been born Frances Fenner on a farm in Iowa and had a junior-college education. She and her husband, Mike, who was fifty-one, had four children: Patricia, who went by Pat, had been born in 1941. Kay came next, in 1942, then Charles, who was nicknamed Chuck, in 1946. Finally there was Maria, born in 1950.

Maria's shell-shocked mother did her best to articulate her youngest daughter's special charm. She showed them Maria's spelling tests—she got 100 in all but one. She took them to Maria's Corner, where all her playthings were. She said Maria had never missed a day of Sunday school and faithfully studied her catechism.

Mike Ridulph, a machine operator at the Diamond Wire and Cable Company, was drained by his night of searching for his daughter through ditches and along railroad tracks, and he could barely speak through his grief. The house was packed with police, reporters, and relatives and neighbors who had come by with trays of food, and he could only run his fingers, swollen from a lifetime of hard physical labor in the factory, through his thick crop of graying black hair, breathing deeply and sighing from exhaustion.

After he'd had a few hours' sleep, Mike went to police headquarters, taking Chuck, his eleven-year-old, with him to await breaking developments. Of the four Ridulph siblings, Chuck was closest to Maria, in age and devotion. He shared a bedroom with her. Her abduction crushed him.

Frances was certain that the kidnapper was not from around Sycamore. She understood her daughter and thought she could explain how Maria might have been tricked: "Whoever took her away hit her weak spot. He played with her." Publicly, she said, "Too many people are saying she might be dead. I don't like to hear that kind of talk, and I don't think it's true. I want folks to help look for my little girl." Privately, however, Frances was saying, "I know she's dead."

In one way or another, virtually the entire city abandoned its regular pursuits to pitch in. Work at Sycamore's three largest factories—Anaconda Wire and Cable, Ideal Industries, and Diamond Wire and Cable Company, which employed Mike Ridulph—essentially came to a halt as workers took the day off to lend a hand. Everyone was assured they would not be docked any pay. Downtown Sycamore was all but deserted. Mothers stayed home and kept their children indoors.

Over at Sycamore High School, education took a backseat; the principal dismissed the senior class so the boys could join in the hunt. Twenty-one Explorer Scouts volunteered. So did the mayor and the entire board of selectmen. A pair of girl's slacks were discovered in a ditch, but when they were shown to Mrs. Ridulph, she said they didn't belong to Maria. She was presented with a bloodstained petticoat that had been found on a farm in Malta, ten miles southwest of Sycamore. It was another dead end; Maria did not wear petticoats. "When they start finding her clothes, we'll know it's too late," Mrs. Ridulph said.

The crime scene at Archie Place was anything but preserved. Nothing had been cordoned off, and overnight, the footprints of Maria and the kidnapper that had been left behind in the snow had been obliterated by the scores of volunteers trudging through the scene. Every trace of the tire tracks made by the getaway vehicle had also disappeared. Surveying the chaotic mess before him, Assistant State's Attorney Boyle said a herd of elephants could not have been more destructive. Maria's doll, which had been found discarded in the snow, was now forensically worthless. By Wednesday morning, so many people had handled it that the chances of obtaining the kidnapper's fingerprints from it were miniscule. Even the mayor, Harold "Red" Johnson, had been photographed turning the doll around this way and that. Nevertheless, after all this fumbling, the doll was placed in a plastic evidence bag and preserved for the crime lab.

Boyle was fixated on the doll. He thought it was the key to everything. On his order, a deputy sheriff drove through the Ridulphs' neighborhood and broadcast another important message over the vehicle's public address system: "We are appealing to the person who placed the Ridulph doll at the point where it was found Tuesday night to identify himself to the state's attorney's office immediately."

Behind the appeal was a distressing question: had somebody planted the doll on the Cliffe property in an effort to divert police away from the true route taken by Maria's kidnapper? Was it possible that "Johnny" had been among the early band of searchers combing the vicinity? It was too chilling to imagine that the abductor could have been, could be living among them—and searching for Maria with them. Another less sinister premise was that a neighbor, to avoid getting involved, had discovered the doll on his property and dumped it elsewhere when nobody was looking.

4

....

A FEDERAL CASE

It wasn't long before local authorities realized that a case of this magnitude necessitated federal resources. On Wednesday afternoon, December 4, a team of agents out of the Chicago FBI field office, headed by Special Agent in Charge Richard Auerbach, arrived in Sycamore as "observers." At 7:00 P.M.—twenty-four hours after the reported abduction, on the presumption that Maria had been transported across state lines, making it a federal crime, they officially took over "Operation Find Maria," as it was now called.

By Wednesday night, every drainage ditch, bush, culvert, bridge, and gully within the radius of Sycamore had been thoroughly explored. Unfortunately, nothing of consequence was found, just a few stomach-churning items like the gouged out eyeballs of a rabbit and a burlap gunny sack containing the carcasses of several kittens that some sick person had unloaded on the side of the road. None of these oddities amounted to a single helpful clue to Maria's abduction.

A squadron of eight airplanes from the Civil Air Patrol was ordered to systematically sweep over the abductor's most likely escape routes, Route 64 to the west and Route 23 to the south.

Whirlybirds skimmed the treetops, as did a U.S. Army Piasecki H-21 helicopter nicknamed the *Flying Banana* for its elongated design.

A light-artillery observation plane from Fort Sheridan, capable of flying as slowly as thirty miles per hour without stalling, also crisscrossed the skies above DeKalb County. Because the temperature on the night of the kidnapping had been 20 degrees, police ruled out the probability of a hastily dug grave because the earth was frozen.

People were encouraged to report any strange occurrence that had taken place in recent weeks that might prove remotely helpful to the investigation. Mildred Whitaker, who lived three blocks from the Ridulphs, informed police that, about a month before, she had caught a Peeping Tom near her house who resembled this Johnny character. Another neighbor said that, on the day of Maria's abduction, he had seen a suspicious 1951 tan Chrysler with "shiny" white sidewalls and a dent under the right front headlight roaming the streets.

Maria's teacher at West Elementary School was Mary Ann Christianson. Only twenty-two years old, she had been teaching for a mere three months and was faced with the task of comforting her class of thirty second-graders now that one of their own was missing.

At 1:30 Wednesday afternoon, Chief Hindenburg took time off from the search to address Maria's schoolmates and distribute a safety pamphlet to them. It warned them, with illustrations, to learn the four don'ts:

1. Don't go with strangers.
2. Don't get in a car with a stranger.
3. Don't accept candy, money, or gifts from strangers.
4. Don't allow strangers to touch you or pick you up.

Hindenburg couldn't help but note how sad the timing was. If only he had given his lecture on December 3.

"It looks like I was a day too late," he said.

That night, Maria's sister Pat watched the local TV newscast that, in those days, started at 7:00 P.M. and lasted fifteen minutes before network news came on (Jim Daley on ABC, Douglas Edwards on CBS, Huntley-Brinkley on NBC). Maria's kidnapping was the lead story, of course, and Pat had a hard time watching her mother on TV making a heartfelt appeal to "Johnny" to return her daughter.

"If the person who kidnapped Maria is listening, it couldn't have been done in malice," Frances Ridulph said on camera. "It was a little mistake. God forgives mistakes. We would, too." Then she spoke directly to her missing daughter, as only a mother could: "Don't cry, Maria. Above all don't cry. Don't make a fuss. We'll be with you soon." Frances knew her Maria was a "screamer," and her nightmare was that the kidnapper would choke her daughter to death just to keep her quiet.

After the broadcast, Pat went up to her bedroom, opened her diary, and with a fountain pen, wrote: "Lord help us." At ten that night, she turned off the lights and tried to sleep.

By Thursday, the third day of "Operation Find Maria," Boyle was profoundly discouraged. "So far we have checked all known sexual deviates and men with records. We have chased down countless clues and we have found exactly nothing."

"I hope it's not a sex crime," Chief Hindenburg said, "but I'm afraid it is."

Sycamore had been gone over "inch by inch," he said, and not a single substantive piece of evidence had been uncovered. The city's frustration reached the level of folly when Hindenburg, accompanied by Mrs. Ridulph and Mayor Johnson, visited a fortune-teller, who made the pointless prediction that Maria would be found dead. For Mike Ridulph, it was all too much. "For God's sake, quit saying she's dead. I know she is alive. No one would have any reason to kill her."

5

· · · · · · · · · ·

THE DOOR KNOCK

Two FBI agents moved into the Ridulph house. They set up a twenty-four-hour command post and slept on a pull-out bed in the den. They also tapped the family's phone. Next to the phone, they left a set of instructions for Mike and Frances on what they should say in the event that the kidnapper called demanding a ransom. The Ridulph children could not believe that G-men were actually living in their home. When Special Agent Bob Wilson told Kay she looked just like the FBI switchboard operator back in Chicago, she tingled. "And Bob said she [the operator] was very pretty," Kay confided to her diary that night. It delighted her to be compared to a sophisticated grown-up from the big city.

Kay wondered whether divine providence was at work. Could it be that Maria's kidnapping was a test of faith? "If only God would bring her back alive," she wrote in her diary. "I think he will as soon as we all begin to show a little faith." Her father was already promising to go to church every Sunday and sit next to Maria. "Boy, if she ever comes back will things be different," Kay wrote. "Now I really appreciate a little sister when I might not have one. Please, God, bring her back and give us another chance. That's my prayer."

The Ridulph house was a whirlwind of comings and goings, what with Pat's and Kay's boyfriends hanging around and neighbors stopping by to see how the family was holding up. It was all too much for Agent Wilson. He also had the legitimate concern that sensitive information might leak out and impede the investigation. Finally, he had had enough, and asked Mike and Frances to stop visitors from coming to the house.

On Friday, December 6, the Ridulph kids were told it was time to go back to school. Kay would have preferred to stay at home. Everybody at Sycamore High seemed to be staring at her. "I felt like Exhibit A all day," she complained. One teacher stopped Kay in the hallway and asked if there was anything new in the case. Kay said there was nothing she could really talk about.

"You've lost all hope, haven't you?" the teacher asked.

Kay could only respond with a firm shake of her head, but she was irked.

As a fresh week of school began, Pat struggled to deal with their little sister's fate, and confided her worries to her diary.

MONDAY DECEMBER 9

The school day sure seems hard. I haven't got much time to do homework and I seem to get further and further behind. I walked home from school today and after supper I went to choir.

TUESDAY DECEMBER 10

Today was dress-up day. I took the car to school. After supper they fingerprinted us.

WEDNESDAY DECEMBER 11

Still no clues today. We saw two movies in history. Went bowling after school. I bowled a 98. I addressed a few Christmas cards. Did homework.

THURSDAY DECEMBER 12

They called for junior and senior boys to go on another search this afternoon. As far as I know there are no real clues. At 8:00 P.M., I went to Teen Town but it was dead.

It also was time for Mike Ridulph to return to work. On his drive to the factory his first day back, he ran into a state-police roadblock. He pulled over, and like hundreds of others driving to and from Sycamore, he had his trunk opened and searched by the police, none of whom recognized him as the father of the missing child they were all looking for. When he arrived at Diamond Wire and Cable Company, his coworkers on the factory floor gathered around him to wish him well, but Mike was inconsolable.

"I'm almost positive Maria will be found dead," Mike told them. "The only thing you fellows can do is teach your kids to be more careful."

In all, sixty FBI agents from Chicago and various field offices across the Midwest were assigned to the Maria Ridulph case. Most of them were staying at the Golden Harvest Motel, just outside Sycamore. Richard Auerbach was in overall command. He was forty-six years old and had a distinguished pedigree, having studied at Harvard before receiving a law degree from Boston University.

Auerbach happened to be politically savvy, having served as executive assistant to the U.S. senator from New Hampshire before he joined the FBI in 1940 as a special agent. Then he climbed up the ranks to special agent in charge, first in Richmond, Virginia; then Seattle, Washington; before his promotion to the Chicago field office. FBI director J. Edgar Hoover had instructed him to transmit daily updates to him on the Maria Ridulph investigation, and interest in the case had reached the White House. President Eisenhower, who had suffered a mild stroke on November 25 that had left him temporarily incapable of articulating a complete sentence, was now back in the Oval Office putting in a full day. He requested that Hoover keep him informed about the case.

This was the halcyon era of the FBI, when the bureau was deemed to be the world's greatest detective agency and its agents were seen as zealous crime fighters, defending the country against the Communist menace. Around Sycamore, the agents were easy to spot in their gray flannel suits—and the hat every one of them wore. They were well mannered, persistent, and crisply professional. When these "men in black" ran an industrial outdoor vacuum cleaner around Archie Place, where Maria had last been seen, it was quite a spectacle to see them literally sucking up any evidence the local cops might have missed. Auerbach called it "spade work."

They went to every restaurant, tavern, filling station, garage, and the bus depot—local hangouts for teenagers and troublemakers—looking for a lead. Recently released patients from Illinois's mental asylums and parolees from the penitentiary and state reformatory who lived in DeKalb County came under investigation. Guests who registered in hotels and motels were checked out. Dentists in Sycamore were asked if they had a patient with strange teeth like Johnny's.

Finally, there was a break in the case. It came through a whiff of information that took two FBI agents to 227 Center Cross Street, the home of Ralph and Eileen Tessier.

The call came to the DeKalb County sheriff's office from a woman who said she had information about the Maria Ridulph kidnapping that she thought the police ought to know about. There was a boy from the neighborhood who definitely needed to be looked into. Deputy Sheriff George Gould took down the information. The boy's name was Treschner, or something like that. The caller didn't know exactly how to spell it. Treschner, she said, was about twenty years old and he had blond hair and lived in the

vicinity of Maria Ridulph. Gould tried to elicit more par-
ticulars, but that was all the caller would say. He asked her
for her name but she said she wanted to remain anonymous.
Click.

Gould was under standing orders to pass all Maria Ridulph leads straight to the FBI. He immediately called Special
Agent Jerome Nolan and relayed what he'd just received.
Nolan was thirty-three and had such a pleasant personality
his friends called him Sunny Skies. He had played high
school football in Wisconsin, was a zealous Green Bay Pack-
ers fan, and had seen action in World War II in the Pacific
theater, in New Guinea and the Philippines. He had joined
the FBI six months after his graduation from the University
of Wisconsin and was assigned to the Rockford, Illinois,
bureau, so he knew the lay of the land in the northern part
of the state.

It didn't take very long for the FBI to figure out that
the name "Treschner" had to be Tessier, because a John
Tessier lived on Center Cross Street, about a block and a
half from the Ridulphs. John was eighteen years old and
had blond hair. In the wave of tips coming in, this one was
deemed interesting and worth checking out.

The knock on the Tessiers' door came two days later. It
was December 8, a Sunday, when Ralph Tessier opened the
door and faced two FBI special agents, Frank Mellott and
David Burton. He told the agents he was not surprised by
their visit. By now, everyone in Sycamore knew that Maria
Ridulph had been abducted by a man calling himself
Johnny. It had been in all the papers. Since they lived so

close to Maria's house and their son John fit the general description, Ralph and his wife, Eileen, had discussed the possibility that he might "fall under suspicion." Given that, and the name factor, it was inevitable that the FBI would come calling.

Ralph invited the agents in.

Ralph was a big galoot, born and raised in Sycamore. Everybody in town knew him from the Ace Hardware store. Eileen Tessier, petite, smart, and articulate, had grown up in Belfast, Northern Ireland, and only had an eighth grade education but she loved books. Mysteries were her favorite. Anything Agatha Christie wrote, she consumed.

Ten-year-old Jeanne Tessier and her sister Katheran, age twelve, were on the couch in the living room where their parents' conversation with the FBI took place.

The agents said they had a few questions about John: where, they wanted to know, had he been on the night Maria had disappeared? The two girls listened to their parents tell the FBI that on the evening of December 3, John was forty miles from Sycamore, enlisting in the U.S. Air Force at the armed-forces induction center in Rockford. Ralph added that John could prove his whereabouts because he had called collect from Rockford at about 7:10 P.M. to say he was "ready to come home" and needed a lift. Frances told the agents that her husband had driven to Rockford and picked John up at approximately 8:00 P.M. and they had come straight home. They were back in Sycamore around 9:00. So John was not in Sycamore when Maria disappeared.

The agents asked to see John's room. The Tessiers obliged, led them there, and gave them permission to rummage through their son's closet. Were they looking for a sweater like the one Maria's kidnapper had been wearing?

After about ten minutes of looking around, Mellott and Burton asked where John was. His parents said they didn't know, and the agents left, saying they'd be back the following day. They needed to talk to John, and he might have to take a polygraph.

Later that night, when John came home, he found his mother in tears.

"What's wrong?" he asked her.

"The FBI was here, and they want to talk to you." She told him that Mellott and Burton had asked them about his comings and goings on December 3. "They want you to take a lie-detector test."

Many years later, John would recall his reaction—cocky indifference. "OK. Well, good. Then we'll get that taken care of."

His mother hadn't wanted him to go near a lie detector. "No, don't do that. Don't talk to them."

"Mom, I don't have anything to hide," he says he told her. "I should go and get it over with."

6

·········

MORNING, DECEMBER 9

Special Agent David Burton arrived at the house and eye-balled John in the flesh for the first time. The teenager was five feet ten or so and had blondish hair with a DA cut. When he smiled, which was often because he was always making wisecracks and joking around, Burton noted a gap in his front teeth. He recalled little Kathy Sigman's descrip-tion of the kidnapper: she'd said he had peculiar teeth, which may—or may not—conform with what he'd observed. So far so good.

Burton asked John if he was ready to go. He said yes, climbed into the FBI vehicle, and asked where they were going. To the Golden Harvest Motel, the command post for the FBI team looking for Maria Ridulph, Burton said.

On the ride over, John chatted with Agent Burton: "He was the nicest guy you'd ever want to meet. A family man, just real nice," John recalled, and they had a pleasant conversation. John said he didn't really know Maria Ridulph. He had seen her around the neighborhood, of course, but the only time he had ever spoken to her was maybe four years before when she was a tot of three. On that occasion, she had been playing on Archie Place, and he was concerned because she was getting close to the corner where his dog, a mixed collie named Laddie the Wonder Dog, had been run over and killed the year before. John told Maria it was too dangerous to be out, and she should go back home. She was a "precious" girl, he said of Maria. "If people could have seen her as I saw her the last time, they would only say one thing: 'Awww.' Because she was just a beautiful big-eyed little child."

John remembered that he knew Maria's sisters, Pat and Kay, but not very well. He had been over to the Ridulph house just once, about two years before Maria's abduction, when Pat and Kay had put on a play and invited the neighbors in to see it. About the only other encounter he had had with the Ridulph girls was when he was walking by their house one day and the two girls were playing jump rope in the driveway. When they spotted him, they launched into a nursery rhyme.

Johnny over the ocean
Johnny over the sea
Johnny broke a bottle
And blamed it on me
I told Ma
Ma told Pa

Johnny got a lickin'
Ha, Ha, Ha

John said he was sure they were mocking him, and it ticked him off. Everybody used to call him Johnny, but he says when he turned thirteen his mother told him, "Johnny's too young for you," and from then on he'd called himself John.

John Tessier had to wonder how much the FBI knew about him. Stories were going around that were on the sinister side. James Cliffe was a handsome youngster who had been voted "Most Photogenic Boy" in DeKalb County and won $50. James often found himself on Center Cross Street getting his hair cut by a man who lived next door to the Tessiers and had a barber chair in his house. A lot of the neighborhood kids went there for a buzz cut because it was so cheap. Center Cross Street was also on James's newspaper route, so he biked through there every afternoon to deliver the *Rockford Register-Republic*. More than once, he claimed, he'd seen John Tessier standing in his bedroom window in his underwear at dusk, just staring out (though John Tessier later denied such incidents ever happened).

"He was a weird cat," James said. John Tessier was into photography, and when he'd expressed an interest in photographing James's sisters, he told them, "Don't go anywhere near that house."

This kind of talk could be dismissed as inconsequential neighborhood gossip. What street in America doesn't have an eccentric in its midst? But it was a more disturbing episode involving John Tessier that had come to the attention of the FBI.

Pam Smith was a pretty and petite tomboy whose father, Roy Smith, was a big deal in Sycamore. Smith owned two Marathon gas stations and also sold air conditioners and home heating systems. The Smiths lived in a nice house with a large backyard at the corner of Exchange and Sacramento Streets. One summer, when Pam was around eight years old, she was playing on the screened-in porch when John Tessier walked up to her and allegedly uttered these words: "Do you want to go for a piggyback ride?"

More than fifty years later, Pam Smith, now Pam Long, could still shake her head at how foolhardy it had been for her to say yes.

"Why I did it, I don't know."

The next thing she knew, John was running down the street at a pretty good clip with little Pam clinging to his back. When "he wouldn't put me down," she said, she panicked and started crying. John kept running for another four blocks until a neighbor, Vince Mulligan, saw what was happening and called Pam's father at the gas station. Roy Smith flew out of his office, jumped into his Chrysler Imperial, and drove around until he caught up with the teenager with his weeping daughter on his back. Smith pulled over, yanked Pam off John's back, then proceeded to give her the scolding of her life.

"Don't you ever do that again! What were you thinking?"

While tears streamed down Pam's face, Smith turned his wrath on John, whom he recognized as the grandson of Eugene Tessier, who owned the house that abutted the Smith property. Eugene was a grumpy old coot, and maybe had a right to be; on too many occasions, baseballs hit by one of the four rambunctious Smith boys had come sailing through one of his windows.

"Never, ever go near my daughter again," Roy Smith warned John. "If I see you do that again, so help me . . ."

John scurried off.

Years later, when asked whether he ever gave Pam Smith a piggyback ride, John Tessier said, "That's just a total fabrication. I would never have done that."

December 3, 1957. Five years had passed since Pam's horrible piggyback ride on John Tessier's back. She was now thirteen, and this being a Tuesday night, she was at Teen Town, a wholesome community center where Sycamore's young people got together. They listened to rock and roll and doo-wop on the jukebox, and sometimes, on special occasions, there'd be live music.

That evening, Pam walked home—Teen Town was just two blocks away—and saw that her father's regular Tuesday-night poker game was going on in the dining room. All his poker buddies were at the table: the town's general practitioner, Dr. Harold Trapp; Jack Haka, who owned the local distributorship for the Schlitz Brewing Company; their neighbor, Vince Mulligan; and several other leading citizens of Sycamore. Pam's mother, Cora, had prepared fried chicken and deviled eggs for the guys and covered the dining-room table with a black oilcloth. Pam said good night to everyone and went straight to her room.

Suddenly, police sirens were wailing, followed by a voice from a police car's loudspeaker notifying the citizenry that a girl was missing and asking them to check every basement and garage on the block. Pam ran downstairs to see that the poker game had broken up and the men had rushed home to see what they could do to help with the search. It wasn't until the following morning that Pam learned the missing girl was Maria Ridulph. It made her sick to her stomach. She knew Maria. Billy, her brother, used to date Maria's sister Kay, and when she visited the Smiths she'd sometimes bring Maria along to play with a litter of rabbits the Smiths were raising in the backyard. They'd been orphaned when the family dog had slaughtered their mother, and it was a struggle to keep them alive. Pam had taught Maria how to use eyedroppers to feed them milk and water. Maria loved those rabbits.

Pam's father told her that until further notice, under no circumstances could she walk the streets of Sycamore alone.

Like everyone in town, the Smith family devoured any and all news about Maria's kidnapping, but one eerie item in the newspapers hit Roy Smith like a punch to the solar plexus: the kidnapper, this "Johnny," to lure Maria away had given her a piggyback ride. That bizarre piggyback ride John Tessier had given Pam a few years back still riled him. Could John Tessier possibly be the culprit? Smith called the police. They'd clearly taken his call seriously; a few days later Pam was at school when her English teacher, Jim

Ballotti, pulled her out of class. Waiting for her in the hallway were two men wearing fedora hats.

The men introduced themselves to Pam and told her they were FBI agents.

"Did you ever get a piggyback ride with a guy named Johnny?" one agent asked.

"Yes. And I got into lots of trouble for it."

They wanted to know when she had last seen John Tessier. At a slumber party not too long ago, she told them. All the girls had gone to the Devil's Drive-in Theater, on Sycamore Road, to see a movie. During intermission, Pam had headed over to the concession stand—and run into John Tessier. She'd rushed right back and told her friends, "Oh, my gosh, that's that creep who used to hang around our neighborhood." John Tessier had a face you could not forget, Pam told the FBI men, and teeth that she could only describe as "odd . . . scary . . . weird."

When Pam got home that night, her father was in high gear. He was positive that John Tessier was Maria's kidnapper.

"They got the SOB," he bellowed. "I just know he did it."

7

·········

GRILLED

December 9: Agent Burton showed John Tessier into the room at the Golden Harvest Motel that had been set aside for his interrogation. That was when John realized this was serious. Another agent, who would later administer the lie-detector examination, was waiting for them.

He got right on John's case. "I know you did it."

John was stunned. He almost said, *You're full of shit*, but thought better of it. Nobody cursed out the FBI, and all he managed to muster was a lame, "I didn't do a damn thing."

For the next hour or so, John recounted every moment of his time from December 2 through December 4 to the agents. They played good cop, bad cop, the bad cop repeatedly getting in John's face screaming, "I know you did it," while John emphatically shook his head. They demanded to know what he had done with Maria, and they kept at it.

Finally, he was hooked up to the polygraph, and Agent Bad Cop told him how the machine worked. He warned John that he had better answer truthfully because the polygraph could detect lies.

The Q&A began, and John stared straight ahead. As he answered every question, he could hear the stylus snaking across the scrolling roll of graph paper. When the session was over, Burton and the other agent must have looked at each other in complete bewilderment. There was no room for ambiguity. The official FBI report typed up later that day and placed in the files read as follows:

> The recorded reactions on the polygraph charts do not reflect evidence of guilty knowledge or implication by TESSIER in this matter. It is believed that he was a proper subject for such a test and would have reacted significantly if he had been involved.

They had been so certain that they had their man.

They had nothing on John. He was free to go. Burton offered him a ride home and, on the way there, was at a loss for words, almost apologetic. He even wondered if the young man could offer any leads for the FBI to pursue. Were there any other suspects in Sycamore they should be looking at? John said that if he thought of anybody interesting he'd be eager to get back to the FBI. When Burton pulled up to 227 Center Cross Street, John said there were no hard feelings. He got out of the car and strode into his house. His mother was enormously relieved to see him.

·········

Despite a polygraph that screamed "not guilty," the FBI was not quite ready to dismiss John Tessier as a suspect. Over the next few days, a team of agents proceeded to check into every aspect of his story.

During his interrogation at the Golden Harvest Motel, he had told the FBI that on December 2—the day before Maria's kidnapping—he was in Chicago getting a physical at the air force induction center on West Van Buren Street. What should have been a routine medical examination ended in disappointment when an X-ray turned up a spot on his lung. He told the air force doctor that he had contracted tuberculosis when he was three but assured the examining physician that the condition was benign. He was told to come back the next day for another round of X-rays. The air force, eager to sign a recruit, handed him a voucher for a night's stay in Chicago. That evening, John found the cheapest place available—a room at the YMCA.

The next morning, December 3, the day of Maria's kidnapping, John said he'd returned to the induction center for more X-rays. The spot on his lung was still present. He saw his future in the military going up in smoke.

"What can I do to fix this?" he asked the recruiting officer. "It has never been a problem."

He was told that if his family physician wrote a letter attesting to the fact that he did not have an active case of TB, his enlistment papers should sail through. He assured the recruiter that obtaining the letter would be a cinch. It was noon. John's train, so his story went, wasn't leaving until 5:15 P.M. With plenty of time to kill, he caught the sights.

Chicago terrified John, a hick from Sycamore who had just turned eighteen. He had been to the city a few times with Ralph but never before on his own. Not knowing his way around, and petrified he'd get lost, a wide-eyed John says he stuck to the Loop, Chicago's main commercial district. At some point, his wanderings took him to State Street, where he says he stepped into an old-fashioned burlesque house and watched a campy vaudeville show featuring slapstick comedians and bawdy dancers. He says he'd never seen anything like it. "That was where I learned the magical things that girls can do with tassels," he recalled with a chortle.

Finally, it was time to catch the train. According to Tessier's account, he headed over to Union Station, which was all decked out for Christmas, and boarded a westbound Illinois Central train to Rockford, the state's third largest city. It left on time, at 5:15, and pulled into Rockford at exactly 6:45. He exited the depot on Main Street and walked to the post office. There, from a phone booth, he placed a collect call to his house in Sycamore (a four-digit telephone number: 3257) and spoke to Ralph, his father.

"I told him I'm in Rockford, I had a problem at the induction center, and if he wasn't busy could he give me a ride home."

John Tessier told the FBI that there were multiple witnesses who could verify his story. Foremost among them was U.S. Air Force Reserve Lieutenant Colonel Theodore Liebovich, who was in charge of the recruiting office in

Rockford. John had run into Liebovich on the steps of the post office building after making the collect call to his father. He told Liebovich that he had just come from having a physical in Chicago and he wanted to "turn in my paperwork."

He said he followed Liebovich up the steps to the air force recruitment office on the third floor. Technical Sergeant John Froom was just closing up for the night. John Tessier handed him his enlistment papers, explained the hiccup with the X-ray, and said he'd be back the next day with a letter from his family doctor. Apparently, he made an unfavorable impression. Froom thought he looked "bewildered" and "acted like a 'lost sheep.'" They shot the breeze for a while; then John said good night and was on his way. The time was around 7:30 P.M. Forty-five miles away in Sycamore, the alarm that Maria Ridulph had disappeared had already been sounded.

John said his next stop in Rockford was a diner across the street from the post office. He ordered a slice of pie and chatted with the waitress. Finally, he told the FBI it was time to head back to Sycamore. On his arrival, he came upon pandemonium in the streets.

That, at least, is the story he related to the FBI. Was it believable?

Special Agent John Roberts Jr. was assigned the task of tracking down the witnesses who could vouch for John Tessier's time frame. On December 10, Roberts put a call in to the Rockford armed-forces recruitment office and spoke to a staff sergeant named Jon Oswald. Based on his conversation with Oswald, everything regarding John Tessier checked out: the physical in Chicago, the spot on his lung, the overnight stay at the Y, John's reexamination the morning of December 3.

Then Agent Roberts also reached out to Lieutenant Colonel Theodore Liebovich (misspelled in FBI files as "Liberwitz"), who thought aspects of John Tessier's story were "difficult to believe." For one thing, John claimed to have been ordered by military personnel in Chicago to report to the recruiting office in Rockford when his train came in, at 6:45. Strange, because no recruitment office stayed open that late, and the people at the Chicago induction center would have known that. Then there was John Tessier's overall conduct. The young man "gave the appearance of being a 'narcotic,'" Liebovich told the FBI. According to the colonel, Tessier confided to him that he had been previously rejected from military service "because he was unstable."

On December 4, while Sycamore's citizens were engaged in the search for Maria Ridulph, John Tessier made his way back to the U.S. Air Force recruiting office in Rockford, with a letter from his family doctor. There, he introduced himself to Staff Sergeant Oswald. Oswald stared at the young recruit; he found everything about Tessier a little off. For one thing, his attire. He wore an "odd colored, flashy shirt"; a string necktie; and a brown jacket made of a "fuzzy" material. There was more. Chitchatting with Oswald, John "mentioned that it was a good thing he was not in Sycamore last night" because of what had happened to Maria Ridulph. Search parties were all over town right now looking for the girl, he informed Oswald and, out of the blue, added that he "would not be considered a suspect because his girlfriend's father was a deputy sheriff." Actually, Jan Edwards's father, William "Harold" Edwards, owned a photo studio in Sycamore, but, part-time, he did shoot crime-scene photos for the police, so what was true was that all the cops knew him.

Oswald's antennae were quivering. He could not help but notice that John had a "slight cut across the upper lip." It looked like a fresh injury, although Oswald would later say the cut was so small it "could have been done while shaving."

The conversation took another bizarre turn, Oswald said, when John, unprompted and without context, pulled out a "little black book" and showed it to him. It contained the names and addresses of a number of young women in Sycamore, along with their bust and hip measurements.

Regarding the little black book, John Tessier would later say, "I think it was a novelty item I might have picked up in Chicago. It was a silly thing so I just filled in some names." Asked why Liebovich would call him a narcotic, Tessier said, "Here is this colonel, he's approached by the FBI, he has to say something bad about this guy that the FBI is interested in, so he can be important. I'm sorry, but I never took drugs, I never smoked drugs, and I was totally in command of my abilities."

Oswald made a mental note of all these peculiarities. Then his phone rang. It was his landlady, Mrs. Grimes, calling with a question. They conversed briefly, and when he hung up, John Tessier asked him, "Is she related to the Grimes girls?"

Barbara Grimes, fifteen, and her sister Patricia, thirteen, had disappeared from Chicago a year before, on December 28, 1956, after seeing, for the fifteenth time, the Elvis Presley movie *Love Me Tender*. Their disappearance was huge news and had triggered one of the largest missing-persons investigations in Chicago history. Elvis Presley had followed the case and issued a statement urging young people everywhere to take care and not stay out late. "If you are good Presley fans, you'll go home and ease your mother's worries." The bodies of the Grimes girls were later discovered off the side of a road in the village of Willow Springs, in Cook County. The case remains unsolved to this day.

Sergeant Oswald said he had no idea whether his landlady was related to the Grimes girls and asked John why he wanted to know. John's response was to launch into a description of the case in great detail. In Oswald's opinion, regarding the Grimes girls, John Tessier was "well read," which he found curious.

To the FBI, this was all very interesting, but what did it add up to?

On December 9, Agent David Burton spoke to Dan Schaeffer, general manager of the Sycamore-Ogle Telephone Company. Schaeffer had been asked to check the records and he was now reporting back that a collect call had been made from a pay phone in Rockford to the Tessier home in Sycamore at 6:57 P.M. The call had been made by "one John S. Tassier"—a spelling error on the part of the telephone operator who had handled the call. The collect call had been accepted by the Tessier family and had lasted just two minutes, until 6:59.

Everything was checking out. John Tessier could not be in two places at the same time. There seemed to be an abundance of evidence backing up the teenager's contention that he had been in Rockford when Maria was kidnapped. And there was the indisputable fact that the polygraph examination had detected no sign of deception when John was flat-out asked if he had killed Maria.

Summing up, the FBI report stated that as far as John Tessier was concerned, "No further investigation is being conducted regarding the suspect."

John was in the clear. The FBI did not even deem it necessary to show his photo to the lone witness of Maria's abduction, Kathy Sigman.

8

....

THE LITTLE WITNESS

Kathy Sigman was under twenty-four-hour police protection. Though she was only eight years old, she was pivotal to any future prosecution. Authorities feared that "Johnny" might attempt to murder the only witness who could identify him. Consequently, in those early days of the investigation, Kathy was never left alone.

She was shown thousands of mug shots but could not pick out the kidnapper, and the pressure she felt to deliver a suspect was crushing for such a young child. Turning page after page of mug shots, she found it beyond belief that there could be so many bad people in the world.

On her first day back at school, Kathy's third-grade teacher, Barbara Hunt, took her aside and consoled her with kind words, but the green-eyed girl found it almost impossible to concentrate on her schoolwork. She couldn't stop thinking about Maria. And to add to her distress, she was frequently pulled out of class to observe police lineups.

One morning when Kathy was late for school, everyone panicked. Had she been kidnapped? Word came back to the principal's office that she was OK—just viewing yet another police lineup. Her mother kept reminding Kathy of the special mission in her life that had been set for her by the kidnapping of Maria Ridulph. Never forget, she would tell Kathy, "You are the only person who knows what Johnny looks like."

As investigators cast around for alternate ways to think about the case, some wondered if it could have been Kathy Sigman, not Maria Ridulph, who had been Johnny's intended victim all along. The theory went: on the night of December 3, Kathy was losing the Duck the Cars game. She just wasn't as fleet of foot as Maria, so when the headlights of the passing cars kept landing on her, she'd lose. Under the rules of the game, the penalty for losing was she had to swing around the streetlight pole at the intersection of Archie Place and Center Cross Street. Johnny, so the hypothesis went, had been prowling around in his car when he drove into the intersection. Only Kathy would have been visible under the streetlight because she was the one who kept losing; Maria would have been cloaked in darkness. When Johnny got out of his car he expected to confront only Kathy. Coming upon two girls instead of one forced the kidnapper to select a victim. Had fate and circumstances chosen Maria and spared Kathy?

These were difficult days for the third-grader. Being

ngled out gave Kathy Sigman a queasy feeling. She knew that behind her back, around town people were calling her "the girl who was with Maria," and it made her feel like an outcast. Her friendships started to fade away, and she got the sense that her playmates had been told by their parents to stay away from her for their own safety. After a while, Kathy couldn't wait to move out of the neighborhood. An evil being was lurking in the shadows there, and she had to wonder if, one day, the bogeyman would come back for her.

In those early days of the criminal investigation, at one point or another, in total, seventy-four men and three women had come under suspicion before they were crossed off the list of suspects.

A twenty-six-year-old passenger on a bus in Wisconsin who had had one drink too many boasted that he knew all about Maria's disappearance. He was thrown into the county jail and released after he'd sobered up and his alibi had checked out.

A twenty-eight-year-old truck driver from Rockford was turned in by his wife for taking indecent liberties with their five-year-old daughter. He came under scrutiny for two reasons: he admitted that he had been in Sycamore on December 3, and when his photograph was shown to Kathy Sigman she had said he "could be" Johnny. He later claimed the state police had given him the third degree in his interrogation.

Then there was the thirty-one-year-old U.S. Marine tech sergeant who was taken into custody in Iowa for beating an eight-year-old girl and binding her hands. When Kathy was shown his photo she reportedly said that he also "could be" Johnny. But he had an airtight alibi.

A Chicago fireman, arrested for pulling a fifteen-year-old girl off a horse, suddenly found himself being questioned about Maria Ridulph. So did a schoolteacher from a small village in Kane County who'd been busted on a morals charge.

A lowlife named Donald Arbuckle became a compelling person of interest when a nine-year-old girl from Rockford who had been missing for twelve hours was found sleeping in his car. She said Arbuckle had taken her to a "cave" at an abandoned military installation outside Rockford. Arbuckle's photo was shown to Kathy Chapman, but at age thirty-four, he was too old to be Johnny—plus he had a rock-solid alibi.

The number of tips coming in slowed to a trickle. Rumors circulated that the federal agents were getting antsy about being stuck in Sycamore for Christmas. Even G-men, it seemed, had family issues to deal with. Special Agent in Charge Richard Auerbach went on a delicate mission. He informed Mr. and Mrs. Ridulph that if the case was ever to be solved, it would probably be by "accidental discovery." He showed them a statement that he wanted to release to the public:

> In view of the lapse of time since the disappearance of Maria Ridulph . . . and in view of the circumstances surrounding her disappearance, it is entirely possible that in the event she is dead her body has been discarded

in a field on a nearby farm. Past experience dictates that carrion birds, such as crows and buzzards, congregate in numbers and feed on decaying matters. It is requested that anyone in the Sycamore area and communities nearby be alert for noticeable gatherings of crows and buzzards. In the event such is noted, it is requested that the location be physically checked for the possible presence of a human body.

Grossly insensitive? Or simply laying out the hard-boiled facts of where things stood? In any event, the Ridulphs agreed to the language, and the statement went out. Privately, Kay Ridulph vented in her diary: "Of all the nerve!"

9

....

THE PHOTOGRAPHER'S DAUGHTER

For John Tessier, it was time to bid his girlfriend a fond farewell.

Jan Edwards was a shapely five-foot-two-inch junior at Sycamore High with blue eyes and soft curly brown hair. *American Bandstand* was her favorite TV show, and on school days she hurried home to catch Dick Clark introducing the hottest rock-and-roll songs. Even before Maria Ridulph's disappearance, Jan's father was worried about her being kidnapped for ransom because he was such a well-known businessman in town. Not only did he own the hobby shop on State Street, a popular hangout, but he was Sycamore's only photographer, which meant he took the yearbook photos for all the high school kids. Harold Edwards was always telling his daughter to be observant. A stern and at times overprotective father, he gave all of Jan's dates a once-over. No way could she date bad boys, only boys with "solid" reputations. Jan's curfew was rigidly enforced: 10:00 P.M. on school nights, 11:00 on weekends.

Jan had been going steady with John Tessier for about six months. She wore his class ring with a yarn of angora to keep it from slipping off her finger. John had never put the moves on her; he was always a gentleman. The high point of their dating life was when John took her to a nightclub in Rockford. She had her hair piled high like a fashion model and wore a sophisticated dress, just right for the occasion. It was the first time she'd been to a nightclub, and it made the seventeen-year-old feel grown up, more like a young woman than a girl. They posed for a photo to commemorate the night.

"We held hands, we may have kissed a little, we talked," Jan recalled. "There was lots of walking around all over town at night. We did that a lot." One thing that was strange about their romance was that Jan never met John's parents, nor was she invited over to the Tessier home on Center Cross Street. Looking back, she found that "very odd." That he came from a Catholic family and Jan had been raised Protestant meant that, in the social conventions of the era, marriage would be out of the question, at least from Mr. Edwards's point of view.

John seemed more into the relationship than Jan, but, as he wondered whether she might be the love of his life, she was already thinking that maybe it was time to move on. Then John informed her that he was enlisting in the U.S. Air Force. One night in early December 1957, John called and asked her if he could come over. Darkness had fallen, and a freezing December wind was whipping through Sycamore. So many years later, Jan doesn't remember how John got there, but she does recall sitting in a car parked in the driveway of her beautiful Victorian house on Somonauk Street on the outskirts of town. It was around 9:30, close to her curfew, but more than fifty years later no one can recall with certainty what the exact date was. It could have been December 3, the night Maria was taken, or possibly December 4. What she does remember is what she and John talked about.

According to Jan, John said he was enlisting in the U.S. Air Force, had been to Chicago "that morning" for his physical, and he was excited that his enlistment was around the corner. Another memory Jan had from that night would prove to be very significant many years later. John handed her a train ticket, explaining that it had been issued to him by the air force. She looked at it and saw that it was a thirty-day open ticket, from Rockford to Chicago. The expiration date on its face was December 30. John told her that he was afraid he'd lose it, and he wanted her to hang on to it for him because she was reliable, and he knew it would be in safe hands. He'd come back for it when he was ready to use it.

Then they chatted a bit, and, of course, Maria Ridulph's kidnapping came up; it was the talk of the town. And Jan knew Maria's sister, Pat, who was in her class at Sycamore High. At some point, for a fleeting moment, it crossed her mind that the suspect's name was Johnny.

"Ha ha; your name is Johnny," Jan joked.

"Yeah, right," he said, shifting the conversation back to the air force and telling her how enthusiastic he was about signing up and starting his military career. He had dropped out of high school and was working as a stock boy at a grocery store. John turned to talk of love. He said he was going to really miss her. Jan said she'd miss him too, but in truth she was trying to let him down easy.

"It came as a relief that I didn't have to break up with him," Jan said many years later. "I was not thinking marriage at all. Period. I was barely seventeen." For someone as pretty and popular as Jan Edwards, there'd be plenty of boyfriends down the road. She and John kissed good night. Then she went up to her bedroom. On her dresser was the photo taken of them at the Rockford nightclub. She looked so grown up. It instantly struck her that it would be the perfect place to store the railroad ticket. She tucked it in the picture frame for safekeeping. That way she'd know where it was when John came back for it. He never would.

Time passed, and at some point, Jan stored the photo, and with it the ticket, in a memory book containing all the keepsakes and treasured mementos of her life in Sycamore. Then she forgot she even had it.

On December 11, 1957, five days after John Tessier's name first came to the attention of the FBI, he said good-bye to his family. There was no going-away party or words of fatherly advice from Ralph, an air force veteran himself. Just a handshake and best of luck. Neither did John's siblings care very much that he was leaving; it was, "Yeah, Johnny's going; bye-bye, Johnny." The only Tessier to shed any tears was his mother, Eileen.

John boarded a civilian plane for San Antonio, Texas, and reported to Lackland Air Force Base for basic military training.

In Sycamore, Christmas shopping was in high gear. The frugal population of the city had withdrawn their savings from the Christmas Club at the National Bank and Trust and loaded up on sensible gifts. The three major supermarkets in town, Piggly Wiggly, King Korn, and Kroger, were jammed with holiday shoppers. In a time of civil rights strife and Cold War uneasiness about the days ahead, small-town America was preparing to celebrate its Christian faith. At Cape Canaveral, a Vanguard rocket stood ready to launch America's first satellite and catch up to the Soviets. Historic days lay ahead.

On Christmas Eve, Mike and Frances Ridulph took Pat, Kay, and Chuck to their grandparents' house. Ridulfo had been the family's original name, which had been Americanized to Ridulph when Mike came to America from Sicily. The Ridulphs celebrated the holiday as they always did, with an Italian Christmas feast. After dinner, Mike and Frances took the kids to St. John, a Lutheran church. Frances, whose background was Swiss and German, had insisted the children be raised Lutheran. Reverend Louis Going delivered a beautiful sermon and asked the parishioners to remember Maria in their prayers.

It had been a good Christmas Eve, but when the Ridulphs got home to 616 Archie Place, something happened.

"We all started arguing and got all upset," Pat wrote in

her diary. "Mom threatened to take her sleeping pills." The fight got bad enough for their next-door neighbor, Meredith Strombom to be summoned. She had been a great friend during these days of crisis and came running right over. So did Aunt Jenny and Aunt Josephine. Frances calmed down. It had probably been inevitable that the past three weeks of intolerable tension would finally come to a head on Christmas Eve. At some point, everyone started to relax again.

The Ridulphs always opened their gifts on Christmas morning, but this night, after the terrible blowup, Mike and Frances decided it would be OK for the children to open their presents early. Of course, the kids jumped at the idea. In quick order, a bounty of gifts lay at Pat's feet: a flash camera, an electric alarm clock, a Samsonite luggage case (which she has to this day), various items of clothes, hand lotion, a stuffed dog, candy bars, ten packs of gum, a white scarf, a box of stationery, mittens, and a mirror with a portrait of Jesus on the back. Kay got a $10 bill, a stuffed dog which she named Larry after her boyfriend, a pink petticoat, hand lotion, gum, ear warmers, and a fancy collar. Mike and Frances had definitely gone overboard on the gifts. It was their way of making this sad Christmas without little Maria special for the other children. Left under the tree was Maria's gift, a two-handled pogo stick bundled in Christmas wrapping paper, just waiting for her. It was a symbol of the great void she had left in their lives.

At the Tessier home, Christmas morning was bleak. They could all breathe easier now that the family name had not been sullied, but it was still a wretched time, with Ralph and Eileen bickering nonstop about money. On December 25, the Tessier children gathered at the tree—a bargain-basement tree, the runt of the lot—Ralph had purchased at the last minute after considerable nagging by Eileen. As usual, the presents, Jeanne recalled, were "the cheapest crap available—whatever hadn't sold out at the hardware store." Nothing was gift wrapped. All the toys—dime-store plastic junk—were just tossed under the tree. It was, in Jeanne's mind, yet another Christmas of failed expectations.

Two days later, the squad of sixty FBI agents that had been searching for Maria Ridulph withdrew from Sycamore. The command post at the Golden Harvest Motel was shut down, and all the agents returned to their respective bureaus. Richard Auerbach, now back in Chicago, announced that, henceforth, all tips related to Maria Ridulph would be handled through the Rockford field office. Life went on for the Ridulph family. That Saturday night, with Pat cheering them on, the Sycamore Spartans beat archrivals DeKalb High, 49–48, to everyone's surprise. On New Year's Eve, Pat babysat for two youngsters, Norma and Kenny, for five hours and got paid $5.

The New Year arrived, January 1, 1958, but no word about Maria. Like the footsteps she had left behind in the snow on the night of her kidnapping—the last physical evidence of her existence on earth—she was still gone.

10

·········

THE WAR BRIDE

February 10, 1946: Ralph Tessier was a lumbering hulk of a GI with big ears that jutted out and pockmarks on his face from childhood acne, just a regular guy from a small town in Illinois called Sycamore who had volunteered for U.S. Army service two weeks before Pearl Harbor and had done his duty in the war against the Nazis. The U.S. Army Air Force staff sergeant had been assigned to the supply depot at Bovingdon Airfield, about twenty-five miles outside London. Bovingdon had quite a history. Clark Gable and James Stewart flew combat missions from there, and it was where General Eisenhower's personal Flying Fortress was based. It was at Bovingdon that Ralph met Eileen, a searchlight operator in the British Women's Auxiliary Air Force.

After they'd been seeing each other for a while, and Eileen became pregnant, she and Ralph were married in

England. Their baby, Katheran, was born on May 16, 1945, eight days after Germany unconditionally surrendered to the Allies.

In the general demobilization of American forces following V-E day, Ralph was shipped home to await his discharge from active service. Now, at last, after many months of dealing with military red tape, he was about to welcome his war bride and his baby.

In a haze of sweat and cigarette smoke, Ralph paced the drill floor at the Seventh Regiment Armory on Park Avenue and Sixty-Sixth Street, in New York City. One GI who was there remarked that his nerves were so shot that it reminded him of D-day.

When the doors opened, there they were, the largest collection of war brides ever brought to these shores: 1,666 women from the British Commonwealth and their 688 children, many of them blond and blue-eyed, an unmistakable genetic marker of their British heritage. A few of the children had come down with colds and rashes during the seven-day voyage on the great ocean liner *Queen Mary*, and there were four cases of measles. All in all, though, considering the postwar wasteland they were leaving behind in Europe, the state of their health was remarkably good.

In the chaos, Ralph found his war bride, Eileen, carrying nine-month-old baby Katheran. And at her side was a towheaded seven-year-old youngster named John Samuel Cherry, the odd boy out. John had been born in Belfast, Northern Ireland, on November 27, 1939. He was Eileen's son from her first marriage, to a British sergeant named Samuel Cherry who had been killed in 1942 at age twenty-three in a German bombing raid on London. For his safety, the boy had lived out the war years with an elderly farmer and his wife on a cattle farm in a town just northwest of London. Now dressed in a sailor suit, John looked like a little lord of the admiralty, shy and small for his age, possibly due to wartime nutritional deprivation. He shook hands with Ralph. Henceforth, he was told, he'd be known as John Tessier, and he was to call Ralph Dad.

The war brides of the *Queen Mary* scattered to all points across the United States. New York claimed the largest number—205 women and 75 of their children. To the state of Illinois went 142 war brides and 56 children.

It took the four Tessiers three days to reach Sycamore by train. Young John soaked everything in, the sights and sounds of this new land overwhelming him. Postwar America glittered with wealth and prosperity. He had never seen a chocolate bar. Somebody offered John a banana, and he didn't know what to do with it.

But Sycamore, tucked away in the northern reaches of Illinois, was not what Eileen had expected. To her dismay, in this part of America, in the middle of nowhere, the streets were paved with anything but gold. And Ralph had led her to believe he came from money, but it was obvious that the Tessiers of Sycamore were struggling just like everyone in Europe was.

When Ralph introduced Eileen to her in-laws, his father, Eugene, was considerate, but her mother-in-law "treated me like trash," she remarked years later. Mrs. Tessier was skeptical about Eileen's personal history. Her story of her first husband's death in the London Blitz sounded sketchy to her. Had this young Irish lass maneuvered her gullible son into a shotgun wedding? She had to wonder.

Then there was the matter of this squirt of a boy, this John Samuel Cherry who spoke with an English accent and was now calling himself Johnny Tessier. Suddenly he was family. Who were his people? And where did he come from?

Ralph moved his wife and the two children into his parents' house on Sacramento Street. He was making $18 a week at the hardware store owned by Lee Hagen, the same salary he'd been making before he'd left Sycamore to go to war in 1941. He wasn't falling down, but he wasn't climbing up the ladder of success either, and now he had a family to feed. To supplement his income, on the side Ralph hand-painted signs for local businesses. Turned out he had an artistic eye along with a good hand. He advertised his services with a simple ad in the local newspaper:

Truck Lettering
Phone 3257
Sycamore, Ill.
R. E. TESSIER

As soon as he could afford it, Ralph bought a lot on Center Cross Street and spent the next year and a half building a small cottage. He did all the brickwork and construction, and a GI buddy installed the electricity. The Tessiers moved into their new home at number 227 in May 1947. Most nights, Ralph drank himself to sleep.

Over time, Eileen got to make friends in Sycamore. She invited the Sycamore Knitting Club to her home for a pleasant social gathering. She'd been raised Episcopalian, but out of deference to her new husband and in-laws, she'd converted to Catholicism and joined St. Mary's Church.

When he was eight, Johnny was walking home after school and stepped out into traffic just as a taxi was rounding the corner. The collision knocked him forty feet down the road and put him in a coma. For a while, it was touch and go; then, after a week, he just woke up, and when he did, he had to urinate so badly he stood up on the hospital bed and peed right on the floor. Some of his family thought he wasn't the same when he got out of the hospital, that the collision had affected his personality.

Johnny tried to fit in, to learn the ways of all-American boyhood. Eileen took him to a rodeo at Chicago's Soldier Field. When he was old enough, he joined the Boy Scouts, Sycamore Troop 2, and learned how to pitch a tent and cook meals. In the fall camporee, his troop earned an A rating for keeping a clean campsite. On Halloween, he helped decorate the store windows in the business district and won a prize. He learned to swim, and after taking a course in lifesaving, he was awarded a safety certificate. A paper route delivering the Chicago newspapers on his bike earned him pocket change. When a neighbor got the first TV set on Center Cross Street, it was a big event, and the family let Johnny and the other kids on the block go over and watch *The Lone Ranger* and *Howdy Doody*.

In quick order, the babies started coming. After Kathy, in 1945, there was Jeanne, born in 1947; Bob, in 1951; Janet, in 1956; and Mary, in 1959. Finally, there was Nancy, in 1960. Nancy's christening was duly celebrated at St. Mary's, but left unspoken was the reality that the baby had been born with cerebral palsy and significant mental impairment. (Nancy Tessier has been institutionalized since she was eleven.) There were seven children in all, stepbrother John being the eldest. And as each Tessier offspring came into being, John saw it not as a blessing but another blow. "You took my mother from me!" he once screamed at his sister Janet.

"From the time I was a baby, Mom was my world," John Tessier recalled in his old age. "A fact that didn't dawn on me until recently is that I had never seen another child until I was seven years old. Never seen another child. I grew up in my own little world, and it took a while for me to fit in when I got to America. I was behind in maturity. But, you know, I caught up quick. They were going to set me back a grade, but Mother wouldn't have it. She got her way."

He hated math but was pretty good at music, art, and history. Charmed by his accent, the nuns at the Catholic school he attended would ask him to sing "When Irish Eyes Are Smiling" and the haunting lullaby "Too-Ra-Loo-Ra-Loo-Ral," which had become enormously popular after Bing Crosby sang it in the movie *Going My Way*. At St. Mary's, where John was an altar boy and sang in the choir, he brought tears to the eyes of the parishioners with his solo performance of "Ave Maria." As time went on, he lost all traces of his English accent, and when puberty hit, in the seventh grade, he regrettably also lost his singing voice.

The fifties were the golden age of sci-fi and fantasy, and

at the Sycamore public library, John got into the stories of the writer Isaac Asimov.

"Why are you reading that crap?" Ralph barked when he saw John with an Asimov book in his lap. John put it aside. Ralph's reproach went to the heart of his issues with his stepson: from day one, Ralph had pegged him as a momma's boy.

Ralph Tessier may have been a limited man, possibly a very ignorant man, and even a bigot, but no one questioned his work ethic. From the hard labor he did at the hardware store, he had the physical strength that his stepson could only envy. John can still remember the day he watched in awe as Ralph pulled a huge refrigerator onto his back and carried it up a flight of stairs without flinching.

When John entered public high school, things started going downhill fast. Latin was a disaster. Taking two years of first-year Latin almost broke his spirit. He had expected it to be a snap because of all his years as an altar boy. Playing high school sports was never an option because the Tessiers couldn't afford the required insurance, so he never tried out.

Then he had a serious run-in with his art teacher, Mrs. Minor. The bell had rung, signaling that class was over. It was around noon, and John wanted to get to the lunchroom fast so he could be first in line. He flew out of his chair and was heading for the door when Mrs. Minor grabbed his shoulders and gave him a little push.

"Sit down; no running," she said.

"Bitch."

He just blurted it out and immediately regretted it. You couldn't talk back to a teacher, much less curse her out, and not expect serious repercussions. She sent John to the principal's office.

"You're done," the principal said.

"That's it? Just like that?"

"Just like that."

John went home and informed his mother that he'd been expelled. It was a jolt for Eileen, and it made John sick to his stomach; he always regretted not being a better son. Then Ralph came home from work and had to be told the bad news. It was especially embarrassing because Ralph had taken Mrs. Minor's class seventeen years before when he'd attended Sycamore High, and she had encouraged his interest in art. Ralph's reaction was, "Go get a job. Welcome to the world. You're not in school anymore—get a job." But his unspoken message was that he was really done with John.

John found work stocking shelves at a grocery store and began thinking seriously about the military, which he considered part of his family heritage. His mother had been a corporal, his biological father a sergeant, and his Irish grandfather a sergeant major in the British army. When he was born in 1939, three months after the British declaration of war against Germany, with the veins in his forehead shaped in a V, supposedly a nurse looked at him and exclaimed, "Victory Baby!" It all made John believe that serving in the military was his destiny, so he bided his time and awaited his eighteenth birthday, when he could legally enlist. He was thinking air force.

With money John had saved over the years from his paper route, he bought his first set of wheels at a used-car dealership—a '48 Plymouth Coupe. It cost $250. It had lousy brakes and the horsepower of a lawnmower, but somehow John could make it go eighty-five miles an hour. Some of Ralph's artistic skills must have rubbed off because John painted winged flames on the fenders. Everybody in Sycamore recognized the wreck with those flames on the side as John Tessier's car. The Coupe became another source of friction with his stepfather. When John got a flat tire, he didn't have a clue about what to do, so he asked his stepfather, who could fix anything, if he could help him change it.

"Hell, no," Ralph said. "It's your car. You bought it. You figure it out."

The Coupe with the flat tire sat there parked for weeks on the tiny patch of grass in front of the house on Center Cross Street. It was a Mexican standoff.

John wasn't the only one looking forward to his birthday; Ralph couldn't wait for him to turn eighteen and get out of the house.

One lazy afternoon, after John had taken up smoking, he had carelessly fallen asleep in bed with a lit cigarette. The smell of the burning mattress woke him in the nick of time, and he instinctively took hold of the mattress and ran down the stairs with it, filling the house with smoke in his wake. He charged out the front door, threw the mattress on the lawn, and stomped out the flames. When he turned to go back inside, there at the door watching everything was Ralph.

They stared each other down.

Then Ralph coldcocked his stepson on the chin.

Even Eileen finally faced it: it was time for her son to go.

"Mom was upset about me enlisting," John recalled. "She thought I wanted to get away from her, but that was the farthest thing from the truth possible. I disappointed her, and I always hated disappointing her. But she knew going into the service would be a good thing for me. I would learn discipline, leadership, work ethic, and the manly things I needed to learn."

John turned eighteen on November 27, 1957. The next day, the Tessiers, along with the rest of America, celebrated Thanksgiving. Now that he was of age, John started the enlistment process. It got a little complicated because for some inexplicable reason, he had never applied for U.S. citizenship, and his legal name was still John Samuel Cherry. Thereafter, events moved quickly. He bid his girlfriend Jan Edwards farewell. On December 2, he went to Chicago to take the air force physical. Maria Ridulph was kidnapped the night of December 3. An anonymous phone tip regarding John Tessier came to the attention of law enforcement on December 6. The FBI came calling on December 8. By the tenth, John had taken the polygraph and been cleared. On the eleventh, he left home and was inducted into the U.S. Air Force.

II

·········

PROM NIGHT

Those first few days of boot camp came as a jolt to John Tessier. First thing to go was the DA cut—shaved off in an instant with electric clippers. The first night in the barracks may have been the most miserable of his life.

Eventually, he settled into a routine. He was instructed in field drilling, marksmanship, and core military values. Academic classes taught him the code of conduct and the distinguished history of the U.S. Air Force in time of war. He could definitely see this military life working out for him. Basic training lasted sixty-three days, at the end of which he was transferred to Shaw Air Force Base, eight miles outside Sumter, South Carolina, and assigned to an automotive unit that serviced a fleet of jeeps and other military vehicles.

One month later, John, "proud as a peacock," was back in Sycamore on leave. Even Ralph seemed happy to see him, and Eileen beamed at the maturing figure the young airman cut in his trim military uniform. He got his little brother, Bob, to put on his Cub Scouts uniform and step out onto the front lawn, then showed him how to present arms and stand at attention. He made him do push-ups and submit to a mock military inspection until something caught little Bob's attention. The nameplate on his brother's uniform read Cherry. Who, he asked, was Cherry? Why didn't it say Tessier? John sighed. It was time to explain the tangled family history to his little brother. That was when six-year-old Bob learned that he and his big brother did not share the same father.

John paid a visit to Jan Edwards, thinking that seeing him in uniform might rekindle the romance, but her cold reception made it clear that the relationship was definitely over.

Young James Cliffe and his buddies from the neighborhood were playing in the schoolyard of West Elementary School, very near where Maria Ridulph had been kidnapped, when a late-model car pulled up. The driver got out and approached them. He wore a fedora, was smoking a cigarette, and had a notepad in his hand. His pencil-thin mustache, the sort Errol Flynn had in movies when he played a debonair gent, reinforced James's funny feeling that this man was passing himself off as somebody he was not. The stranger introduced himself as a newspaper reporter from Chicago, but he just looked too young to have a job like that. When the man started asking questions about the Maria Ridulph case, wanting to know if there were any fresh leads, twelve-year-old James really got rattled. Then this character did something unforgettably weird. To take notes on what the kids were telling him, he stuck a filtered cigarette up a nostril so he could free his hands.

It hadn't registered to James Cliffe until that moment that there was something oddly familiar about this fellow. James scrutinized his face, then it hit him: it was John Tessier, the neighborhood "creep" who James said he sometimes saw standing in his bedroom window in his underwear at dusk, just staring out. (Years later, when asked whether he ever posed as a newspaper reporter, John Tessier said, "Not true.")

That evening, James was at the dinner table with his parents and four sisters when he said, "I saw Johnny Tessier today, I think. He was asking questions about Maria Ridulph." He now had everyone's attention.

"He was pretending to be a reporter," James said. "He took out a cigarette and put it in his nose!" When his father shot him a skeptical look, James really unloaded on him. "Hey, I couldn't make that up! You'd better check that guy out."

Mr. Cliffe went to the phone and called the city desks of the *Chicago Tribune*, *Sun-Times*, *Daily News*, and *Herald-American*. He also reached out to the *Morning Star* in Rockford. He asked the same question of everyone: had any of their reporters been in Sycamore earlier that day working on the Maria Ridulph story? They all said no. Then Cliffe called the Sycamore police.

....

The year 1958 was shaping up to be a prosperous one for the city of Sycamore.

Anaconda Wire and Cable was expanding, and the asphalt-paving giant, Barber Greene, was opening a new million-dollar plant on the outskirts of town. The Texaco station at DeKalb and Sacramento and the Economy Variety Store had been spruced up, and in the downtown shopping district, a new shoe-repair shop and a women's apparel store had opened for business. Sycamore Bowl had moved to a fancier facility on South Sacramento Street. The population of the city had grown to 6,999 souls, up 111 from the previous year. Three new housing subdivisions were under construction, and the voters had approved a $1 million referendum to build a new high school. A senior at Sycamore High had signed a contract with the Detroit Tigers, and another player on the baseball team had signed with the San Francisco Giants. These boys were the pride of the city. The future looked bright for Sycamore.

This was also the centennial of Sycamore's founding, in 1858, and a four-day celebration was planned over Labor Day weekend to mark the anniversary. It was going to be the grandest parade in Sycamore's history.

"What's in the future for Sycamore?" asked the local newspaper, the *Sycamore True Republican*. "With each and every day our future looks brighter." Unfortunately, the 100-year-old *Sycamore True Republican* had only ten years left in its existence—it ceased publication in 1968.

Now that the FBI had returned to Chicago, the state police and the sheriff of DeKalb County, Alf Deisz, had been running the Maria Ridulph investigation, with assistance from local Sycamore cops. Deisz was tall and brawny, with a double chin and outsize waist.

"I think Maria is alive and well and I'm not ashamed to admit it," Deisz said. He offered this line of reasoning: "The girl's disappearance doesn't follow the pattern of kidnappings by sexual deviates. When a deviate picks up a child, he usually disposes of her body fairly soon after, and not far from where he picked her up. Also, he isn't too careful about where he gets rid of the body." Deisz even wondered if Maria had been taken by a "child-hungry" couple who were raising the little girl as their own. If only. It was certainly the best-case scenario.

Deisz set about obtaining Maria's fingerprints, sending crime-lab technicians to the Ridulph home and Maria's school with the mission of lifting a complete set of the missing girl's fingerprints from various sources: her desk, books, toys, bathroom mirror, inkwell—any objects that she had come in physical contact with. Prints were also taken from a greenhouse Maria visited regularly (she loved flowers). The sheriff wanted to be ready in the event that "a pretty brunette may turn up twenty years from now and say she is Maria Ridulph."

No one in Sycamore was forgetting Maria. At the Jane Fargo Hotel barbershop, Maria Ridulph remained the number-one topic of conversation. And a hard lesson had been learned, so everyone was on the lookout. Children were less trusting, and new rules were set down. Maria's abduction was definitely changing the way Sycamore's youngsters were being raised and where and how they played. Closer tabs were kept on everyone. People were locking their front doors now. Some folks were thinking about moving to another town before the bogeyman awakened and returned.

On January 21, 1958, twelve inches of snow blanketed Sycamore, and all the schools in town were shut down for two days. It was a long, hard winter, but spring brought with it renewed vigor in the hunt for Maria.

In April, the ice on Sportsmans Lake finally thawed. The eight-acre body of water—three feet at the shallow end, twenty-one feet at its deep end—remained the only location in Sycamore that had not been thoroughly searched. It took six centrifugal pumps to drain the lake into the Kiswaukee River—an arduous and painstaking undertaking. Sportsmans Lake was spring fed, and the pumps struggled to overcome the inflow. The water receded at the rate of only two inches every three hours. At last, the water level was low enough to get a good look at the bottom. Searchers wearing hip boots waded on the silted lake floor looking for anything, maybe even Maria's body, but the hunt turned up nothing but a bike and a woman's pocketbook. No one really expected to find anything; everyone knew that with the water warming, the body would have floated to the surface. Unless, of course, it was being weighed down on the lake bottom.

Observing all this activity from the shore were Maria's parents, Mike and Frances.

"Maria is still alive," Mike told a reporter. "She has been gone so long that if something happened to her, evidence would have turned up by now." Endorsing Sheriff Deisz's theory about the case, he said, "I think some couple that lost a child has taken her. I know it would be easy for a couple to pick her up and love her and not want to bring her back."

Saturday, April 26, was a big day in Sycamore. It was prom night. Frances Ridulph had driven her daughter Pat forty-eight miles to the A. C. Steiner Dress Shop, in downtown Plainfield, to buy a formal dress for the prom. It was a very special dress, "gorgeous," in fact, Pat thought.

The morning of the prom, Pat put in a shift at the drive-in restaurant where she worked part-time. At 2:30, she went to get her hair done. When her date came to pick her up, she was good to go. At the time, she was juggling two boyfriends, a boy named Brian and a Sycamore High senior named Phillip Fleetwood. Phillip was her prom date.

When the young man arrived, he shook hands with Mr. and Mrs. Ridulph, then handed Pat her corsage, a yellow rose together with an orchid, tied with green-and-white ribbons. It matched her floor-length mint-green dress perfectly. Phillip was serious-minded and considerate and was thinking about becoming a teacher. Like everyone in town, he had not forgotten Maria and was in the process of assembling a scrapbook of all the articles written about her kidnapping that he was planning to present to the Ridulph family as a keepsake. Pat's parents liked Phillip a lot.

Phillip and Pat drove off in his car, and their first stop was a pre-prom party at a friend's house; then, at 9:00 P.M., they arrived at the prom with the other kids. The theme was "Sayonara," the Japanese word for *farewell*, and also the name of a popular Marlon Brando movie that had come out a few months before, about a U.S. Air Force major who falls in love with a Japanese woman. It was going to be a long and wonderful night, with an after-prom party to follow over at the Elks Club. Pat expected to be dancing until four in the morning.

As Pat mingled with some friends, one of her teachers pulled Phillip over to a corner to have a private chat. Pat saw Phillip nodding, taking in what he was hearing. What were they were talking about, Pat wondered. Then Phillip came back and said he had something to tell her. The teacher had just given him some upsetting news.

They had found a body.

12

·········

THE MUSHROOM HUNTERS

Mr. and Mrs. Frank Sitar had driven 275 miles from their farm in Hopkins, Minnesota, to the northern reaches of Illinois for a no-frills spring vacation. Frank Sitar was a fifty-seven-year-old retired farmer. He and his wife had been coming to Illinois for many years to hunt mushrooms.

The Sitars crossed the state border and stopped for lunch in the town of Elizabeth in Jo Daviess County, which the locals pronounced *Davis*. At the coffee shop they inquired about a good place to hunt mushrooms, and their waitress happened to know the perfect spot—it was about two-and-a-half miles east of Woodbine. The Sitars were given precise driving instructions: stay on Route 20 until they reached the railroad underpass, just before the road started to curve west up a hill. The place was called the Herman Bonnett woods. You can't miss it. A farmer named Ray Cahill owned the land, but he wouldn't mind letting a nice couple on vacation onto his property.

Late April was a great time for hunting mushrooms in northern Illinois. The first morels of the season would be springing to life out of the moist, blackened earth. Morels are among the most distinctive-looking genus of mushrooms in existence, with a delicate honeycomb flesh prized by gourmet cooks and French chefs, although it didn't take much skill in the kitchen to make a delicious meal from morels, breaded and fried, or just plain sautéed in butter with a sprinkle of salt and cracked pepper.

Following the waitress's directions to the Cahill property, the Sitars took a leisurely drive east on Route 20 until they saw the railroad underpass and pulled over into the graveled wayside stop on the state road. They got out of their car there and proceeded to slog deep into a thicket of brush and trees.

They had gone about three hundred yards, eyes glued to the earth looking for mushrooms, when they saw something strange. At first, Sitar thought it was abandoned game, maybe a deer. They got a closer look. *Dear God*. It was a small body, lying next to a downed evergreen tree, and jammed under a rotting log. Mrs. Sitar gasped. The Sitars didn't touch a thing. They hurried back to their car, drove to the nearest pay phone, and called the local sheriff. It was 2:30 on Saturday afternoon, April 26, just about the time Pat Ridulph was getting her hair done for the prom.

The sheriff of Jo Daviess County, Emma "Two Gun"

Grebner, was Illinois's only female sheriff. She rushed to the scene, joined by the county coroner, James Furlong, who owned the funeral home in Galena.

Observing the remains, Furlong and Sheriff Grebner saw that the body was lying face up with the head slightly tipped. The right arm was crossed over the chest and the right leg was slightly bent. The shoulder-length hair with brown bangs was still in place, but it was the only feature that could possibly identify the body as having once been an adorable little girl named Maria Ridulph. From the body's decomposing condition, it was evident that she had been there in the woods all winter. Her rib cage was partially exposed. This was not normal decomposition. Animals must have gotten to the body.

Sheriff Grebner realized this must be the child who had been kidnapped in December down in Sycamore, more than a hundred miles away. It had to be Maria Ridulph, the only young girl recently reported missing in northern Illinois. Grebner and the coroner drove back to the county seat in Galena, at which point Furlong called his counterpart in DeKalb County and communicated the fact that a body had been found that in all probability was the Ridulph child.

Maria's body was transported to the sheriff's garage next to the county jail in Galena. She still wore her checked shirt, cotton undershirt, and brown socks, but her coat, pants, shoes, and other garments were missing. The remains, along with Maria's clothes, were spread out on a sheet on the floor, and a twenty-five-year-old photographer, Jim Shaffer, was called in to take photos. Shaffer took a deep gulp. The brown socks still on Maria's feet really got to him.

Shaffer worked for the *Dubuque Telegraph Herald*, but every now and then he helped out the sheriff because Jo Daviess County didn't have the budget for a police photographer. Schaffer was civic-minded and never billed the county. He did it as a favor, and it also built up his police contacts. He took pictures with his Swiss-made camera, a single-lens reflex Hasselblad, one of the most expensive cameras in the world. When he was done with his work, Maria's body was taken to the Furlong Funeral Chapel. A preliminary autopsy was conducted there by the coroner. Furlong ruled out a blow to the head as the cause of death. No visible skull fracture or broken bones were evident. There was no sign of Maria having been stabbed, shot, or strangled. Due to the advanced stage of decomposition, however, the cause of death was impossible to determine. A dentist from Galena examined the teeth. He noted three fillings in the lower molars and two in the upper. A photostat of Maria's dental chart would later show the fillings to be identical to Maria's. A one-and-a-half inch scar on the ball of Maria's left foot was also recorded. She had once cut herself while playing in the rain after a storm. Now there was no question about identity. Later, a pathologist was brought in from Rockford to conduct the official full-fledged autopsy. One distressing fact that emerged from the discovery of the body and the autopsy was that not a single clue as to the killer's identity was brought to light.

• • • • • • • • •

The call to Mike and Frances Ridulph came from Assistant State's Attorney James Boyle. He said he needed Mike and Frances to go with him on a "long ride." He refused to say much more, except that they should get ready; he'd be right over. The phone rang again. A newspaper reporter was calling. He had gotten a tip that he needed to check out. A body had been found near Galena, and he was hearing that it was a girl, but as he understood it, the approximate age was ten or eleven. Mike thanked him. It was more information than he'd gotten from Boyle. Based on the reporter's description, the Ridulphs were pretty convinced that, because Maria was seven years old, this would be another wild-goose chase. But the news made fifteen-year-old Kay Ridulph sick. She ran to the bathroom and got weepy. A few minutes later, a police vehicle pulled up. Mike and Frances got in, and only then did they realize that this could be the real thing; in the car they found DeKalb County's four top law-enforcement officers: James Boyle; his boss, State's Attorney Carl Swanson; Sheriff Deisz; and Chief Hindenburg. It was a grim two-hour ride northwest to Galena. On the way, the Ridulphs were given additional information, all terrible. The remains were that of a little girl who had been wearing brown anklet socks at the time of her death. Frances braced herself. She always knew those brown socks Maria wore the night of her abduction would one day factor in the identification process. They were brand new. Maria had worn them for the first time on December 3, 1957.

When the Ridulphs got to Galena, they were driven straight to the home of Sheriff Emma Grebner, who briefed them on where things stood. It was the news the Ridulphs had been dreading for 144 days. Frances wanted to view the body to make a positive identification. She insisted that she had to see Maria one last time to be sure it was her child. Everyone wanted to spare her the ordeal, but Frances could not be dissuaded. Finally, Mike spoke up. What good would it do? he asked his wife. He was very firm, and Frances finally backed off. It was agreed that positive identification could be legally determined by showing the clothes found on the body to Maria's parents.

As the Ridulphs sat in Sheriff Grebner's parlor, the first item of clothing was brought in. It was a little girl's black-and-white checked flannel shirt, with a patch on the left elbow.

Frances choked back her tears. "I did that myself," she said, pointing to the patch that she had sewn onto the sleeve. "I took the patch from a shirt of Kay's." It was definitely Maria's. There was no doubt about it. The brown socks were also displayed to the Ridulphs. Having never been laundered, their trademark was still visible.

"We've been expecting this," Frances said. There was nothing left for the Ridulphs to do. Showing them more clothing from the body would just add to their pain. A police officer was assigned to drive Mike and Frances back to Sycamore. On the way, they tried to talk through their grief.

"There's one thing I would still like to know," Frances said. "I would like to know how she died. They've got to catch that man. They've just got to get him." They didn't get to their neat white-framed house on Archie Place until five in the morning. Only then did Frances burst into tears.

At dawn's early light, Boyle, Deisz, and Hindenburg were taken to the Cahill farm to check out the crime scene for themselves. Boyle, for one, couldn't believe the body had been removed before he'd had a chance to examine the remains. In any event, the first thing he observed was a jerry-rigged pasture gate consisting of three wires, just west of the zigzag in the road where the Sitars had parked. Boyle wondered whether this was how the kidnapper, with Maria's body presumably in the trunk of his car, had made his entry. Tire tracks would not be visible because the earth had been frozen in December. The body must have been placed in the woods either on the night she was kidnapped or in the days thereafter. It was impossible for anything amiss to have been seen from Route 20. Only serendipity had brought the mushroom hunters there.

"Awfully good hiding place," Boyle remarked.

Everything Boyle was hearing about the remains, especially the missing pants, reinforced his conviction that the killer was a menace to other children and was likely to strike again.

"The man we are seeking is definitely a sex deviant," he stated.

Hindenburg put in his two cents. He deduced that whoever hid Maria's body must have been familiar with the lay of the land. One more thing: the body must have been placed there during the daytime because no one could have found such a good hideaway in the dark.

All day Sunday a platoon of twenty-five state troopers, reinforced by civilian volunteers, searched the woods. They were told to be on the lookout for Maria's missing corduroy pants and her black-and-white saddle shoes with zippers, tan coat, and undergarment. Nothing was found. Indeed, all that resulted from the effort was a traffic tie-up on Route 20.

I3

....

MARIA COMES HOME

Sycamore rallied to comfort the grieving family. Operating on no sleep, Mike and Frances attended Sunday services at the Evangelical Lutheran Church of St. John, where Maria had gone to Sunday school and attained a perfect attendance record for three years running. They bowed their heads as they heard Reverend Going, the pastor of St. John, ask the congregation to pray for the Ridulphs. Discovering Maria's body represented the end of a long road, and a spiritual and physical defeat for Sycamore. Mayor Harold "Red" Johnson spoke for everyone when he said, "In some ways it's a relief that her body has been found. But now we must get the killer."

Kay took it very hard. As a family, the Ridulphs decided the time had come to dismantle Maria's Corner, where the little one kept her toys and books and her tests from school.

Also, there was her pogo stick, the Christmas present still in its wrapping that Maria never got to see. It was just too heartbreaking a reminder of her death.

On Sunday night, Maria went home. A hearse carrying her body returned her to Sycamore via Route 20, then Illinois State Roads 26 and 64. It took just over two hours to make the journey. In all likelihood, it was the same route Maria's killer had taken, only in reverse.

In the ongoing investigation, chaos prevailed. Richard Auerbach, still in charge of the Chicago FBI field office, failed to send a single agent to Galena, though he said the agency stood ready to lend any technical assistance if asked.

"We're officially out of it," Auerbach said, noting that under the Federal Kidnapping Act of 1932, the FBI had no legal jurisdiction because Maria had not been transported across state lines. From where Maria's body was discovered, Wisconsin sat just twelve miles directly north, and Iowa, fifteen miles due west. It was a devastating accident of geography that the nation's preeminent law-enforcement agency could no longer be involved in the case.

The Illinois state police put Lieutenant Ray Kramer in charge of the investigation.

"It's going to be a difficult case," Kramer admitted. "We don't know how, when, or where she died."

Police Chief Hindenburg was on his way out. After he'd complained about outside interference in the way he was running his department, a feud with Sycamore's Mayor Johnson had cost him his job. Hindenburg was fifty-four years old and well liked in Sycamore as an all-around decent man, but he had very few of the qualifications needed to be point person in a homicide investigation, especially one that was the focus of national attention. Prior to his appointment as police chief, he had served as an army sergeant in World War II, then worked in maintenance at Sycamore High for fifteen years. He also drove the school bus. He'd been chief for only a year when the mayor let him go. Just the same, because of his knowledge of the Maria Ridulph case, he was named a special police investigator for a thirty-day period. A city vehicle was placed at his disposal, but he was given no funds to finance any out-of-town travel. One factor in Hindenburg's favor was that he truly wanted to bring Maria's killer to justice.

Dysfunction reached its peak when Sheriff Emma Grebner and Sheriff Alf Deisz, her counterpart in DeKalb County, started bickering with each other in public. Deisz was furious because he thought that Grebner had botched the handling of Maria's remains. In his opinion, the body had been too hastily hauled off to the county garage before his office and the state police could dispatch crime-scene experts to the location. Who knows what evidence had been destroyed in the removal process? It was police ineptitude at its worst. Grebner was deeply offended by his criticism and didn't appreciate being pushed around in her own county.

Reached at home on Sunday night, April 27, Sheriff Grebner told a newspaper reporter that she had no special plans just yet to investigate Maria's murder, because she was cooking dinner!

"I'm getting supper in the kitchen," she said. "I have other things to think of at the moment."

Sheriff Grebner pointed out that there was very little "sinning" taking place in Jo Daviess County. Not many ex-cons lived up her way and she could not remember the last case involving a child predator.

"There's not much use in getting excited. It doesn't look like the girl was killed in my county."

Deisz couldn't believe the woman's indifference. In his opinion, there had to be some connection between Maria's killer and the secluded dumping grounds where the body had been hidden.

"Why did he pick the place he did?" Deisz wondered. "A very good place, incidentally. We believe he did it because he knew the area well." He said all signs pointed to the killer being a "sex maniac from the Galena area."

Sheriff Grebner was an interesting character. At age forty-seven, she was in her fourth year in office, having won election twice. With her horn-rimmed glasses and floral print dresses, she could pass for a schoolmarm, but with that holster-ready six-shooter she carried, Annie Oakley was more like it. A newspaper profile once described her as a "real gun-totin', badge-wearing sheriff." But, undeniably, she was out of her depth in the Maria Ridulph case.

"This is the biggest case we've had since I took office, and I don't like it," she conceded. Her husband, Lawrence, who she succeeded in office when he couldn't run for reelection because of term limits, was now her chief deputy. He pretty much ran the department, while Emma was content to answer the phones and work the police radio. All this would prove laughable except for the fact that, technically, Emma Grebner was in charge of the investigation because she was chief law-enforcement officer in the jurisdiction where the body was found. As Hugh Hough, a future Pulitzer Prize–winning crime reporter for the *Chicago Sun-Times* put it, "Only Maria Ridulph's kidnapper could have been happy" about the squabbling.

Governor William Stratton of Illinois finally had had enough. It was time for the grown-ups to step in. Four days after the body was found, all the lawmen involved were ordered to the State Building in Chicago. The gathering signaled that law enforcement at the highest state level was now in charge. The superintendent of the state police announced that henceforth the highly regarded Emil Toffant, a Mob-busting lieutenant in the criminal-investigation section, would be running the Maria Ridulph case. Assisting him would be State Trooper Michael Frankovich, reassigned from the stolen-car division. A pledge was made to pick up every ex-con, known sex offender, and "moron" in northern Illinois for questioning. Basically, the state police were starting over from scratch.

Sycamore said good-bye to the little girl who was now its most famous citizen.

At a wake Monday night, two hundred mourners filed past her white casket, which had been personally picked out by Frances. Within, Maria lay on a bed of plush lambskin, certainly a caring mother's handiwork to make her child's journey comfortable.

The next day, Maria's second-grade classmates from West Elementary School came as a group to pay their last respects.

The funeral was held on Wednesday, April 30, 1958, under a warm spring sun. At 1:30 in the afternoon, the funeral procession formed in front of the Ridulph house. Mike and Frances and the Ridulph children climbed into a Cadillac and were driven to the Evangelical Lutheran Church of St. John.

When they got there, Lieutenant Emil Toffant of the state police and twelve plainclothes troopers were standing outside, observing and scanning the face of every man entering the church. Some of the mourners were also photographed by a state police photographer who was on the lookout for men with blond hair and pale complexions. Would Johnny be deranged enough to attend the funeral of the child he had butchered? Not such a preposterous notion if you believed that he had been among the volunteers searching for Maria the night of December 3.

Eight FBI agents were also in attendance, not as investigators, but to mourn. They had come to know the Ridulphs during the early days of the kidnapping, before they were pulled off the case.

Kathy Sigman was also there, wearing white shoes, bobby sox, and a fifties formal coat with a Peter Pan collar. All the lawmen were keeping a watchful eye on the eight-year-old girl, the only witness who could identify Johnny. For the time being, Kathy was once again under twenty-four-hour police protection. Chief William Hindenburg had really stirred things up by saying he believed Kathy was in mortal danger.

"She's the only person who can identify Johnny," he'd said, and he'd asked school authorities to put two teachers on the job watching her movements during recess.

Kathy attended the funeral with her parents and, hovering behind her at all times, James Boyle. He never left her side. She was his most precious and only witness. Without her, there was probably no case.

Every seat in the church was taken, all three hundred. A spray of white and pink carnations mixed with sweetheart roses adorned the casket. First to enter were Mike and Frances, followed by their children Pat, Kay, and Chuck. Frances shook her head, murmuring, no, no. Mike helped her to the front pew.

Reverend Going's sermon had special meaning because he had offered spiritual guidance to the family throughout the kidnapping ordeal.

"All hope and pray that the criminal will be apprehended and that he will receive the punishment the authorities authorize," he told the mourners. He also expressed concern for the soul of the killer. "No one can have peace while his conscience is weighted with the knowledge of this great sin. He must make his peace with God and man." In her grief, Frances had seen to every detail. She requested the hymn, "Jesus Loves Me" because it had been Maria's favorite. It was sung by the president of the First National Bank of DeKalb, who had a beautiful voice. Frances had also selected the four teenage pallbearers who carried the coffin out of the church to the hearse. They were classmates of Pat's and Kay's from Sycamore High School.

Maria's final resting place was Elmwood Cemetery, only three blocks from her house. Her parents had seen to the purchase of four plots: for Mom, Dad, and Maria, who was to be buried between them. The fourth plot was set aside for Chuck. Pat and Kay were left out on the presumption that their final resting places would be determined years in the future once they had married and had their own children.

"Dust thou art, to dust returnest," said Reverend Going at the gravesite.

"Chuck didn't cry at all," Kay wrote in her diary that night. "I was really proud of him."

The list of suspects grew apace. With Sycamore no longer the predominant center of attention, it now seemed as if the killer could be from remote northwestern Illinois or possibly from Wisconsin or Iowa.

A twenty-seven-year-old motorist from the city of Pontiac, Illinois, arrested on a drunk-driving charge, kept mumbling "I didn't mean to do it," when he was locked up in the county jail. No big deal, until it was determined that he had once lived in Sycamore, two hours away. At six feet with blondish hair, he fit the general description of Johnny. Could it be? Once he sobered up, he denied any involvement, and there was nothing to hold him on.

Interest turned to a drifter answering Johnny's description who had hitchhiked his way to the tiny village of

Hazel Green, Wisconsin, on the night of December 4 or 5—nobody could remember the exact date. Encountering the town marshal, he asked for shelter and ended up spending the night in jail because there was nowhere else to sleep. The next morning, he was seen having breakfast at Jen's Cafe, looking strung out and complaining how hard it was to find work these days. What struck the marshal was the vagrant's age. Usually hobos were much older. Hazel Green was 250 miles from where Maria's body had been dumped, but, suddenly, tracking down this drifter became a hot lead for Illinois law enforcement.

A thirty-two-year-old vagrant walked into a coffee shop in Milwaukee and blurted out that he had killed Maria Ridulph. He threatened to kill the waitress unless she called police. When cops got there, he changed his story to say that it was his old cellmate from a prison in Vandalia, Illinois, who had confessed to killing Maria. Later, the vagrant said he had made everything up because he was broke and needed a place to sleep.

Word filtered down from the prison grapevine that the police ought to check out an organist who had played a nightclub engagement in Rockford on December 3. It became the "best tip yet," and the musician was an active suspect because of his prior history as a sex offender.

Suspects materialized only to be briskly cleared. There were at once too many and not enough potential perpetrators. The net was widening and yet, perversely, going nowhere.

....

Time marched on. In September 1958, William Hindenburg was critically injured when a car driven by his sister-in-law swerved into the wrong lane of traffic and was hit broadside by another vehicle. Hindenburg, who was sitting in the passenger seat, died a month later. In December, Sheriff Alf Deisz left office. A few months later, Richard Auerbach of the FBI Chicago bureau was reassigned to run the FBI's San Francisco bureau. The sole original investigator remaining on the case was James Boyle.

December 3, 1958, marked the first anniversary of Maria's kidnapping. All the Chicago and Sycamore newspapers ran retrospectives. "Nothing has been found yet," Boyle was quoted as saying. "Nothing may ever be found." The probe ground on, the *Chicago Tribune* reported, "but the trail seems very cold."

December 3, 1959: It was the second anniversary, and yet another newspaper retrospective. Lieutenant Toffant remained on the case, assisted by four state troopers, down from twelve troopers the previous year. More than two hundred suspects had been quizzed, and twenty-nine volumes of reports accumulated. But work seemed to be winding down.

December 3, 1960, the third-year anniversary. Boyle was still around.

"There have been at least fifteen or twenty men who matched the kidnapper in almost every detail." But no arrests.

December 3, 1961. A fourth anniversary headline said it all: *Bitter Night Memory Fades.*

....

Sycamore did all it could to enshrine Maria's name. A Maria Ridulph Memorial was mounted on the side of the new municipal building. It was an eight-foot-square map of the city highlighting all of Sycamore's schools, parks, and churches and other points of interest. It was hoped that the memorial would immortalize the name of the little girl in the hearts of Sycamore forever. There was unanimity among townspeople knowledgeable about local history that the kidnapping had been the most significant event in the city's century of existence.

The Ridulphs appreciated everything. Thousands of letters offering condolences had been sent to the family from all over the United States. The Ridulphs read each one and cherished them all. Among them was this letter, postmarked Sycamore, and mailed on Sunday, April 26, 1958, the day after Maria's body was found.

Dear Francis [sic] and Mike,

We heard last night of the discovery of little Maria's body and with all your friends and neighbors our hearts are heavy with sorrow for you.

There are no words to comfort you I know. Just try and remember that what you saw was not really your little Maria, but just the poor shell of her body. I know your lovely little girl is well and happy in Heaven with Jesus and his Blessed Mother. Our prayers are always with you and a candle burns on the Altar of Our Lady in Church to bless and comfort you. Your burden is too great to bear alone but our Savior who bore all our burdens will help you. And always remember that now you have a little saint in Heaven to pray for you too.

God bless you.
Sincerely
Eileen and Ralph Tessier

BOOK II

14

·········

THE SIXTIES

A year passed, and then another, and then many more, and the mystery of who murdered Maria Ridulph remained unsolved. It was the shadow that hung over Sycamore.

December 30, 1961, saw the marriage of Pat Ridulph to her beau, William "Bill" Quinn, a handsome fellow from the tiny village of Towanda, Illinois, population four hundred, whom Pat had met at Illinois State University, where she was majoring in education and minoring in accounting. The *Sycamore True Republican* reported that the wedding was "of much significance" to the city, a deft way of acknowledging Maria's place in local history without referring specifically to her tragic murder in the typically breezy wedding announcement.

Maria would have been eleven had she been alive to attend her sister's wedding.

Kay was a student at Northern Illinois University, and

in the fall of 1960, Chuck, at the age of fourteen, left for prep school at Concordia College, in Milwaukee. It was operated by the Lutheran church, and he intended to study for the ministry.

Remembering it many years later, Chuck said, "I have been asked many times if the tragic loss of my sister had influenced my decision to study for the ministry. I can only say this: I don't know. But this I do know: the kidnapping and murder of Maria, without any doubt, changed and influenced who I was from the very moment she was taken from us.

"Maria was kidnapped when I was eleven. By the time I was thirteen, I was drinking at every opportunity, sometimes even going back to school after drinking some wine during lunchtime. By the time I was fourteen, I was drinking on a regular basis. By the time I was sixteen, I was drinking on a daily basis. I have been asked if Maria's tragic death led me to alcohol, and many times people have commented that it is no wonder that I drank because of the pain which this brought into our lives. But to that question I can truthfully say that I had a tendency to like the taste of wine and its effect even before Maria was gone. Did this event influence my preexisting problem with alcohol? Here again I can only say that Maria's murder influenced my very being.

"During my junior year at Concordia College my drinking was out of control. All I did was drink. I was kicked off the basketball team for drinking, which was a major blow to me, and still bothers me to this day. My grades took a nosedive, and I was asked not to return. It was a different time then, and alcohol was not really considered to be the addiction that it is today. My drinking was not seen as anything more than unacceptable behavior. I was seventeen.

"I enrolled for my senior year of high school at the Sycamore High School. I continued to drink daily, often times intoxicated by midday at school. My journey to the ministry was on hold, to say the least.

"In September of 1963, I met a girl who was new to Sycamore at a party. There was a lot of drinking going on, which was usual for my senior class, and Betty and I really hit it off. Our first official date was at her brother's wedding. There was a lot of drinking at the reception, and after we left, I was drunk, and I took her to the cemetery to see Maria's grave. It was dark, and in my drunken state, I couldn't find the grave. What a first date. In December, we were secretly married with the aid of a Kane County clerk, which was not using very good judgment to say the least. Betty was sixteen. I was seventeen. It was six years after I was considered a child, six years after Maria's murder."

In 1963, the Tessiers also celebrated a wedding, that of their eldest daughter, Katheran, the girl born in England who had sailed to America on the *Queen Mary* in 1946 with her war-bride mother and half brother Johnny. The groom was Wayne Fetzer, just out of a three-year hitch in the U.S. Army and now servicing vending machines in Sycamore. The wedding took place at St. Mary's and received prominent coverage in the *Daily Chronicle* as, at the time, Katheran was working for the newspaper's "Women's

Page." The reception for two hundred guests was held at the Veterans of Foreign Wars meeting hall.

The same year Katheran got married, her sister, Jeanne, who was a junior at Sycamore High, applied to be a foreign-exchange student. If selected, she'd spend the summer living with an Italian family on the island of Sardinia. Dizzy with excitement, she couldn't wait to tell her parents, but their response was not what she'd expected. "They called me an idiot," Jeanne remembers. "They said I was never going to be picked, and even if they chose me I didn't have any money to go." A few weeks later, she got the good news that she had been accepted, and to finance her trip, she set up a table at school and sold her pastel-chalk drawings. On June 20, she left Sycamore for New York City, where she boarded the ocean liner *Seven Seas*, bound for Europe. An American Field Service representative met her when her ship docked at Rotterdam and escorted her to Italy and her host family. She got back to the United States on September 10, unfortunately five days too late to be at her sister's wedding.

Jeanne was invited by the Sycamore Rotary Club to give a lunchtime talk on her Sardinian adventure and described the island's tropical climate and generous people, who, she said, "lean to Communism." That fall, she played the Grand Duchess in the Sycamore High School production of the Kaufman-Hart comedy *You Can't Take It with You*. Behind the scenes, she also supervised makeup. In December, she won a $25 U.S. savings bond from the Northern Illinois Gas Company in a "Voice of Democracy" contest. For her sixteenth birthday, her friends threw her a surprise slumber party and gave her a ski jacket they'd all chipped in for.

It seemed to everyone in Sycamore that Jeanne Tessier was an intellectually gifted standout destined for exceptional achievement. Amazingly, in such a small town, where it was hard to keep a secret, no one suspected that inside the Tessier home at 227 Center Cross Street, monstrous things were happening.

Jeanne was just a toddler when her father, Ralph Tessier, the well-liked hardware-store salesman who everyone in town called Popeye, would hold her in his arms and "finger" her with his dirty, calloused hands. Ralph called it "tickling," but Jeanne tells a very different story in her self-published memoir *Unspoken Truth: A Memoir of Abuse*.

The cruelty of her parents toward her, Jeanne says, was sustained and unrelenting: a "sudden slap" for no reason; an "animal meanness" that she says devoured, "chewed away" at her self-esteem. Just the sight of her would throw her parents into an inexplicable rage. One or the other would scream at her, "Wipe that look off your face!" It would mystify her—*what look?* "What was this look of mine that they hated so much? My mother seemed most of the time to hate the sight of me."

All his life, Ralph Tessier had borne a grudge against educated and wealthy people. A nice couple who were fellow churchgoers at St. Mary's once invited him and Eileen to have dinner with them. In Ralph's opinion, they were full of themselves, "holier-than-thou," and he was doing a slow burn when the conversation turned to the vexing problem that faced all young parents—babies crying in the middle of the night. As the mother of seven, Eileen could speak to the practical side of it. Ralph, however, saw it another way. To him, a birth was not a wondrous event but, in his words, "another goddamn mouth to feed." That evening, he must have been feeling particularly ill-tempered, or maybe he had had too much to drink. Eileen sat there, mortified, hearing her husband say that he never had trouble with his children crying because all he had to do was take a piece of string, tie it around their throats, and turn and twist it until they couldn't breathe. Their holier-than-thou hosts were speechless; was he kidding or serious?

When the couple got home, Ralph, feeling very pleased with himself, recounted what he'd said to Jeanne.

"That shut them up good," he told her, laughing demonically.

Something Jeanne had heard when she was around ten was another story he'd told for shock value. His wife was pregnant, and he took her on a motorcycle ride around the neighborhood, deliberately driving over bumpy gravel roads in the hope of terminating her pregnancy because he didn't want another baby. Jeanne quickly calculated the timeline.

"That would have been me," she said.

Jeanne slept in the attic, which had been converted to a bedroom she shared with her sister, Katheran. Sometimes she'd kneel at the window at night and pray that somebody would see her, "recognize my misery," and come to her rescue. She could see herself vanishing from sight, just like Maria Ridulph, but she had to wonder whether her family would even notice she was gone. Maria's kidnapping had made her understand a fundamental truth: the world was a dangerous place where not even little girls were safe.

The worst of Ralph's sexual abuse of Jeanne took place when the Tessiers rented out their house on Center Cross Street and moved to a dreary unincorporated community known as Clare, just outside Sycamore. It had a post office, general store, bar, a cluster of about twenty houses, and not much else. Ralph had quit the hardware business because he was so fed up with working for his boss, Mr. Hagen, and he'd gotten a job managing the Clare general store. The Tessiers lived in an apartment above it. It was a woeful time for the family because the new place was a comedown from Center Cross Street; everyone was just miserable there, and when Ralph got a part-time job driving the school bus, Jeanne and Katheran were embarrassed.

Early one summer day, when Jeanne was around six, she put on her favorite cotton dress, one she loved because it wasn't a hand-me-down from Katheran, and it made her feel pretty. For whatever reason—it could have been that she had run out of clean underwear, "a frequent occurrence," Jeanne says, or perhaps she just liked the sensation of the cool breeze on her bare bottom—she was naked under her dress when she flew down the flight of stairs above the general store. Ralph, who was working in the store, leered at her. He had a "hunger" for young flesh, Jeanne says.

"I know what you want. I know what you're looking

for," he said, taking her by the arm and dragging her into the cornfield behind the store. He threw her down on the dirt and climbed on top of her. When he was finished, Ralph went back to the store, leaving Jeanne bloodied and in tears, and her dress in tatters. She ran back upstairs—and straight into her mother. Eileen wanted to know what had happened. Jeanne told her everything.

"She lost her mind," Jeanne wrote of her mother in her memoir. Eileen screamed and hit her, bellowing, "Liar! Liar!" Then she pulled the torn dress off Jeanne and left her naked, in her room. Jeanne never saw the dress again.

Not long thereafter, following another terrible day of being whipped with the buckle end of her father's belt, Jeanne decided to write a letter to her parents telling them how much she hated them and saying she never wanted to see them again. She folded the letter and boldly marched down the steps, handed it to Ralph and Eileen, and went right back upstairs to her room. Several minutes later, she heard her father calling her. She walked out of her room and saw her parents standing at the bottom of the landing. In his hand, Ralph menacingly twirled her letter. Eileen was standing right behind him. Jeanne bounded down, and Ralph waved the letter in her face.

"Do you know what we're going to do with this?"

Jeanne shook her head, no.

"We're going to take this to Father Cain and let him see what kind of girl you are to say such terrible things to your parents. We're going to give it to him and let him deal with you."

Father Cain was a hard disciplinarian, and Ralph, probably aware that Jeanne was terrified of having any dealings with the parish priest, definitely hit the right button. But little Jeanne, even though she was on the brink of bursting into tears, managed an indifferent shrug.

"Alright then, that's what we'll do. We'll let Father Cain take care of you," was Ralph's pronouncement.

He made a fussy show of placing the note on a top shelf in the kitchen. "I'm going to leave it right here where you can't get at it, and when I'm good and ready, I'm going to give it to Father Cain and let him give it to you." Then he ordered Jeanne to go back to her room. That talk with Father Cain never happened, of course. The brainy third-grader had outbluffed her parents.

A few weeks later, Jeanne used a chair to climb to the top of the refrigerator and reach the note, which was still on the shelf where Ralph had put it. Then she jumped down, took it to her room and hid it in a secret place behind the chimney. Only years later did Jeanne come to fully realize that Ralph would never have risked taking her to Father Cain for fear of what family secrets she might blurt out.

The Tessiers moved back to 227 Center Cross Street. Ralph got his job at the hardware store back. In those days, Eileen was working part-time as a proofreader at the *Daily Chronicle,* and Ralph, who very often came home for lunch, would be alone in the house with Jeanne, especially in the winter, because she was susceptible to bronchitis and was frequently too sick to go to school. On other days, he'd insist that she skip school, even when she was feeling fine. As Jeanne relates in her memoir, "My father kept me home to fulfill his own dark needs." One consequence of Ralph's sexual abuse was a severe kidney infection, when she was nine years old, from "collateral damage from a too large member in a too small frame." His unspeakable acts of incest escalated during the summer, Jeanne says, after which Ralph would rush over to the ice-cream store and bring her back a chocolate malt—a twisted reward for being such a good girl.

15

....

HOMECOMING

John Tessier mustered out after four years of service in the U.S. Air Force, most of it stationed in Japan, and returned to Sycamore. Of course, he didn't have much going for him, and he lacked a trade, which would have helped his prospects. For a while, he worked for the local phone company, then his aunt Mary, who was Ralph's sister, pulled a few strings and got him a job at the General Electric plant in DeKalb, where she worked as a secretary. Her boss at GE held her in high regard (she was state champion in speed typing), and since her nephew was just out of the military, he was happy to give him a break. John was put to work repairing motors on the factory floor.

Now that he had a job, John also got reacquainted with his old high school chums. One was a fellow named Dennis Twadell. Like John, Twadell had completed his military service, in his case, in the U.S. Navy. They had had a lot in common growing up in that they were both skinny—Twadell stood six feet three and weighed about 160 pounds in high school—and they'd both worked as stock boys after dropping out of high school. Twadell also lived with a stepfather he didn't get along with, George Meier, who happened to be a former Sycamore police chief.

"I just didn't see eye to eye with my stepdad," Twadell said. "Whenever I did something out of bounds, it got back to him because he was a cop. I'd come home and he'd say, 'I need to see you out in the garage.'" That meant Twadell was about to get the crap beaten out of him. Over the years, Twadell says, he'd sustained broken noses, a dislocated shoulder, and had had several teeth knocked out by his stepfather.

"Ralph Tessier and my stepdad were two of a kind," Twadell continued. "John was over at my house quite a lot after his run-ins with Ralph, pissing and moaning about getting socked around."

Twadell was living in a one-room apartment on Syca-more Street when he heard that John Tessier was back in town, and they'd meet over a few bottles of Budweiser on a Friday or Saturday night, usually at the bar at the Jane Fargo Hotel or Burgee's restaurant, across the street from the county courthouse.

On a Saturday morning in the spring of 1962, at the Elks Club, John Tessier ran into a guy playing pool. His name was James Gassaway, and they started hanging out together. Gassaway was a country boy from a West Virginia steel town who looked like Conrad Twitty. Like John, he'd served in the U.S. Air Force, and had ended up in Sycamore after an air force buddy connected him with a job at a factory making lawn sprinklers. Later, he worked at Anaconda Wire and Cable. He found Sycamore to be a nice place to settle down, flush with factories and manufacturing plants and hospitable to able-bodied men fresh out of the service.

"You'd quit a job one day and get a job the next," recalls Gassaway. "Jobs were plentiful in those days."

When he'd first relocated to Sycamore, Gassaway had lived in a boardinghouse. Then he heard about two brothers, Terry and Mike Glen, who were looking for a roommate to share expenses at their house at 751 Carlson Street. It was a narrow 900-square-foot house with three small bedrooms, plus a couch in the living room. Like the house, Terry Glen was compact, standing about five feet six. His brother, Mike, had served as a U.S. Air Force air-traffic controller in France. Mechanically inclined, in civilian life, Mike had found work as a draftsman. For some reason, he went everywhere by taxi and had no desire to own a car, very unusual in car-crazy America. Mike Glen was smart and good-looking, almost too good-looking; his friends used to tease him, saying he was too pretty to be a boy, which he didn't appreciate at all.

Guys were always coming and going at 751 Carlson Street, the roommate situation being fluid and subject to continual turnover. So when Terry Glen got drafted (he became a Green Beret) and more space became available, James Gassaway and John Tessier signed on. The rent, with utilities, was reasonable, about $80 a month split four ways. Another guy, Floyd Tucker, who everyone called Gator, was also in and out, depending on where else he was able to hang his hat.

Gassaway found John Tessier to be a personable guy, good company and quite intelligent, though at times maybe a little conceited; John seemed to think he was smarter than just about anybody else. There were quirks in John's personality that grated on other people but amused the laid-back country boy from West Virginia. Once, they were drinking Old Style beer at a restaurant in Sycamore, and at almost two in the morning, John ordered home fries and a raw egg from the kitchen. When it arrived, he cracked the egg open over the warm fries and let it cook. He offered Gassaway a taste: not all that great, not too bad either, in Gassaway's opinion.

Because John had grown up in Sycamore, he took the lead in showing Gassaway around. They went on a double date to see Gregory Peck in *The Guns of Navarone*, which they thoroughly enjoyed, and afterward they all went for burgers and malts. At a house party in Rockford, Tessier introduced Gassaway to a girl he was dating, an Illinois State University student named Sonja Carlson. By coincidence, her last name was the name of the street John was living on. Sonja was a lively blonde of Swedish descent, a tad on the chunky side but with a really pretty face, sassy hair, and a bubbly personality. She and John had met at a Rockford dance hall where Sonja had gone with a girlfriend, and John had been attracted to both. "It was a coin toss who I was going to be involved with. They both seemed to like me," Tessier recalled, but the way things worked out he ended up dating Sonja.

Gassaway also had brought a date to the house party, a local girl named Bridget, who would later become his wife. Everyone was having a grand time just talking and drinking when out of the blue John started singing the Johnny Mathis ballad "Chances Are." Gassaway was stunned—who knew Tessier had a great voice? To the locals who'd only known the gawky teen as the neighborhood "creep," it seemed he'd come into his own. Apparently the U.S. Air Force had worked its wizardry; he was brimming with self-confidence.

Life at 751 Carlson Street, inhabited by a bunch of young single men, was pretty much like anyone would expect it to be. The house was always a mess, and except for an occasional burger or a steak, nobody cooked. Mike Glen was in charge of the rent and keeping track of who owed what. Basically, he managed the place. Like a lot of fellows in the early sixties, he was a Hugh Hefner wannabe who read everything in *Playboy* magazine that was related to carnal knowledge and pop culture. Like a faithful *Playboy* reader, Mike also played Dave Brubeck records on the hi-fi turntable and listened to satirist Mort Sahl's comedy albums.

During the workweek, it was pretty quiet on Carlson Street, but on Friday and Saturday nights, the place got busy, and things went a little crazy. Word got around, and Carlson Street became an after-hours watering hole where, after the bars in Sycamore had closed, everyone gathered. People would start dropping by to shoot the breeze and have a couple of beers at two or three in the morning, so the Glen brothers built a bar just inside the front door.

Around this time, John got into a scrape that could have landed him in serious trouble. In October 1962, he and his roommate Floyd "Gator" Tucker took a drive out to Sportsmans Lake for some target practice. John and Gator had history. They had been classmates at Sycamore High and once gotten into a nasty fight in the gym. What the fight was about no one can remember, but fists flew, and John found himself getting pounded. Luckily, there were other students there who pulled Gator off John before he was seriously hurt. Later, Gator and John made up, but their encounters had always seemed edgy. Now, happenstance had thrown them together as roommates in the same house.

On this particular day in October, Sportsmans Lake was deserted and desolate. The draining of the lake during the search for Maria Ridulph's body was now a distant memory. John carried his .22 caliber Colt pistol; Gator, who worked in construction, had brought a rifle with him. They were shooting cans when John turned to reload his weapon with his back to Gator, but it was a clumsy maneuver and, without warning, as he was pulling back the hammer, the gun slipped from John's hand and fired. A bullet hit Gator in the left thigh. John carried Gator piggyback, screaming in pain, to the car and drove to Sycamore Municipal Hospital. Gator, worried that he could lose his leg, kept shrieking at John to drive faster, but John stubbornly kept to the speed limit.

It turned out to be a clean wound because no bone or major vein or artery was hit—the bullet had gone right through. John tried to downplay the mishap, telling everyone that the doctors had patched Gator up with "two Band-

Aids and he was done," but in fact, he felt truly foolish because he was usually so careful around firearms. Gator was plenty pissed. Because gunplay was involved, the Sycamore police were notified, and they questioned both men at the hospital. An incident report was written up, but the matter was declared an accident, and the case was closed.

In the spring of 1962, Jeanne Tessier was sitting on the front porch at 227 Center Cross Street when a car pulled up that she had never seen in the neighborhood. It was a really cool-looking red convertible, and it took a moment for her to realize that the driver was her half brother John. Since John's stint in the U.S. Air Force, Jeanne hadn't seen much of him. He'd only stop by with a duffel bag every now and then and ask his mother to do his laundry.

When he was stationed in Japan, Jeanne had received a strange letter from John. To her it read like a love letter.

"When my mother read it, she declared it rubbish and threw it away," Jeanne says.

Jeanne hopped off the steps and asked her brother if that snazzy red convertible was his car. No, he said, it belonged to a buddy. She asked him to take her for a ride; she'd never been in a convertible. John wasn't eager to accommodate her.

"Please, just a short ride," Jeanne pleaded. "Just a ride around the block."

Finally, John relented. Jeanne climbed into the passenger seat, and John hit the accelerator. Just like that, his demeanor changed. He drove in dead silence but with "great intensity." Some sixth sense told Jeanne she was in danger.

"I realized I had made a terrible mistake," Jeanne recalled many years later.

John turned left on DeKalb Avenue, took another left on Charles Street, and made his first right on Carlson Street. In all, the trip took less than two minutes, a distance of about three-quarters of a mile. Then he drove straight into the driveway at 751 Carlson Street.

According to Jeanne's memory from that day, John told her to follow him into the house. He led her to one of the bedrooms. Although the sun was out, the curtains were drawn, and the bedroom itself was very dark and dank. The only piece of furniture was a cot.

"He told me to get on the bed, and he took my lower clothes off of me and he raped me," Jeanne wrote in her memoir.

Not a word was spoken, Jeanne says. As she tells it, at some point she heard voices coming from somewhere inside the house. John was still on top of her completing the act when the door to the bedroom was flung open. Jeanne couldn't see who the men were, but there were at least two of them there, perhaps three.

Jeanne wrote: "Without hesitation, he offered me to them."

"Hey," John called out. "Hey, guys, this is my sister. Do you want a turn?"

After John climbed off Jeanne, she says two of the men took their turns. One made her roll over on her stomach and entered her from behind. Then, Jeanne says, the other man went in "for sloppy seconds." When they were done, Jeanne found herself alone in the room with a third man who she thought she recognized as the brother of a class-mate from Sycamore High. It could be that through this superficial connection a common bond of humanity was forged, because the man sat with her for a little while and never touched her, until he finally told her to put on her clothes.

What happened next was a blur. Jeanne staggered out of the room and found herself in the daylight with the sun still shining brightly on Carlson Street. Not knowing which way was home, she walked until she found a landmark she recognized as the entranceway to Elmwood Cemetery, the cemetery where Maria Ridulph was buried, and it oriented her.

She knew she could get home from there.

She made her way back to 227 Center Cross Street, the setting of so much misery at the hands of her father, but that today was a safe haven. Much to her relief, no one was home. She headed straight for the basement and put all her clothes in the washing machine, along with some other clothes she found on the floor. Then she stepped into the basement shower stall and stood under the hot water until it was gone, "trying to wash away what had just happened to me." When she got out, she wrapped herself in a bath towel, went up to her bedroom, and fell asleep.

As Jeanne tells the story: "My half brother Johnny had sex with me for years . . . I was his for a very long time, when it suited him, when his hunger found no other outlet than me, who was close at hand.

"The injuries he inflicted run so much deeper than those of my father and are so much harder to speak of, because my half brother screwed not just my body but my mind. I was a child desperately in need of love and Johnny used that need in me to satisfy his own. At times he even suggested that we might run away together and live where no one would know we were kin. He was a Jekyll and Hyde; all words of love and tenderness on approach, telling me he couldn't help himself, begging me please, please, please to let him do the deed, promising kindness, gentleness, sweetness, but when aroused, delivering mindless animal rage. This pattern, which was set so early and so clearly, made me a coconspirator because I allowed myself to surrender to his words. As a result, I hated and blamed myself for our relationship for many years. Each time I gave myself to him or allowed him to take me, I was left feeling brokenhearted and utterly betrayed.

"I will never fully recover from the harm he did to me."

John Tessier refuses to discuss his relationship with Jeanne except to say, "Jeanne and I were very close." Asked about the allegations that he raped her at 751 Carlson Street when she was fourteen, Tessier would only say, "She's lying her ass off."

It was time to move on. After a year or so at the GE plant, John Tessier decided that Sycamore was "not the place where I was going to make my mark." Working in a factory made John feel like a cog in a wheel, an inconsequential part of a giant, impersonal assembly line.

"I wanted to do something that I could be proud of and it wasn't going to be in Sycamore."

John once again signed up for military duty, not the U.S. Air Force this time but the U.S. Army, with the understanding that he would be assigned to army intelligence, sent to Officer Candidate School, and commissioned a second lieutenant. Once more, John said his good-byes to the Tessiers, and to his new girlfriend, Sonja Carlson. Marriage with Sonja was definitely on the horizon. On January 23, 1963, Sonja's parents—her father worked for Sunbeam, the electronic consumer-products company; her mother was a domestic—published an announcement in the local newspaper:

Mr. and Mrs. Thursten Carlson of Rockford
are announcing the engagement of their daughter,
Sonja Marie, to Pfc. John Tessier, son of Mr. and
Mrs. Ralph Tessier of Sycamore, who is stationed at
Fort Knox, Ky., and in February will enter the
Army Intelligence School at Baltimore, Md. An
early spring wedding is being planned.

The army had other plans for Tessier. After he completed intelligence school at Fort Holabird, Maryland, in June 1963, John received orders that he and his company were being deployed to South Korea. He called Sonja.

"We should postpone the wedding. They're sending me to Korea for a year."

Sonja would not hear of it. "I'm coming out tomorrow," she informed her fiancé. They were married by a justice of the peace in Baltimore, on June 10, 1963. Immediately afterward, the new Mrs. John Tessier flew back to Rockford. John telephoned his mother from Baltimore to say that he and Sonja had eloped. The next morning he boarded a plane to San Francisco, the first stop on his way to South Korea, and soon, Vietnam.

16

....

LOOKING FOR A FACE

Ten years after the bogeyman calling himself Johnny had taken Kathy Sigman's best friend, Maria Ridulph, Kathy was now a young lady of eighteen. She no longer lived on Archie Place. Her parents, eager to take their leave of the neighborhood and its memories, had built a new house in a subdivision north of town.

On a Sunday morning in November 1967, Kathy was babysitting her two sisters, who had been born in the years following the kidnapping; Cindy in 1959 and Julie in 1961. They were being raised in the manner of the postkidnapping generation of Sycamore youth, with tighter restrictions imposed by more watchful parents who were always alert and keeping close tabs on their whereabouts. In just a few days, Sycamore would be marking the tenth anniversary of Maria's abduction, which the town fathers had decided to make a low-key event.

Kathy took her sisters to the Welcome Lanes bowling alley, in the city of DeKalb, that morning. The place was almost empty, and she was surprised when a young man settled into the bowling lane next to theirs. He said that the manager had told him he had to share a scoring alley with the Sigman party of three.

The young man introduced himself as Mike Chapman. He was eighteen and had just dropped out of the Illinois Institute of Technology, which meant losing his student deferment from the draft. Now he was living back home and thinking about whether to enroll at Northern Illinois University or enlist in the U.S. Air Force and get his military obligations over with. In 1967, the Vietnam War was raging. More than 11,600 American military personnel would be killed that year, and the number would climb to 16,500 in 1968.

Mike and Kathy got to talking, and Mike said he'd just broken up with a girl he'd been seeing who went to the University of Chicago. To help him get over the breakup, he'd treated himself to a new pair of bowling shoes and a new ball, which he was trying out for the first time. Kathy thought Mike had an engaging personality, and even their small talk was easygoing. At some point he asked, "Are you seeing anybody?"

"Nope."

Mike asked Kathy for her number, and three days later, he called and asked her to go out that Friday night. They went to the State Theater in Sycamore and saw Audrey Hepburn and Albert Finney in *Two for the Road*—and they never dated anyone else again.

Mike had been raised about ten miles from Sycamore in the village of Malta, population about a thousand, and just 350 or so houses in the village. His mother, Charlotte, was curious about this young lady her son was seeing, and when Mike told her the girl's name was Kathy Sigman, Mrs. Chapman did not look pleased. The Chapmans had no substantive connection to the Maria Ridulph case, just an unpleasant memory of a stressful time. The gravesite of Charlotte Chapman's eighteen-month-old nephew, who had died from an accidental overdose of aspirin in 1957, was in Elmwood Cemetery, coincidentally right next to where Maria was buried. On the day of Maria's funeral, in 1958, the crowd of mourners who were there to pay their respects to the Ridulphs trampled over the little boy's grave, adding to the anguish of his mother, Charlotte's sister. It was just an unfortunate no-fault incident, but Mike's mother still seemed to have hard feelings about it.

Mike was heading out the door to meet up with Kathy when his mother spoke up.

"You know, that's the girl who was with Maria Ridulph."

Mike said he knew all about it, and, more to the point, it didn't matter.

Later that night, when Mike told Kathy about his conversation with his mother, Kathy sighed, "It'll never go away." She told Mike that whenever she walked down a street or passed a stranger in Sycamore, in DeKalb, in Chicago, on vacation—anywhere she happened to be—she'd conditioned herself to scan the faces of strangers. She was looking for Johnny. As her mother had once told her, "You are the only person who knows what Johnny looks like."

As Kathy kept an eye out for Johnny, Mike Chapman took on a special duty of his own.

"She spent her life looking for a face. I spent my life trying to watch her back. I knew somebody was out there who would want to hurt Kathy. I just knew there was always that potential."

Kathy Sigman and Mike Chapman were married in San Antonio, Texas, on January 13, 1969. The next day, Mike reported for basic training at Lackland Air Force Base.

Janet Tessier was eight days shy of her first birthday when Maria Ridulph was kidnapped, in 1957. Consequently she had no memory of Maria, yet as she was growing up, people in Sycamore were still talking about her kidnapping, and Janet was inexplicably drawn to the story. Janet often went to the movies on Saturday afternoons with her sister Mary. She was a fan of cheesy horror films like *The H-Man* and *Mothra vs. Godzilla*, dubbed over from the Japanese. Her other favorite was low-budget horror westerns. Imagine her glee when *Billy the Kid vs. Dracula* and *Jesse James Meets Frankenstein's Daughter* played at the State Theater on the same double bill.

Following an afternoon at the movies, Janet and Mary would walk around the corner to Holiday's ice-cream parlor and treat themselves to a ten-cent vanilla cone or root beer in a frosted mug. Then, with police headquarters right there, the girls would duck in to check out the latest wanted posters on display in the basement. Janet imagined herself as a girl detective going after bad guys, and Maria Ridulph's poster, featured on the police corkboard, intrigued her. Perhaps it was simply because the little girl from Sycamore who had been taken too soon was the city's most famous citizen. When she stood before Maria Ridulph's poster, Janet would close her eyes and ask God to find the bad man who killed Maria.

Janet, like her mother, loved books, especially detective stories, and read Nancy Drew and Encyclopedia Brown and later Eileen Tessier's collection of Agatha Christie mysteries.

When the TV series *The F.B.I.* began its long broadcast run on ABC in 1965, Janet became a hard-core fan. She'd sit in the living room at 227 Center Cross Street with her parents and watch it every Sunday night. She really got a kick out of the closing segment, when the star, Efrem Zimbalist Jr., would ask Americans for their assistance in tracking down that week's most-wanted fugitive.

One night, while everyone was enjoying *The F.B.I.*, Eileen Tessier said something completely unexpected. Out of nowhere, she blurted out that the FBI had once been to their house.

Janet turned to her mother. "Really? What were they doing here?"

"It was because of Maria Ridulph."

"Why were they here?"

Janet could tell her mother didn't want to talk about it and almost certainly regretted bringing it up. "Well, they had to investigate everybody's house," Eileen said.

Eileen clammed up, and everyone went back to watching the show.

17

··········

WASHINGTON STATE

The army sent John Tessier to Vietnam in 1969 and assigned him to an infantry company in a hotbed of North
Vietnamese infiltration. Second Lieutenant Tessier figured
he had a life expectancy of maybe three months. When he
got to A Shau Valley, the action was bloody, and they took
too many casualties. Hamburger Hill, so named because
American soldiers were chewed up like hamburger, was
fought in 1969 in the A Shau Valley along the border of
Laos. His first day in-country, Tessier boarded a helicopter
to link up with his unit in the jungle. Ten minutes into the
ride, the helicopter was flying sideways.

"What's going on?" he asked.

"We're being shot at."

John Tessier was dismayed by the political leadership in
Washington, who, in his opinion, "wouldn't let us win the
war." When a soldier in his company was killed in action,

and as the young man's commanding officer he had to send his condolences to the soldier's mother, it really got to him. In his letter, Tessier wrote that the war wasn't worth the loss of her son's life because "we shouldn't be here." It was probably a violation of military protocol but Lieutenant Tessier sent it anyway.

John served in Vietnam with distinction and was awarded a Bronze Star. When he returned stateside, he was promoted to captain. He was reunited with his wife, Sonja, and the young army couple moved into a small apartment outside Fort Sheridan, in Illinois. It was great because the base was close to Sycamore and also to Sonja's parents in Rockford. Sonja had given birth to two children, a son they named Sean and a daughter, Christine. Then John was transferred to Fort Lewis, in Washington State. Mount Rainier was a revelation, he said, and crossing Puget Sound in a ferry took his breath away. It was a dreamland of mountains and clean air and rivers. He wasn't crazy about the state's liberal politics, but he put that aside and told Sonja, "I am never leaving here."

With the fall of Saigon, the Vietnam War was over, and the army went through a reduction in force the consequences of which were if John remained in the military, he'd be reduced in rank to sergeant. Understandably upset, he resigned his commission and applied for a position as a police officer in the city of Lacey, population about 40,000, ten miles from Olympia. With his military career in two branches of the armed forces and that Bronze Star for heroism in Vietnam, plus his recent graduation from the King County police academy, John Tessier was eminently qualified for employment in law enforcement, and then some. That first year, he worked the graveyard shift. His monthly take-home pay was $536.

In the meantime, his marriage to Sonja was coming to an end. In court papers, she stated that the split came about because "I learned of my husband's involvement with another woman." Fidelity issues aside, there was never-ending squabbling over money. "He spends more than we earn," Sonja told the court, and as an accountant at a local community college, she knew whereof she spoke. It infuriated Sonja so much that John was making noise about buying a boat, which she maintained "we could ill afford," that without telling him she withdrew $4,000 from their joint savings account to keep it out of his irresponsible hands. John retaliated by withdrawing the remaining $1,500. He was so irate with Sonja, it was he who filed for divorce. And it got really nasty.

Sonja accused John of harassing and abusing her and filed for a restraining order that prevented him from entering their home except to pick up the children for visitation. When the marriage was dissolved, John walked away with a red couch, an end table, a lamp, and a dresser, as well as his 1969 Buick plus snow tires and his Yamaha motorcycle. Sonya was awarded the 1973 Pinto and the simple 1,300-square-foot house on Willowood Place in Tacoma, Washington. Not much to show after twelve years of marriage.

In November 1974, the Lacey police chief called Officer Tessier into his office. He knew John was having money trouble with the divorce and asked him if he'd be interested in moonlighting. John said sure. The chief said a lawyer he knew was looking for a reliable man who could work private security for a "millionaire's daughter." For some reason, the woman thought her life was in danger. Tessier went to see the lawyer, who made a "very nice offer." Tessier took the assignment.

The woman in question was a twenty-three-year-old student, "Sally" (Sally is not her real name, as she stipulated that her real name not be used), who was studying nursing at Pacific Lutheran University.

Sally was living in a dorm on the campus of the liberal-arts college outside Tacoma when someone broke into her room and pocketed her cash. Then an expensive suede suitcase with leather corners was stolen from a storage space set aside for her in the basement; it had been a gift from her father and bore his initials. When Sally told her father about the thefts, he hit the panic button. Was somebody targeting her? Dad, a wealthy industrialist, called his lawyer in Washington State, who, in turn, reached out to the police chief of Lacey and asked for a recommendation. And that is how John Tessier came to enter Sally's life.

John's first step was to get Sally to a secure location. He went to her dorm, helped her pack up all her stuff, loaded it into her Pontiac Firebird 400, and temporarily moved her to a hotel in Tacoma. He checked in to an adjacent room, all expenses paid by Sally's father. She was grateful to her dad, of course, but also a little embarrassed. Was this not overkill?

For the next week, Tessier, working off-duty plain-clothes, drove Sally to class and watched her from a discreet distance to make sure she wasn't being followed. He also used his law-enforcement connections to run background checks on her friends. Everybody checked out clean. After a week or so, Sally and her father came to the conclusion that there wasn't any threat. Hiring a bodyguard to ensure the physical safety of his daughter had been an act of love by an overprotective dad with unlimited financial resources. Even John Tessier had to agree that she was in no danger. He put a call in to Sally's father.

"Look, I really enjoy the money, I enjoy the job, but you don't have a problem. She's fine."

Tessier and Sally said good-bye, and they parted company with a handshake.

After several days had passed, John called Sally and asked her out. Considering his financial woes, he must have thought he'd won the lottery: rich heiress, no boyfriend, obviously into cops. For her part, Sally was grateful for the professional way he had handled his bodyguard assignment. She also thought he was attractive and had to confess that the shoulder holster John carried was an incredibly seductive badge of masculine strength. Plus, that he was in law enforcement and he'd achieved the rank of captain in the army made her feel safe in his company. The age difference—John was twelve years her senior—was not an issue for her.

Sally had long light-brown hair, which she pulled away from her face with a barrette. She wasn't very sophisticated, and she didn't think she was particularly attractive, so she was flattered by the attention John showered on her. He told her he was divorced, and he was honest about the financial nightmare he faced, paying his ex-wife Sonja alimony plus monthly child support of $150 on a small-town cop's salary. He was also open with her about the fact that he was seeing another woman.

Their first date, dinner at a restaurant overlooking Puget Sound in Tacoma, launched their whirlwind romance: in no time, John had moved into her one-bedroom apartment near the Pacific Lutheran University campus.

When things were turning serious, John decided to tell Sally about the Maria Ridulph case. She was a little girl who had been murdered in his hometown of Sycamore, Illinois, he said, and for a very brief time he had come under suspicion before the FBI had concluded that "it could not have been me." He described it as the "worst experience of my life," and he was telling Sally, he said, because he thought it was only right that she know. Sally took in what he'd said and very quickly dismissed its relevance. It seemed inconceivable to her that John could have kidnapped and murdered a seven-year-old girl. *Inconceivable.*

Sally knew she'd have to tell her father about her relationship with John Tessier, but it never seemed like the right time. Fate intervened when her dad stopped by for a visit and found a man's shaving kit in the bathroom. Dad didn't say a word, but Sally was conscience-stricken that he'd had to find out that way.

"I wanted to keep John in my life," Sally stated. "I thought I'd lose him to a girlfriend who was sexually active. John was my first man. He was the one I wanted to give up my virginity. I was in love with him. I wanted to marry him." They had met in November 1974. Two months later Sally told her parents she was getting married.

John, deeply concerned that Sally's father would try to talk her out of it, wanted to hurry things along.

The task of organizing a large formal wedding in a matter of weeks fell completely to Sally. There was so much to do. She selected the venue, a Methodist church in Olympia. Then she got the invitations in the mail. At the Tacoma Mall, she bought a gown and veil at David's Bridal. Eileen Tessier, John's mother, flew out for the wedding, while Ralph stayed in Sycamore. Sally made a home-cooked dinner for Eileen, and afterward Eileen kept her future daughter-in-law company in the kitchen while Sally did the dishes. They were getting to know each other when, in passing, Eileen brought up the Maria Ridulph case.

"Yes, I know all about it," Sally said. "John told me."

The subject was dropped. Thinking it through later, Sally said, "She wanted to make sure I knew before I committed to the marriage."

The day of the wedding was January 7, 1975—only four days after John and Sonja's final divorce decree came through. John wore a tuxedo with a ruffled shirt, and two police officers from Lacey served as his best man and groomsman. To save a little money, the wedding was held on a Thursday, and the reception was at the Evergreen Inn. John had invited the entire Lacey police department. Little round tables were set up at the restaurant so the guests could circulate, and there was a buffet dinner and a band that played live music. Through it all, Sally's father had a sour expression as he looked on, but he loved his daughter unconditionally, even if he suspected that she was making a big mistake. Sally was grateful that her parents were able to get through her wedding day without incident, and, of course, Dad paid for everything—including the two-week dream honeymoon in Hawaii.

"Let's face it; he spoiled me," Sally now says.

Sally got to know John's children; Sean was seven and already playing the guitar, and Christine was three and a cutie-pie. She also met Sonja, who she found to be pleasant and always well put together. But John couldn't stop complaining about how much the divorce was costing him. Behind Sonja's back he called her the Beast.

For the Fourth of July holiday in 1975, the newlyweds flew to Sycamore so Sally could meet the rest of John's family. Even Ralph made a good impression, and she thought he had a winning way. Four of John's half siblings were there: Katheran, Jeanne, Robert, and Mary. Only Janet was absent, and, in an aside, John told his new wife that his half sister Janet was a hippie and a chronic runaway.

Sally thought Sycamore was a pleasant working-class town though she was surprised that Eileen and Ralph had found the wherewithal to raise seven children in so tiny a house. Overall, Sally thought to herself, she was fortunate to have married into such a fine family.

Everyone went to a July 4 picnic, which was fun, except that Jeanne Tessier wouldn't sit at the table with the rest of the family and spent most of the day sulking and kicking a ball around the park. She kept her distance from John and, from Sally's perspective, seemed alienated. It seemed very strange to Sally. What was Jeanne's story, she wondered.

....

The John Tessiers bought a big white dog with a sweet temperament. Sally would throw her arms out and say, "Give me some sugar," and the dog would put his paws over her shoulders and give her a bear hug. They named him Sugar Bear. John was talking about moving up the chain of command in the Lacey police department. Someday, he told his wife, he'd make detective. It was a stable middle-class existence, with John earning a steady paycheck with full civil-service benefits and health insurance. The marriage seemed to be working. Then one afternoon John came home and said he had resigned from the force. Sally was thunderstruck. As John explained it, it was a matter of principle: he'd refused to play the political games he had to play to get promoted, and he just got fed up. It sounded a little fishy to Sally, but she held her tongue. She was non-confrontational by nature and wanted the marriage to work out so, for the moment, she let it ride.

They sat down and talked things over. What, Sally asked, did John want to do with his life? John was direct: he wanted to go into business for himself and open a photography studio. It seemed that there had been a photographer back in Sycamore who lived in a beautiful Victorian house, and John wanted a life like that for himself.

"I figured it would take a couple of years for a new business to get out of the red and turn a profit," Sally recalled. "I thought, OK, give it two years and if it didn't work out he'd have to get a job." In the meantime, Sally, who was still in college, would bear the cost of all the household expenses. She had an independent income from investments her father had made in her name; plus, her dad was always willing to help out.

John converted their garage into a darkroom and built a small studio in the house, but, unfortunately, very few clients came knocking, and John decided he needed to be closer to a large metropolitan hub. Thanks again to Sally's bighearted father, the Tessiers made a down payment on a nice clapboard house in the Seattle suburb of Lakewood. It had three bedrooms, two bathrooms, and a fence for the dog. John rented office space in the historic Perkins Building in Tacoma and waited for his business to grow.

At first he focused on commercial photography, shooting ads for products and services, sometimes using a model when the ad called for a touch of eye candy. He brainstormed ways to build his business from scratch and started shooting head shots for singers, dancers, actors, and other performing artists. He found dancers in particular a pleasure to photograph because they really knew how to work their bodies. It was impossible to shoot a graceless pose when the subject was a dancer, John told his wife.

The steady stream of beauties turning up at John Tessier's studio really got to Sally. What wife would not feel apprehensive under the circumstances? One day her father called from Los Angeles to give her a heads-up that John was stepping out on her. Someone had seen his son-in-law taking a drop-dead gorgeous woman to lunch at Tony C's, a trendy restaurant downtown. Sally assumed it was either one of her dad's sales reps from the Seattle branch who had chanced upon John and ratted him out or her dad had hired a private detective to tail her husband. She didn't ask and, honestly, she didn't want to know. *Tony C's, of all places.* It made her blood boil. He's having lunch at Tony C's with a hot chick while she's paying all the bills and living on peanut-butter sandwiches and tuna casserole.

Still, Sally didn't say a word. She decided to wait and see. Not long thereafter, John called to say he was working late. When he got home, Sally was waiting up for him. It turned out that he'd gone out with some friends to a bar with live music and dancing. What really ticked Sally off was that he kept saying what a great time he'd had. She started to imagine all sorts of scenarios and wonder what had become of the good man she'd married with the career in law enforcement.

John found himself so broke he couldn't meet his monthly child-support obligations. Sally wrote a personal check to cover them.

"That's the last time," she told him. "I'm not going to do it again."

When Sonja Tessier received the check and saw who'd signed it, she called Sally to thank her.

It didn't stop. John asked Sally to make a mortgage payment on an empty lot he owned in Bear Lake, where he hoped to build his vacation house.

Absolutely not, Sally told him. "It has nothing to do with me," she said, shaking her head for emphasis.

Then John said he was thinking of calling Sally's father and asking for a loan. Sally put her foot down. Under no circumstances would she let John make the call. Enough already. She made up her mind. The time had come to have it out with him. Sally braced herself for the showdown. She was sitting on the sofa when John came home from work. He got a beer from the refrigerator and came over to join her.

"You've got a really nice setup here, haven't you?" she asked him evenly.

John blinked. He hadn't seen this coming.

In her head, Sally had formulated a list of accumulated grievances, which she proceeded to recite out loud in emasculating detail.

"You've got me paying your bills. You're paying nothing." Her tone, she realized in retrospect, was contemptuous, even mocking. His masculinity offended, John pitched the beer bottle across the room. It hit the fireplace mantle and shattered. Sally got up and ran into the bedroom, shutting the door behind her. In their three years of marriage, it was the first time she'd seen him lose it like that.

"I was downright afraid of him," she would say later. "He had a brown belt in karate. I didn't want to be the next thing he picked up and threw against the wall. I didn't want it to escalate." The fit of rage reminded her of a story she'd heard about John, that when he was married to Sonja he was accused of punching a wall so hard he left a hole the size of his fist in the plaster. Sally called a lawyer, and they worked out an exit strategy. Meanwhile, she and John continued to sleep in the same bed. Sometimes they even had sex.

Sally sighs, remembering. "People are complicated. Part of me still loved him. I was afraid of him, but I still loved him."

With everything in place, and following the script she'd worked out with her lawyer, Sally sat John down and laid it out for him without any sugarcoating. "I'm filing for divorce. You need to start looking for a place to live." It was, after all, her house, which her father was paying for. She gave John a deadline and warned him that if he didn't move out by then, he'd face the public shame of a court-ordered eviction. She served John with official papers, but weeks passed without him showing any sign of leaving. It was starting to look like John wasn't going anywhere.

Finally, the deadline for John to vacate the premises arrived. Sally's stomach was in knots. It was a Saturday morning. She waited for him to get in the shower and called her father in Los Angeles for a quick pep talk. Then, while John was still in the shower, she packed a few overnight belongings and drove off with Sugar Bear. Meanwhile, sheriff's deputies arrived to escort John out of the house. A few weeks later, John was permitted to return to collect his stuff. He showed up with two buddies. Sally was so afraid she stayed on the phone with her father the entire time they were there, giving him a blow-by-blow of what was happening. She had a loaded revolver in her pocket just in case.

A full year passed. Sally decided to sell the house and lost all contact with John, though she heard some gossip that he was a mess, and Sonja had moved back to Illinois with Sean and Christine. Then a collection agency called looking for John. The collector told her that he'd shuttered his photo studio.

"Oh, you mean he's not a photographer anymore?"

"No, he's working as a policeman."

It was news to Sally.

As she was going through the house one last time before the closing, she came upon a box of John's socks that he'd neglected to take with him when he moved out. She figured he was hard up and the decent thing was to return the socks to him. She drove over to the apartment where she knew he was staying and left the box at his door. Wouldn't you know it: John heard somebody futzing around, opened the door, and saw Sally. They had an awkward exchange, and Sally saw a guy in the apartment who evidently had been practicing karate with John. John took the box and said good-bye.

That was the last time Sally saw him.

18

....

MICHELLE

The sequence of events that brought Officer John Tessier into the life of a fifteen-year-old high school freshman named Michelle Weinman began when she was sentenced to after-school detention for smoking on campus.

Michelle lived in the town of Milton, Washington, population 7,000, about the same size as Sycamore in 1957 when Maria Ridulph was kidnapped.

She was an indifferent student with a troubled home life. Her mother had been killed in a car crash in Tennessee when Michelle was two. She never knew her biological father. Her mother's widower had remarried and formally adopted her when she was six. He moved the family to Milton, where he drove a truck and painted houses.

"I was not *his*—and he reminded me of that a lot," Michelle would say.

No one who knew her was surprised when Michelle

skipped detention and spent the afternoon listening to music with her ex-boyfriend instead. She didn't think anybody at school would notice.

Michelle hurried back to school in time to be picked up by her stepmother, Donna, at the prearranged hour.

"How was detention?" Donna asked when Michelle got into the car.

"Kinda lame, really boring."

It was a trap. The school principal had called Michelle's parents to let them known that she hadn't shown up for detention. All hell was about to break loose.

When she got home, Michelle was told to call her father at work right away.

"How was detention?" he asked.

"OK, fine."

"Look here, you little bitch," Michelle says her father told her. "I'm coming home and I'm going to kick your ass."

Many years later, when she was asked about this incident, she said, "All I kept thinking was my dad's coming home to kick my ass. I'm outta here. I took off."

Michelle was on the run. She slept a night in the cabin of an abandoned semitruck. Then the mother of her best friend, Dorothea, allowed Michelle to stay with them for a few days until her parents calmed down. One thing Michelle knew for sure was she didn't want to go home. She and Dorothea were at a 76 gas station trying to figure things out when Dorothea had an idea.

"Hey, there's a cop I know, and I think he'll take us in."

Dorothea dropped some change in the pay phone,

reached the cop, and spoke to him for a few minutes. Then, with a wink, she handed the receiver to Michelle.

The police officer said his name was John Tessier, and she could stay with him.

Tessier had joined the Milton police force following his divorce from his second wife and the collapse of his photography business in Tacoma. Now he was forty-three years old and on the phone with Michelle Weinman, arranging for the teenage runaway to move in with him and his girlfriend, a woman named Lane. They spoke for a few minutes. It was such a big step that Michelle said, "I should ask my dad."

"I already spoke to your dad. He said it was OK," Tessier said.

That sounded strange, Michelle thought. How had Officer Tessier communicated with her father? How had he even known of her existence? But she put it out of her mind.

Dorothea got her mother's permission to stay at John and Lane's temporarily to make Michelle feel more comfortable about the living arrangement, and the girls spent the next two weeks there in Lane's apartment. Michelle said, "We trusted John. He was a police officer."

Tessier was great. He drove Michelle and Dorothea to and from school every day and even took them to dinner and the movies. He encouraged Michelle to broaden her tastes, saying, "I'd like to take you to the ballet." They were passing a record store at the mall when Michelle saw a poster for Joan Jett and the Blackhearts. Their song "I Love Rock 'n' Roll" was a huge hit.

"Oh my God! I love that song," she said.

"I'll get it for you," Tessier said. "But you have to promise you're going to be good."

"I'll be good."

Tessier was like a father to Michelle, but some would say he acted more like a boyfriend. He gave her driving lessons in his patrol car, and she got pretty good at it.

"Can I turn on the siren?"

"Sure, go ahead." She couldn't believe she was getting her driver's education from behind the wheel of a cop car.

Tessier even taught her how to apply makeup, and he was very particular about what she should wear.

"You know, Michelle, when you do your eyelashes, make sure you use brown mascara and black mascara on the tips." He never asked how she was doing in school or whether she'd done her homework.

All the attention she was getting from Tessier did make her wonder, but the fact that his girlfriend was living with them kept her uneasiness in check. One thing she found incredibly creepy was John's insistence that every night before the girls went to sleep, he kiss them good night—on the lips.

"When John kisses you good night, does he put his tongue in your mouth?" Dorothea asked.

"Ugh, gross," Michelle answered. She was more worried about Tessier taking advantage of Dorothea because Dorothea was physically more mature and outgoing than she was.

Then one day, Tessier and Lane had a big blowup, and she kicked him out of her apartment. Apparently, she'd found out that he was seeing another woman. He was definitely doing very well with the ladies in town. Besides Lane, there was a woman named Genevieve and a talented artist named Joan Painter who he dated a few times, though it never went beyond holding hands. He and Joan Painter had a lot in common in that they were artistically inclined. On a date at Dave's Restaurant in Milton, he surprised Joan when he handed her his self-portrait, sitting naked on a chair, one knee up, the other leg extended to cunningly cover his private parts. His body had been oiled up like a professional bodybuilder's at a contest, and he was flexing his muscles. *My goodness*, Joan thought. It was a hell of a photo to be showing to a woman he'd just started dating casually. *What a strange duck*, she thought.

"Here, why don't you paint it someday?" Tessier handed Joan the self-portrait.

With Lane gone from the scene, Michelle and Dorothea ended up in the bachelor pad Tessier was renting: unit number 11 in an apartment complex on Twelfth Avenue in Milton. The walls were bare, and there were two clean mattresses without box springs on the floor for the teenagers. By now, Dorothea's mother wanted her home, but Dorothea talked her into letting her stay because she didn't want to abandon Michelle.

Michelle says she was alone with Tessier when he told her to spread out on the floor. "I'm going to teach you how to give a massage." He said it was an excellent skill to have and suggested that when she became an adult, she might want to consider working in a massage parlor. She didn't think much of that career advice but got into position, flat on her stomach. Suddenly, she says, Tessier was lifting her shirt and rubbing her back. Then he pulled her pants down a bit.

"You really need to concentrate on the muscles in the buttocks if you want to be a good masseuse," he told her.

He told Michelle that his living situation with her and Dorothea was causing all sorts of murmurs at the Milton police headquarters.

"You know, they think I'm crazy," he said.

"Why?"

"Because I have you living with me."

Two weeks passed.

A new woman Tessier was dating lived in a one-bedroom apartment about three blocks from his place. Sometimes the two girls spent the night there, sleeping on couches in the living room.

On March 7, 1982, Tessier's girlfriend had to be hospitalized—something to do with "female problems," Tessier explained. So Tessier, Michelle, and Dorothea slept in the girlfriend's apartment that night. Around one in the morning, Michelle was asleep on the couch when she says she was awakened by Tessier whispering something in her ear. She was in her pajamas, covered with a blanket. The next thing she knew, Tessier was pulling off her pajama bottoms. She didn't cry out, Michelle says, because her voice was frozen in fear. Then Tessier allegedly performed oral sex, after which she says he forcibly inserted his fingers into her vagina. He kept saying he wanted Michelle to come with him into the bedroom, and she kept shaking her head, saying, "No, no, no." Finally, he gave up and left her alone, but he was very annoyed with her.

Dorothea had slept through the incident. Michelle woke her up. She was in tears, "bawling like crazy."

She told Dorothea, "John was just doing stuff to me."

"What?"

"Dorothea, he was going down on me."

"Oh my God, what do you want to do?"

"I want to leave."

"Michelle, it's the middle of the night; where are we going to go? We have school tomorrow."

Michelle pulled her blanket up to her chin and stayed awake the rest of the night. The next morning, Tessier rounded up the girls and drove them to Fife High School "as if nothing had happened," Michelle says.

Michelle couldn't stop crying. She went to her first period class but couldn't concentrate. Heading to second period, she crossed paths with a boy who yelled something disgusting, along the lines of, "Did you go down on John?" Michelle broke into sobs. The gossip mill was already churning. Did everyone at school know? She ran to the girls' bathroom and was trying to pull it together when the school's guidance counselor came in looking for her.

The counselor had one question for her: "Is it true?"

Michelle told her everything.

The counselor took Michelle to her office, where she stayed for the rest of the day. Going back to Tessier's apartment was, of course, out of the question. She pondered calling her father, but she just couldn't go back there either.

Another student, Monica, came by to see how she was doing and offered to let her stay at her house for the night.

Monica's family lived in a well-to-do neighborhood of Milton, and her mother extended a warm welcome to the traumatized freshman. These surroundings gave Michelle a taste of the kind of tranquil family life she had never experienced. Then the doorbell rang. Three uniformed officers from the Fife police department wanted to speak to Michelle Weinman. They were shown into the dining room, where Michelle sat at the end of the table. She gave them her statement but had trouble articulating the words because she was getting the impression that these cops were sticking up for a fellow officer. They all knew Tessier from the Milton police force and referred to him by his first name.

At the end of the interview, Michelle was taken to a crisis clinic for wayward teenagers in Tacoma. She was there about three weeks when, at last, her father reached out to her, and they had a heart-to-heart talk over the phone.

"Michelle, I'm going to come for you. We're going to get counseling and family therapy."

For the first time, Michelle wondered if maybe things could work out. Arrangements were made for her dad to take her home. Anything was better than this hellhole she was living in. On the appointed day, she packed her bag, excited to be reuniting with her family, but her dad never came. All she was told was that there had been an unavoidable delay. Another few weeks went by, and still no dad showed up. Finally, she was informed that her father had signed documents declaring her to be a ward of the state.

She couldn't believe it. It was official: she was now an orphan. A series of foster homes followed, maybe fifteen in all that she was sent to until she reached the age of maturity. Once, after she fled an especially wretched foster-family situation, she was incarcerated at Remann Hall Juvenile Detention Center. Every year a court-appointed guardian ad litem would track her down and check on her whereabouts and well-being. All her formal education ceased.

Tessier was in a terrible fix, and this time it was something he couldn't talk his way out of.

He was arrested for the offense of statutory rape and released from the Pierce County Jail on his own recognizance. His dismissal from the Milton police department promptly followed. There had been no love lost between Tessier and Milton police chief Harold Burton. Tessier had been a stone in Burton's shoe since joining the force. Bill collectors were always calling looking for Tessier, and Burton had to field complaints about inappropriate behavior, mainly that Tessier would tell tasteless dirty jokes to diners at a restaurant during breaks. In Tessier's personnel file, Burton wrote:

"Five incidents have been brought to my attention involving local women." One woman said Tessier had invited her to move in with him after Tessier busted her for drunk driving. Another woman Tessier was dating had a prior arrest for prostitution, and to Burton's embarrassment, Tessier brought her as his date to a party thrown by the town. A seventeen-year-old waitress complained that Tessier took a photo of her posing topless for a mock *Playboy* layout.

"Tessier is not very well liked by his coworkers," the chief wrote in Tessier's personnel file. "He is consistent in screwing up." Now the Michelle Weinman incident. Tessier was out of there.

One year later, in March 1983, he pled guilty to the lesser charge of communication with a minor for immoral purposes. He faced a year in the county jail and a $1,000 fine, but the sentence was suspended and the fine reduced to just $350.

In a statement to the Washington State superior court judge presiding over the case, Tessier was asked to write in his own words his version of what had happened between him and Michelle Weinman:

> With the parents' permission I took in two runaway girls and cared for them with the help of my girlfriend and her mother. At her request [Michelle] I gave her a massage and touched her sexually. I did not have the intent to commit the action and ceased when I realized the seriousness of my actions which constituted a crime. I regret my actions and the problems it has caused.

In an interview, Tessier offered this further explanation.

"I didn't even want Michelle Weinman near me. I knew she was trouble. She ran away and I said, 'Come in; you can live with me and my girlfriend until you figure something out.' There was no rape. She lied, lied, lied. And what did happen was an accident."

Tessier didn't want to talk about Michelle anymore except to say, "I'm not gonna tell ya what happened, but it was an accident. And it never should have happened. I didn't have the resources to fight it. And I didn't stand a chance against the jury, I knew that, so I just said, OK, I'll plead to a misdemeanor. And the judge agreed, and I was told not to get in trouble for a year."

Tessier left Milton—effectively driven out of town, just like Michelle Weinman says she was. The big city of Seattle beckoned.

BOOK III

19

....

VICAP

"I know who killed Maria Ridulph."

Detective Patrick Solar tried to make sense of what the woman sitting in his office was talking about. Every small town in America had somebody like her: the local busybody who dialed 911 when she saw a neighbor's dog pooping on the sidewalk. Or the chronic complainer who found a suspicious package in a garbage can on Main Street that turned out to be a discarded burrito. Sycamore, Illinois, also had its share of cranks.

On a Saturday afternoon in 1982, a woman had walked into the Sycamore police department and insisted on speaking with the chief of police, Robert Huber. She was well known to him, so he asked Detective Solar to do him a good turn and listen courteously to whatever screwball story she'd come there to tell this time and send her on her way.

It took no time for Solar to surmise that she had mental-health issues and was, in his words, "way out there." The long and short of what she told him was that she thought her husband, who had a history of domestic abuse, had murdered Maria Ridulph: "I know he did it," she said.

Solar had joined the fourteen-member Sycamore police department two years earlier, after graduating from Northern Illinois University and working in retail at Kmart for a year. He'd started off as a uniformed patrolman, issuing traffic tickets, breaking up bar fights, and dealing with the usual domestic disturbances. After only a year, he'd been promoted, assigned to the detective division, a division that consisted of a single detective, Patrick Solar.

Now here he was, listening to this woman tell him that she knew who killed Maria Ridulph. *Interesting*, he thought. *But who was Maria Ridulph?*

Solar had grown up in Antioch, on the border of Illinois and Wisconsin, so his knowledge of Sycamore's history was limited. It was the first time he'd heard the name Maria Ridulph.

Solar slipped out of his office and went to see Chief Huber.

"Who is Maria Ridulph?" he asked.

Huber sighed. "Yeah, that's a notorious case." He gave Solar the basic background, how some twenty-five years earlier, a seven-year-old girl who lived on Archie Place had been kidnapped and murdered. Solar was intrigued. It sounded more interesting than the usual break-ins he'd been dealing with.

"I'd like to look up the case file."

"Well, there really isn't one."

"What do you mean?"

Huber dug around and handed Solar a thin folder. "Here's the file. Don't go nuts." Solar looked through everything the Sycamore police had on Maria Ridulph, and it wasn't much: newspaper clippings about the crime from 1957 and 1958, and just one original document. It was a scrap of paper stating "Possible missing child on Archie Place" and noting the time when the first call reporting Maria's disappearance had come in on the night of December 3, 1957. As a historical document, it had a certain cachet, but it was of limited investigative value.

"If you want to entertain yourself, go for it," Huber said, but he also made it clear that any work Solar did on the Ridulph case would have to be conducted during his downtime.

Solar was able to dismiss the woman's accusations against her husband in short order. It could not be true, Solar reasoned, because he was in West Germany serving in the U.S. military the night Maria was kidnapped. He couldn't have done it. But the case piqued his interest.

Not long after, a commissioner on the Sycamore Fire and Police Commission came in to see him.

"Hey, a friend of mine told me he has a suspect in the Maria Ridulph case."

Solar thought that was odd. This was the second tip about Maria Ridulph that had recently come his way. He chalked them up to the time of the year; anniversary dates of famous crimes had a way of stirring things up. Solar asked the commissioner what he had.

It concerned a guy named Johnny who lived on the outskirts of Sycamore. "An odd bird," the commissioner said. Not much to go on, but Solar took down the man's full name and said he'd check it out. He called the FBI in Washington, D.C., and asked a clerk in the office of the Central Records System to look up the files on Maria Ridulph. When the clerk got back to him, he told Solar, "There are twenty-four volumes. What exactly do you want?"

Solar gave the clerk the full name of the odd bird named Johnny and asked if the suspect popped up anywhere in the files. The clerk promised to look into it.

A month later, he was at his desk when the phone rang.

"Is Detective Solar around?" It was the FBI clerk informing Solar that his inquiry had hit a brick wall because the FBI had no index of suspects related to Maria Ridulph and didn't have the manpower to read through thousands of pages of investigative reports on the case.

"Look," Solar said, "can you just send me the whole file?"

Much to his surprise, the clerk said yes.

It took several weeks for the FBI to copy the documents stored on microfiche. Finally, Solar received a large box. It was a disorganized mess. He read and sorted everything and put it all in chronological order. He found it taxing work but engrossing.

From what Solar gleaned, FBI director J. Edgar Hoover himself had been calling the shots from bureau headquarters in Washington—not a surprise, as President Eisenhower had asked to be kept informed of any progress in the case. Hoover's Teletyped instructions to Richard Auerbach, the special agent in charge of the Chicago FBI field office in 1957 and 1958, were all over the files. So were memos from another high-ranking FBI official, Associate Director Clyde Tolson, Hoover's companion and long-rumored homosexual lover.

What struck Solar was the breadth of the FBI bureaucracy, the massive number of interoffice memorandums that were generated to document irrelevant minutiae. A culture of micromanagement seemed to have trumped solving a missing-child case receiving national attention.

John Tessier, AKA John Samuel Cherry, was one of eight men the FBI had seriously looked into in 1957. The bureau's top polygraph examiner had been sent from Washington to conduct his test and had eliminated him as suspect; the suspect's timeline also seemed to clear him.

Solar's next move was to request the files of the Illinois state police. In time, he received about 300 pages—not nearly as many as he'd received from the FBI. He found it intriguing that when the state police officially took over the case, in 1958, investigators had put together a list of Sycamore residents who had enlisted in the armed forces around the time of Maria's kidnapping. The working theory was that the kidnapper may have signed up for military service to legitimize his getting the hell out of town. Five young men from Sycamore had fit the suspect list, and John Tessier was at its top. But, once again, he had been dismissed from further inquiry because he had passed the FBI lie-detector test—and he had an alibi.

Reading the files, Solar came to understand why the murder had remained unsolved: the investigation had bounced around from agency to agency; no one had taken ownership of it. The initial probe had been handled by local Sycamore police, who were ill-equipped and inexperienced. The FBI had commandeered the case but pulled out when it lost jurisdiction, in 1958. When the state police finally got involved full-time, the case was cold as ice. What a shame, Solar thought, and so unfair to the Ridulphs.

Solar filled out a twenty-five-page questionnaire detailing everything he knew about the Maria Ridulph case and mailed it to the FBI operations center in Quantico, Virginia. There, the information was ingested into the Violent Criminal Apprehension Program (ViCAP) mainframe computer, the largest repository of major criminal cases in the United States. Criminal behavioral analysts used ViCAP to ferret out patterns and "signatures" that could correlate one crime to another. Could Maria Ridulph have been murdered by a serial killer? ViCAP might hold the answers.

Solar waited for a hit.

Nothing came.

He waited for years.

There came a day when Chief Huber sent Solar to pay a visit to Ralph Tessier. Solar recognized the name—Ralph was John Tessier's stepfather. He had a sign-painting business, and for years the Sycamore police had engaged him to paint identifying letters and numbers on the sides of squad cars. But these were lean times, and Chief Huber had decided to use vinyl stickers to save about $300 a year. Considering the long business relationship that Ralph had had with the department, Huber had asked Solar to give Ralph the courtesy of letting him know about the budget cuts in person. When Solar pulled up to 227 Center Cross Street, he found Ralph in the front yard working on a sign.

"Hey, Ralph, how ya doing?" he called out.

Ralph grunted and went back to work.

So much for niceties. Solar laid out the new direction the police department was going in. "We're trying something different with the squad cars this year. We're not going to be able to use you."

"Why the hell not?"

"It's more cost effective to use stickers."

"What does the mayor think of this?"

Solar explained that as far as he knew, the mayor was on board.

After Ralph used some colorful language to let Solar know what he thought of the new policy, Solar drove off thinking, *What a surly old coot.*

Over time, Solar was promoted to the rank of lieutenant, and there was talk that he was in line to become the next chief of police.

More time passed. Then, in 1996, he got the call he'd been waiting for. It was from the FBI.

"We've got a hit on your ViCAP."

The lead was coming out of the state of Pennsylvania.

20

....

THE TRUCK DRIVER

William Henry Redmond had been committing monstrous acts of brutality since the 1930s. At the age of sixteen, he confessed to choking an eight-year-old girl from Ohio. Thinking she was dead, he buried her under a pile of stones and concrete blocks. By some miracle, the girl, Esther Strickland, regained consciousness, struggled her way out of her grave, and identified Redmond as her attacker. Redmond was arrested and confined to the Boys' Industrial School. In 1938 he was transferred to a state mental hospital, where he remained until his release, in 1943.

Redmond drifted around the country finding itinerant work with railroads, carnivals, and trucking companies. In April 1951, he was operating the Ferris wheel for a traveling carnival that had set up camp in the town of Trainer, Pennsylvania, and so another little girl never made it home.

The body of eight-year-old Jane Marie Althoff was discovered in the front seat of a truck parked on the carnival grounds. She had been asphyxiated. A smudged greasy handprint was discovered on her underwear, and there was a candy-bar wrapper tucked inside her boot. Had the candy been used to lure her? Every worker at the carnival, including Redmond, was fingerprinted. When police arrived to question Redmond, he was gone. He hadn't stopped to collect his last paycheck. Over the years, police lost track of him.

The murder of Jane Marie Althoff, like Maria Ridulph's, languished in files for three decades until it caught the attention of Pennsylvania state trooper Malcolm Murphy, who was assigned to the cold-case squad. Modern technology had enabled Murphy to positively match the greasy fingerprint to Redmond's; then, it became a matter of locating Redmond, which Trooper Murphy proceeded to do via state motor-vehicle records.

Redmond was found to be living in Grand Island, Nebraska. Murphy traveled there in January 1988 to arrest him, and found a decrepit sixty-six-year-old misfit at death's door. Redmond was bent with age, had deep creases on his weathered face, and was afflicted with heart disease and emphysema. Murphy cuffed him and hauled him on board the *California Zephyr* for the train ride back to Pennsylvania. Murphy later testified that as the train was hurtling through the state of Iowa, Redmond was making a full confession. According to Murphy, Redmond said he had put his hand over Jane Marie Althoff's mouth until she suffocated because she had been "pestering" him for a ride on the Ferris wheel.

Redmond pled not guilty to Jane's murder and hired a smart defense lawyer who somehow persuaded a state judge to release him on $1 bail, on grounds that he was "already a day away from death." Redmond returned to Nebraska, supposedly to await his trial, but in actuality to meet his maker, which he finally did in a nursing home in 1992 at age sixty-nine, never having gone to trial.

"Tell me about your case," Solar said after introducing himself on the phone to Trooper Murphy, of the Pennsylvania state police.

Murphy was not surprised by the call. Since his man Redmond's arrest, he'd received several inquiries about him. It seemed that police departments from the Midwest to the mid-Atlantic states were trying to clear their unsolved child murders. They were looking at Redmond because of the itinerant nature of his work history and claims that he had allegedly boasted to another inmate, "They may have me on this one but not the other three."

As Murphy laid out all the information he had about William Henry Redmond, Solar got to thinking. *Could it be? Had he finally found Maria Ridulph's killer?*

When it was Solar's turn, he told Murphy what he had on Maria Ridulph. His account made Murphy's hair stand on end:

"Redmond is your guy," he said.

Solar had to agree. Redmond could very well be Maria's killer. One working theory about Maria's kidnapper had been that he was a truck driver who was passing through Sycamore when he came upon Maria. Since all known local sex offenders in DeKalb County had been eliminated as suspects, the truck-driver hypothesis was really all they had to work with. Center Cross Street, where Johnny took Maria, was actually a section of a heavily trafficked state arterial roadway known as Route 23, running 126 miles through northern Illinois. Commercial truck drivers traversed Route 23 to connect with Route 90 to the north or Interstate 80 to the south. *A truck driver made sense.*

Solar spent the next few weeks focusing on Redmond. One big issue was the age discrepancy. Redmond would have been thirty-five at the time of Maria's abduction, about fifteen years older than the man Kathy Sigman had described. Plus he was dark-haired and muscular, not blond and thin like Johnny. But Redmond's teeth were said to be peculiar in shape, just like Johnny's. Solar also had information that placed Redmond in Chicago in December 1957, when he was reportedly employed by a trucking concern. And Redmond was said to have a fondness for wearing the style of clothes that jibed with the multicolored sweater Johnny had worn. Figuring he had nothing to lose, Solar telephoned Redmond's common-law wife, Mercedes, and asked her straight out whether Redmond had ever mentioned killing a little girl in Illinois in 1957.

"He didn't have anything to do with that," she told him. "He believed in God." Of course, Redmond had gone to his grave denying responsibility for the asphyxiation of Jane Marie Althoff, so his wife's denial didn't mean much to

Solar, who was so confident he had his man that, had Redmond been alive in 1997, he would have gone to the state's attorney and asked for a grand jury indictment.

It was time to notify the Ridulphs and give them closure.

Lieutenant Solar got on the phone to inform Chuck Ridulph of some startling developments in the investigation of his sister Maria's murder from forty years ago.

"I want to sit down with you and your family and share this information with everyone," Solar told Chuck.

They had met once before to discuss the case. At the time, Chuck had owned a country bar in Virgil, Illinois, called Beak's Place, "Beak" having been his nickname in high school. The bar was about eight miles east of Sycamore, on Route 64. One Sunday afternoon in 1990, a woman had come into the bar with her adult daughter and asked to speak with Chuck. She said she had information about his murdered sister, Maria.

"She gave me a convincing story indicating that her husband had killed Maria," Chuck said. "She said she was compelled to tell me since the police officials refused to listen to her."

Chuck had reached out to one of his regular customers at the tavern, Gordon Plunket, a detective with the city of DeKalb, and asked him what he should do with the tip. Plunket made a few calls and put Chuck in touch with Pat Solar of the Sycamore police. Solar invited Chuck over to the police department, where he told Chuck that he'd been working on the Ridulph case on his own time for many years. It was, Solar said, a "passion project." He told Chuck he was aware of the woman's claims and assured him that her story had been thoroughly checked out, and her husband had been ruled out as a suspect because he was in West Germany, serving in the U.S. armed forces, on December 3, 1957. Chuck thanked him, and things ended there. Chuck found Solar to be sincere and well-meaning, and he appreciated his efforts in keeping the case alive.

Now it was 1997, and a lot had happened in Chuck Ridulph's life since he'd last spoken with Solar. For one thing, he'd gotten out of the bar business, having sold Beak's Place. He'd also returned to Concordia College, now Concordia University, to study for the ministry. This is Chuck Ridulph's story, told in his own words:

"In 1963, I was an alcoholic, a teenaged husband, secretly married, and no longer studying for the ministry. My first priority was beer, then cigarettes, and lastly food. I had come a long way—a long way in the wrong direction.

"On July 16, 1966, my wife and I had a daughter and named her Maria Annette. Oh, what a beautiful child. I was twenty. It was nine years after her aunt Maria was murdered.

"I continued to drink daily. The thought of becoming a minister was a distant memory. I had remarried, adopted my wife Georgia's two-year-old daughter, Diane, and she became my own. In October of 1980, I purchased a country bar in Virgil, Illinois. I remember, when my daughter Maria was only a few months old, I had a short-lived life as a part-time Electrolux Vacuum Cleaner salesman, and had gone to this same bar attempting to sell a vacuum cleaner.

I did not make a sale, but the owner was successful in getting me drunk.

"I named the bar Beak's Place. It was a family bar and we ran it as a family. My wife, Georgia, worked during the day, and I worked during the night with my daughter Diane working there once she turned sixteen. It was here that I got sober and my life began to change once again.

"In December of 1987 I had an aneurysm burst and I almost bled to death. The doctor told me that it was a result from prolonged alcohol abuse, which had thinned the walls of my blood vessels, and that if I continued to drink I would die. I was in the hospital for several days, and the day I was released, I went to my first AA meeting. I was forty-one years old. I again divorced on September 14, 1988, and my daughter Diane and I continued to operate the tavern. On July 18, 1993, I married again. My wife, Diane, was the mother of one of my daughter Diane's best friends from high school as well as an old classmate of mine.

"With my sobriety came new life. I renewed old friendships: childhood friendships with some of those who were closest to me when Maria was kidnapped, and friendships with some of my classmates when I was studying for the ministry, one of which was Reverend Paul Koester, of West Allis, Wisconsin, the guy who replaced me in the starting lineup when I was kicked off the basketball team for drinking.

"And, in the fall of 1994, I went back to what had now become Concordia University Wisconsin to again study for the ministry, not even knowing where it would take me.

In 1997 I sold the bar, and in 1998 I was installed as deacon of my home church of St. John in Sycamore."

Chuck's journey into the ministry may have been along a crooked path, but he says he knew "God's hand was always there gently prodding."

Chuck notified his parents and his sisters Pat and Kay that Lieutenant Pat Solar wanted to meet with everyone. All the Ridulphs gathered in the situation room at Sycamore police headquarters to hear what Solar had to say. Mike Ridulph was now an old man of ninety-one but still sharp. Frances was eighty-four. When tragedy besets a family, some marriages are strengthened. Regrettably, Mike and Frances had never recovered from the grief of their youngest child's murder, which had intensified existing friction. The couple had divorced in 1963. Pat was now a fifty-six-year-old mother of three. Kay, the talented singer in the family, was fifty-five and had raised three sons. She and her husband, Larry—her boyfriend from Sycamore High—worked long hours as the owner-operators of two gas stations and convenience stores.

Solar introduced himself and asked if anyone wanted coffee or soda. Then he faced the Ridulphs and presented the evidence. He told them that he believed William Henry Redmond, a truck driver from Nebraska, was responsible for Maria's slaying, in 1957. He said Redmond had smothered an eight-year-old girl at a carnival in Pennsylvania in 1951 and had blabbed to another inmate that he'd killed a little girl and had never been a suspect. Solar said he believed "this second little girl was Maria." He showed the Ridulphs the boxes of files that he'd accumulated since 1982. When he started to read to them from the original autopsy report, Chuck asked him to stop.

At the end of his briefing, Solar said that, in his opinion, he'd solved the case. He looked at the Ridulphs.

"How do you feel about this?" he asked.

Their reaction was not what he'd expected.

"What difference does it make?" Mike Ridulph barked. Even if this animal Redmond was the killer, he was six feet under and couldn't be brought to justice.

Frances echoed the same sentiments.

Chuck, Pat, and Kay were all skeptical of Solar's conclusions. Pat wanted to know why Redmond's name wasn't John or Johnny.

"The killer most likely would not have used his real name," Solar answered.

Pat nodded her head. She understood what he was saying, but what about the age discrepancy? Redmond was thirty-five in 1957, and Maria's kidnapper was supposed to be in his late teens or early twenties. Plus the physical description wasn't even close to Kathy Sigman's account from 1957.

"An eight-year-old's recognition of age cannot be depended on," Solar replied.

Chuck wasn't buying it either. "It just doesn't make sense," he said.

The Ridulphs were grateful for Solar's enthusiasm, but they wondered whether he had deluded himself into thinking Redmond was the killer. In Chuck's assessment, the ambitious police lieutenant had good intentions, but he may have "wanted it too much and had overlooked obvious flaws in his investigation."

The meeting ended with Solar saying that as far as he was concerned, the case was closed. The Ridulphs were invited to examine the evidence so they could see for themselves why he was convinced Redmond was the killer. They left the meeting still deeply skeptical.

Not long thereafter, the *Sycamore News* of November 5, 1997, broke the story in a banner headline: *Ridulph Murder Case Is Closed*. Solar was interviewed by the paper and posed for a photo at Maria Ridulph's gravesite.

At their home in the city of St. Charles, Illinois, Kathy Sigman Chapman and her husband, Mike, were confounded. The lead paragraph in the *Sycamore News* read:

The 40-year-old case of Maria Ridulph's kidnapping and murder was officially closed last week thanks to Sycamore Police Lt. Pat Solar's 15 years of work and research.

Kathy was now a middle-aged woman of forty-eight and the mother of three children, the oldest being twenty-three; the middle child, twenty-one; and the youngest, nineteen. Impossible but presumably true, after forty years it was finally over. Since she was eight, Kathy had made it her mission to study the faces of strangers, looking for the bogeyman named Johnny who'd taken her best friend. Now, in 1997, she could finally end her search.

"We assumed the case was over. After 1997, I quit looking," Kathy says.

Lieutenant Solar found the language in the *Sycamore News* article excessive and a little embarrassing. He says he never said the case was officially closed. The story lacked nuance, and he was worried that people might think he was grandstanding because he was positioning himself to become chief of police. He had had enough and packed away his files on Maria Ridulph. He didn't want to hear about it anymore and focused his free time on studying for advanced degrees in police science. Eventually, he'd earn a master's degree and a PhD. He was pretty certain the Maria Ridulph case was a dead end and could never be solved with any degree of certainty.

Practically speaking, all of Sycamore was now of the opinion that, in a random act of child abduction, Maria had been kidnapped and murdered by a truck driver from Nebraska named Redmond who had been passing through town.

No one seemed to be considering what, in police work, is a fundamental article of faith: the people you have most reason to fear are the people who live close to you.

Always, so it's said, look at the guy who lives next door.

21

....

DEATHBED CONFESSION

Eileen Tessier was dying.

In September 1993, Eileen's daughters had gathered in the lobby at the Rush Presbyterian–St. Luke's Medical Center, in Chicago, where she was undergoing treatment for cancer. A tumor the size of a baseball had been discovered on her pelvic bone, and it had metastasized. Eileen's physician, Dr. George D. Wilbanks Jr., told the family there was little he could do to prolong her life. He had discussed the diagnosis with Eileen, and she was "adamant" that she didn't want any further surgery or extraordinary measures taken to prolong her life. Dr. Wilbanks informed them all that she had perhaps three months to live.

Everyone in the lobby teared up. Dr. Wilbanks had first treated Eileen for a rare form of cancer of the vulva, in 1980. After surgery, chemotherapy, and radiation, she had been considered cured. Now, fourteen years later, there was nothing further that could be done. Even Dr. Wilbanks, a distinguished cancer researcher, was in tears.

"She's a brave woman. I'm proud to have served her. We got her fourteen good years."

As children do in times of family crises, Eileen's four girls came together to share the burden of caring for her in these final weeks.

Eileen returned to 227 Center Cross Street to live out however many days she had left at home. All her children took turns caring for her, but the reality of geography meant that most of the burden fell on Mary, who was thirty-four and living in Batavia, just east of DeKalb, and Janet, who quit her job at a bookstore in DeKalb to help out.

Thanksgiving 1993 was a sad time for the Tessiers. They knew it would be Eileen's last, and the family made every effort to make it a special occasion for the dying war bride. All seven of her children, except the institutionalized Nancy, returned to Sycamore for the holiday, even her first-born son, John, who was in from Washington State. At the house, he was leaning against the refrigerator, videotaping his half siblings and all his nieces and nephews as they came in the door. Janet, the family hippie, now thirty-seven, floated in wearing a long flowered dress with boots and her hair done up. She smiled at the assembled family—then saw "the idiot with the camera."

"Turn that fucking thing off," she told John.

Without appearing to be at all offended, he put the camera down and gave Janet a bemused look.

Jeanne Tessier was facing this Thanksgiving celebration

with trepidation. The last time she had seen John was Thanksgiving 1980, thirteen years before. She was a newlywed then, and she and her husband, Mike Barone, had moved into their first home, an old farmhouse in DeKalb not far from the campus of Northern Illinois University. All the Tessiers were coming over to their house for the holiday dinner, but Jeanne made it clear to her parents that John wasn't welcome. That Thanksgiving morning in 1980, Jeanne was in the kitchen working hard, preparing the turkey and side dishes for the large family gathering. There was a knock on the side door, and when she opened it, she saw her parents standing there with John.

"I told you he could not come here."

"Come on, Jeanne, let me in," John said, and repeated it a few times.

"I don't ever want to see you in my house."

Jeanne's husband came over to see what the commotion was. He was in the dark about the family history and the repellant acts of incest that his wife's father and half brother allegedly subjected her to when she was growing up in Sycamore. She wanted Mike to stay close by in the event that the situation deteriorated and she needed him to physically remove John from their property.

John tried to calm her down. "Don't talk to me like that, Jeanne."

Jeanne locked eyes with him. "John, you destroyed my life. I don't want you here. Now leave. And do not come back for dinner."

And he left.

Now, thirteen years later, it was another Thanksgiving at the Tessiers, and John was back. It was a rough time in Jeanne's life because she'd recently separated from her husband. Eileen, the matriarch of the Tessier clan, was lying down on the couch. Everyone was aware that she was nearing the end, and her daughters had arranged for her parish priest from St. Mary's to come over and say mass, a very special honor for devout Catholics. They gathered around the couch, her children, their spouses, and all the grandchildren. First, the priest renewed Eileen and Ralph's wedding vows for their fiftieth anniversary. When Eileen had learned her condition was terminal, in September, she said all she wanted was to live for this moment, her fiftieth anniversary. Now, she said, she could die in peace.

As Jeanne observed the ritual, she could sense someone's presence behind her, standing too close. It was John. To her complete stupefaction, she says, John put his hand on her crotch and squeezed. *During mass at her parents' house. With the parish priest in the room.* She quickly moved away, Jeanne says, and didn't say a word about it to anyone, relieved that at least no one had witnessed John's shameful behavior.

Not long after Thanksgiving, Eileen was admitted to Kishwaukee Community Hospital, in DeKalb.

What happened next would change many lives, and make history.

Janet Tessier and her sister Mary were in the hospital room keeping each other company as Eileen rested in bed. An IV line dripped morphine into her arm, and soothing hymns were playing because when Eileen passed on, her children wanted her to leave earth on the wings of a heavenly choir. Janet was reclining in a lounge chair at the foot of the bed, flipping through a magazine, chatting with Mary in a soft whisper so as not to disturb their mother. All at once, in an unexpectedly strong voice, Eileen called out, "Janet!"

The sound of her mother's voice jolted Janet out of her seat and straight to Eileen's side.

"Mom, I'm right here."

The social worker at the hospital had explained the end stages of life, and Janet braced herself, wondering whether this was it. She looked into her mother's face; it was luminous, from a light that seemed to come from within her. "Mom, I'm right here. What's the matter?"

Eileen's body somehow worked itself into a tightly coiled state, and with her bony little hand, she grabbed Janet. She said, "Those two little girls who disappeared. John did it. John did it."

For just a moment, Janet wondered what she was talking about. Then it clicked.

"Mom, are you talking about Maria?" The second girl must be the witness, Kathy Sigman, Janet thought.

Eileen struggled to continue. "Yes, the two little girls. John did it. You have to tell someone. *You have to do something.*"

Janet and Mary exchanged looks. Mary silently mouthed the words, "Oh, shit."

Janet tried to reassure her mother. "Don't worry, Mom. I'll take care of it. Don't worry."

Eileen's body settled back into her bed, and Janet encouraged her to rest. When they were sure she'd slipped into a deep sleep, Janet and Mary went to the cafeteria for a cup of coffee. They just stared at each other.

"What do we do now?" Janet asked. It had never once occurred to her that her brother John could be responsible for Maria Ridulph's murder—not until now. "I knew he was an evil son of a bitch," she remarked years later, "but not this."

Mary's knee-jerk reaction was to tell Janet to forget the whole thing. Her primary commitment, as Mary saw it, was to protect Eileen and preserve her dignity in death—in her words, to "let her go in peace." Unspoken were other serious issues. For one thing, the disgrace that an investigation would bring to the Tessier name. And who knew what the legal implications could be? Had Eileen just confessed that she had lied to the FBI, in 1957, when she backed up her son's alibi? Had her deathbed confession made her, and perhaps even Ralph, accessories after the fact to the kidnapping and murder of a seven-year-old girl?

Janet reached out to her sister Jeanne, who was living in Kentucky, and her advice was similar to Mary's. Even with everything John had done to her in the past, she told Janet, "Mom's dying. Don't say anything. We've got to deal with Mom dying."

One week later, Eileen lapsed into unconsciousness.

Janet couldn't stop thinking about her mother's dying declaration. Facing her last waking moments on earth, she believed that Eileen had been driven to speak the truth. As

Janet saw it, an exceptional duty had been passed on to her by her terminally ill mother. To remain silent would be, to her thinking, a dishonor to her mother on her deathbed. So Janet did what she had to do. She called the Sycamore police and said she had information concerning the Maria Ridulph case. A few days later, a detective from the police department came by to talk to her. Janet doesn't recall the name of the detective. She was living in Section 8 housing at the University Village apartments in DeKalb. She told him the story. He sounded interested and said he'd like to interview Eileen.

"You can't. She's in a coma."

According to Janet, the detective told her that, without Eileen, there was no point in pursuing the matter. When asked about Janet's account of her exchange with the detective, Lieutenant Patrick Solar said, "It wasn't me. I would have handled it differently." He said there were three detectives assigned to the squad in late 1993. No police records exist of Janet having made the call, which Solar says doesn't surprise him. "They may have filed a report; they may not have."

The detective's reaction left Janet dumbfounded. But she felt she had done her duty and fulfilled the promise she had made to her mother. It was time to move on.

Eileen Tessier died on January 23, 1994. The funeral took place four days later, with more than three hundred people in attendance. Her son Bob arranged for Irish bagpipes. Eileen would have liked that.

Word got back to John Tessier in Washington that it

would not be a good idea for him to come to Sycamore for the funeral, that he would not be welcome. And so, he was not present when his beloved mother was laid to rest.

Her casket was lowered into the grave, and with it, so it seemed, her family secrets.

22

·········

REVELATIONS

The passing of her mother sent Janet Tessier into a tailspin of grief that she says she tried to deflect with pot, hallucinogens, and shots of vodka. Reflecting on the state of her life at the age of thirty-seven made her wonder how she had messed everything up so badly.

"I hated the smallness of Sycamore. I wanted to be somebody. A great folk singer–songwriter maybe, or a writer. I had dreams, insanely grandiose dreams of what I was going to be. But no discipline."

She gave up her apartment in DeKalb and moved to Madison, Wisconsin, where she had a job lined up at a company that distributed textbooks. She got fired, she says, for being a "total jerk." Her ex-husband, Joe Alberti, sent their nine-year-old daughter, Mary, to live with Janet in Madison, but she sent the child back.

"I wouldn't take my daughter down with me," she said.

Evicted from her apartment, she lived in a car. Then, on Saturday, July 29, 1995, she stepped into a clubhouse in Madison to attend her first AA meeting. Two men sitting at a table drinking coffee saw the newcomer wandering around, looking a little lost.

"So, young lady, what do you know?" one of them asked her.

Janet stared him down. "I don't know anything."

"Well," he answered, "that's the beginning of wisdom."

It was the kind of smart-ass comment that made her want to tell the guy to get the hell out of her face. But then she realized it was just what she needed to hear. She opened her arms to the AA community, which, in turn, embraced her, and that evening gave her a kick start on her road to sobriety. "When you first get sober, you learn it's not about you," one of her AA sponsors told her. "And then, eventually, you learn it's all about you."

Janet moved into a cheap room at the YWCA and found a job doing something she'd never considered before; she became a taxi driver. She learned the geography of a new city and enjoyed the back-and-forth repartee with the dispatcher on the car radio. She got a kick out of picking up and dropping off all kinds of passengers and chasing down fares. The work suited her because she liked to be in constant motion; somehow, it destressed her. It took Janet three months to nail the street grid to where she didn't require a map. First, she drove a silver sedan for the Madison Taxi Company, then dispatched taxis for Union Cab. Life wasn't bad.

....

All this time, she couldn't get her mother's deathbed declaration about Maria Ridulph out of her head. When she
was a little girl staring at Maria's poster in the basement of
the Sycamore police department, and later, watching *The
F.B.I.* on Sunday nights, Janet had developed a bond with
the slain child. Could it be that she, of all people, held the
key to solving Sycamore's greatest mystery? All her life,
she'd considered herself a problem child, the family screwup
and chronic runaway who smoked dope and dropped out
of high school. Now she was beginning to understand that
when her dying mother had blurted out, "John did it," she
had thrown Janet a lifeline. Janet knew she had to do *something* more with the information. She couldn't just sit on
it. In her fourth year of sobriety, she decided to try to revive
interest in Maria's murder again; this time, she called the
FBI's Chicago field office and asked to speak to an agent.
When she was connected, she told him her story.

The reaction was no different than it had been in 1994
when she reached out to the Sycamore police. Once again,
she was shocked by the complete lack of interest, this time
by the FBI. The agent was polite enough but advised her
that she should communicate with the original jurisdiction,
in this case, the Sycamore police, and relay the information
directly to them. Janet tried to explain that she'd already
tried that approach, but the agent said it was the best course
he could offer and wished her luck.

When she told her sister Jeanne about her call to the

FBI, Jeanne just said, "Would you just let this go? The case is too old."

In the summer of 1999, Mike Ridulph was tilling his garden when he felt a sharp pain in his side. He thought he'd pulled a muscle, but it turned out to be terminal liver cancer. Mike kept his mind alert playing cards at the Elks Club every day, and four weeks before he died, he got his driver's license renewed. He lived to be ninety-four, and he was buried at Elmwood Cemetery next to his slain daughter, Maria.

Frances Ridulph also lived to the age of ninety-four. She died in 2007. Her final resting place was, as she wished it to be, Elmwood Cemetery, on the other side of Maria.

Ralph Tessier, after his wife's death, sold their house at 227 Center Cross Street and moved to Minnesota to live out his final days with his eldest daughter, Katheran, and her husband, Joe, a psychologist. Ralph died in 2008 at the age of eighty-nine; the official cause of death was listed as Alzheimer's disease and congestive heart failure. Katheran arranged for Ralph's cremation in Minnesota, then joined her siblings in Sycamore. They went to the cemetery where Eileen was buried and scattered their father's ashes over her gravesite. John didn't come to that funeral either. It was a plain ceremony for a man whose ship had never come in.

23

....

THE BULLDOG

Janet Tessier was living in Louisville with Jeanne when she got a call that she never expected. Jim Lemberger was a taxi driver she knew from Madison, Wisconsin, and he was wondering if Janet would be interested in moving back to Madison to care for his mom, who had suffered a nasty fall at home and needed a part-time companion to help out with simple chores and keep an eye on her welfare. The job paid $200 a month, plus free room and board. It was just what Janet was looking for. She moved into Alma Lemberger's place, and every morning she'd make the old lady a light breakfast of oatmeal and orange juice, and later a sandwich for lunch. Then Janet would catch a few hours sleep and head back to the cab company for the start of her 8:00 P.M.-to-4:00 A.M. graveyard shift. This became her well-ordered existence.

Alma had advanced arthritis and failing eyesight, but

she was self-sufficient and even painted landscapes and still lifes and sold them through art galleries in Madison. Sometimes she and Janet got on each other's nerves, but Alma appreciated the good care Janet was giving her.

Alma had another son, a computer salesman named Mark Lemberger, who lived in Columbia, South Carolina. He had taken four years off to research and write a true-crime book, which was published in 1993. *Crime of Magnitude* was the story of the murder of seven-year-old Annie Lemberger, in the year 1911. Had she lived, Annie Lemberger would have been Mark's aunt. Annie was abducted from her bedroom in Madison. Three days later, her body was found in a lake. A neighbor, John "Dogskin" Johnson, confessed to the crime but retracted his guilty plea and claimed he'd been railroaded. He was sentenced to life, but after a ten-year stretch in state prison, his life sentence was commuted by the governor, and suspicion fell on Annie's father, Martin, although no charges were ever brought because the statute of limitations for manslaughter had expired. In his book, it was Mark Lemberger's contention that Johnson really did commit the crime, and Mark set out to prove his grandfather's innocence. The book received solid reviews; *Publishers Weekly* called the writing "deft."

In June 2008, Lemberger and his wife, Penny, flew up from South Carolina to celebrate his mother's ninetieth birthday. Mark and Janet Tessier had often spoken to each other on the phone, but this was their first meeting in person. He thought she was an interesting character with her friendly smile, bemused crinkles at the corners of her eyes, and a strong voice that filled a room. "She had been knocked around some, but she was intelligent and she took good care of my mom."

Alma lived in a spacious two-bedroom apartment. A painter's studio had been set up with an easel in the sunniest room, and dozens of Alma's artworks were stacked against the walls. It was a great little space. Mark saw that, like any proud mother, Alma Lemberger had displayed his book in a place of honor in the living room, on a marble table, so she could make a big fuss about it when her neighbors stopped by for tea or coffee.

Alma and her daughter-in-law Penny were going out to lunch one day, strictly for the ladies, and they invited Janet, too. Janet declined because she had a bad cold, and she was left alone in the apartment with Mark Lemberger.

Striking up a casual conversation, Janet said she'd read *Crime of Magnitude* and been struck by the similarities to Maria Ridulph, in that both cases involved the murder of a seven-year-old girl from another time. That Lemberger had written a book about an enduring mystery from the turn of the century prompted Janet to tell him about her family secret from long ago.

"I have this problem that I'd like to talk to you about," she began.

As Lemberger recalls the conversation, Janet said she had information about the murder of a girl from her hometown. She said that just before her mother died, in 1994, she had in so many words confessed to falsifying an alibi to the FBI concerning the whereabouts of her son John on the night of the murder in 1957. Janet said that on her deathbed her mother had "demanded" that she, Janet, "do something."

"I'm scared that he's guilty," Janet told Lemberger. "But I'm afraid of doing the wrong thing. He's also a scary guy. He frightens me. He's a threatening guy. There's a ferocity about him."

She said her brother John currently lived in Washington State. Lemberger pointed out that living so far away probably minimized the potential personal danger to herself if she betrayed him to the cops.

Janet said she was at a loss as to what to do, and she leveled a string of sensible questions at Mark: How would she go about informing the police? Could the case ever be solved? What's the hardest thing that she'd face if the police got involved? As Janet spoke, she became overwrought, plainly aware of the implications for herself, her siblings, and her brother, who, after all, was still family. It wasn't only implicating John Tessier as the killer but also her late parents as accessories.

Lemberger listened. In his evaluation, he said, Janet had a moral obligation to notify the police. "Call the jurisdiction that handled the case," he told her.

Janet shook her head. "You don't understand. I did."

"Well, do it again." Family secrets are toxic, he told her. Cold cases do not rest in peace. He had learned that reality during his research for *Crime of Magnitude*. He explained the huge obstacles that awaited her. "It's going to be a very hard thing to dig up all that information. You're going to need somebody really tenacious. That's going to be the hardest part. There are going to be so many interpretations and questions. You'll need to find a detective with the tenacity of a bulldog."

The conversation with Lemberger resonated in Janet's mind, and on September 11, 2008, while Alma was taking a nap, she surfed the Internet and found the official website of the Illinois state police. After being rebuffed by the Sycamore police and the FBI, she figured trying the state police was her last option. She sent this e-mail on the tip line.

> Sycamore, Illinois. December 1957. A seven-year-old child named Maria Ridulph vanished. Her remains were found in another county several miles away in early spring of 1958. I still believe that John Samuel Tessier from Sycamore, IL . . . was and is responsible for her death. He is living in the Seattle/Tacoma Washington area.
>
> I've given information to the person responsible for the cold case in Sycamore. I've done this a few times. Nothing is ever done.
>
> This is the last time I mention this to anyone. What information I do have makes Tessier a viable suspect, and worth looking into. I'm not going to keep doing this over and over. It's exhausting and it dredges up painful, horrible memories.

At 1:04 P.M., Janet took a deep breath and hit Send. It had been fourteen years since Eileen Tessier's deathbed confession, and fifty-one years since Maria's murder.

Later that night, she stepped out for some fresh air,

looked up at the sky, and spoke to her mother, who she knew was in heaven.

"OK, Mom, if anything comes of this, it's going to be up to you and God. I can't keep doing this."

Two days later, her cell phone rang. It was Illinois state police Captain Tony Rapacz, commanding officer of Zone 1, which covered DeKalb County.

Janet was flummoxed. "Really?" She had convinced herself that her e-mail to no one in particular at the state police had probably landed in somebody's catchall in-box and gone unread.

Janet and Rapacz talked for about forty-five minutes. First, he wanted to get a sense of who she was. When the twenty-five-year police veteran first read her e-mail, he'd been struck by the sense of frustration expressed in those last lines. *"This is the last time I mention this to anyone. . . . I'm not going to keep doing this over and over. It's exhausting and it dredges up painful, horrible memories."* His cop instincts told him this was worth checking out.

The first thing Janet told Rapacz was that she had been one year old when Maria was kidnapped. Right away, he thought, *Crackpot.* Then Janet related how her mother had made a deathbed confession in 1993. *OK*, he thought, *it's getting better.*

"I can't promise you anything, but we're going to try," he told Janet.

"You've got to try."

"I know. I was afraid you were another crackpot when you called."

"Do you think I am?"

"No."

Rapacz asked Janet where she lived. Outside Madison, Wisconsin, she told him. Would she mind driving to Elgin, Illinois, to meet with some investigators from the state police? Janet said sure, but wondered whether anything could really come of a case that was so many decades old.

"Let me tell you something," Rapacz said. "We don't let go. I'm putting my bulldogs on this."

24

·········

A COLD CASE

While she was making the hour-long drive to the Illinois state police barracks, Janet tried to stay calm. She was expecting very little, probably a perfunctory meeting and a quick thank-you for coming.

The barracks building, at 595 South State Street in Elgin, was a grim and intimidating structure with a tall flagpole out front flying the American flag. Janet went to the main entrance and found it was locked, but there was a bell for visitors. She rang it. A voice came over the intercom.

"Can I help you?"

Janet replied, "I have an appointment with Special Agent Brion Hanley."

"Just a minute; he'll be right there."

When the door opened, she came face-to-face with Brion Hanley. His tie and crisp wrinkle-free white shirt and khaki pants suggested that he didn't want to think about what to wear in the morning; he just wanted to get to work. Hanley had a crew cut, a stout body, and a heavy face. In another life, he might have been the high school football coach. He was a nine-year veteran of the state police, the last three working out of Zone 1 as a special agent investigating homicides, sexual assaults, and other major crimes. When he worked undercover, he wore college football jerseys and his baseball cap turned around and gnawed on a wad of chewing tobacco in the corner of his mouth.

Janet shook hands with the agent and followed him down a long corridor to a conference room, where four other investigators were waiting. Janet tried to steady her nerves, but it was hard not to be intimidated by the presence of these case-hardened lawmen. Captain Rapacz was there, and so was an out-of-shape guy with a mustache and thinning hair who was introduced as Larry Kot, the criminal intelligence supervisor. Technically, Kot was not a police officer at all but a civilian employee of the state police. Consequently, he didn't carry a badge or gun. Janet could tell he was probably the smartest guy in the room. She could not have known that he also possessed a photographic memory.

On the table, there was a box that contained the state police files on the Maria Ridulph case.

They offered her coffee, then got right down to business and asked her what she knew. She gave them a rundown of her family history and her suspicions regarding her half brother, John Tessier. She described in as much detail as she could recollect her mother's deathbed declaration fourteen years earlier. One important fine point in her story came when she told them that there had been a witness to Eileen's confession who could corroborate everything she was saying—her sister Mary Hunt, who had been present in the hospital room with her. Janet stuck to the straightforward facts. She knew that her credibility was on the line, so she kept her voice level and businesslike. All this time, Hanley was watching her intently. He would be the go-to guy, the lead investigator, should Captain Rapacz determine that it was worth assigning manpower to this cold case.

It seemed to Janet that the detectives were in the very early stages of developing a behavioral profile of John Tessier because they wanted to know what she could tell them about John's state of mind. "Do you think he could have a bipolar disorder?" Rapacz asked.

The question struck a nerve with Janet; it was the only time during the interview that she turned prickly. It so happened that she had been diagnosed with bipolar disorder herself, and she knew a lot about the subject matter.

"No," she said emphatically, "he is not bipolar. I know a lot of people with bipolar disorder, and none of them behaved as John behaved. He is a sociopath."

Sociopath.

There was dead silence in the conference room as the term hung in the air.

At the end of the hour-long meeting, Janet was exhausted but relieved. The state police officers thanked her, and Rapacz said he'd get back to her. It wasn't at all a brush-off. In fact, as Brion Hanley escorted her out of the barracks and they said their good-byes, she saw the look of stern resolve on the special agent's strong face. It told Janet that the cold case was finally going to warm up.

On the drive back to Wisconsin, Janet could barely breathe; her throat was tightening. She was worried that she was going to break down on the highway, and it took everything she had to hold back her tears. Only when she got to Alma Lemberger's apartment did she permit herself the release of a flood of emotion. Alma asked her how it had gone, but Janet didn't want to talk. She had to process what had happened. One notion dominated her thinking: *They believe me.*

"Most of my life, I've felt just such a loser. I've been a pariah, and I've always felt that I've failed immensely. Intellectually, I know that's wrong, but I've battled with a sense of inadequacy all my life. The moment I left that meeting, I knew they were taking what I had to say very seriously."

A few days later, Captain Rapacz called Janet to inform her that the state police department was officially proceeding with the investigation. Not long after that, Brion Hanley followed up, asking her for the names and phone numbers of all her siblings. Janet asked him how the case was proceeding.

"I eat, sleep, and dream this investigation," he told her.

She had found her bulldog.

Janet braced herself for the backlash from her family. She knew she had to break the news to Jeanne first.

The dead silence on the other end of the phone and the even tone of Jeanne's voice when she finally spoke told Janet that her sister was not happy Janet had contacted the state police. Once you involve law enforcement, she warned Janet, you never know which way the wheels of justice could turn. Jeanne had a sinking feeling.

When they got off the phone, Janet wondered if they'd ever speak to each other again.

25

·········

THE TRAIN TICKET

In October 2008, when the Maria Ridulph investigation was officially reopened, fifty-one years after her abduction and murder, Sycamore was a changed place.

Giant manufacturing plants like Anaconda Wire and Cable and Diamond Wire and Cable, which had employed Mike Ridulph, were long gone. Ace Hardware, where Ralph Tessier had worked, was out of business, and only one shoe store remained when there had been three when Maria was alive. The Great Recession hit Sycamore hard. It used to be a rarity to see a foreclosure notice in the *Daily Chronicle*. Now half a dozen a week was the new normal.

The bowling lane where Chuck Ridulph hung out in his youth had become a warehouse, and the card shop that once sold paperbacks was history, having reestablished itself as an appliance store. Kroger on Sycamore Road was now a Salvation Army thrift store. The town took a big hit when the local Kmart closed. Even so, Sycamore's population had grown 45 percent in the years after the turn of the millennium. It now stood at 17,500 citizens.

A new generation of law-enforcement officers had taken over the Sycamore police department. Lieutenant Solar had finally made chief, not in Sycamore, but in the neighboring city of Genoa. When Maria was kidnapped, the Sycamore police department had eight men on the payroll. That number stood at forty in 2008.

Brion Hanley and Larry Kot got down to work. One of their first tasks was to check out John Tessier's alibi. The old FBI documents indicated that a collect call had been made from a pay phone in Rockford, forty miles away, to the Tessier home in Sycamore at 6:57 P.M. on December 3, 1957. The call had come from a "John S. Tassier"—an apparent spelling error on the part of the local telephone operator. The call had been accepted by the Tessiers and had lasted only two minutes, until 6:59. Obviously, John Tessier could not have been in two places at once. No wonder he'd been cleared by the FBI.

The FBI files also contained an interview with Ralph and Eileen Tessier in which they backed up their son John's alibi. Ralph had told the agents that John had called collect from Rockford to say he was "ready to come home" and could he get a lift. According to the Tessiers' story, Ralph had driven to Rockford and picked up John at approximately 8:00 P.M. and they had come straight home. They were back in Sycamore around nine, at which point John had gone to his girlfriend's, Jan Edwards, around 9:20 and stayed with her until 10:30.

Hanley and Kot knew that if there was any hope of nailing John Tessier, they had to crush his so-called ironclad alibi. This was Kot's handiwork. Analysis. Doing the math. Connecting the dots.

It took months to collect all the paperwork from the archives of three law-enforcement agencies. There were thousands of pages to study and evaluate. Digging through the old state police files, Kot came across a report dated July 27, 1958. That would have been three months after the mushroom hunters found Maria's body. It was quite eye-opening.

The very first sentence declared, "We feel certain facts may have been overlooked." Specifically, the report stated, Maria Ridulph's abduction had taken place earlier than everyone believed.

In those first desperate moments following the kidnapping on December 3, 1957, when Maria's mother, Frances, was out of her mind with worry, she told police that her daughter had gone outside at 6:30 P.M. and come back for her rubber doll at 6:40. Three neighbors also reported seeing Maria and Kathy playing at around 6:30. But Kot started to wonder whether the kidnapper himself had thrown everybody off track by injecting false data into the order of events. When Kathy Sigman ran home to fetch her mittens, she asked Johnny the time. He told her it was 7:00 P.M. Everyone went with that timeline. But Kot was now looking at a state police report that moved it up. It stated that Maria had left the house at 5:50 P.M. and come back for her rubber doll closer to 6:02 P.M. How could it be so precise? Because Frances said she drove out of her driveway at 6:05 P.M. to take her daughter Kay to a music lesson. And a heating oil deliveryman, Tom Braddy, told police that he saw Maria Ridulph and Kathy Sigman at 6:00 P.M. playing at the corner of Archie Place and Center Cross Street. When he completed his delivery, fifteen or twenty minutes later, he drove past the intersection but didn't see the girls.

Kot put together a minute-by-minute log that covered three walls of his office, and as he did, he reached a pivotal deduction: Johnny had kidnapped Maria no later than 6:20 P.M. Given that Rockford was forty miles away, John Tessier could have dashed down country blacktop roads with Maria dead or alive in the trunk and made it in time to place the collect call to his home at 6:57 P.M. even in the snow. There was no way of knowing what telephone booth the call had been made from. It could have been in downtown Rockford near the post office, or it could have come from a pay phone on the outskirts of town that had a Rockford phone code.

That phone call made by Tessier, it now seemed to Kot, was looking more and more like somebody had been trying to establish an alibi.

Hanley had to find Jan Edwards, and it was easy enough using public records to track her down at her new home in Bradenton, Florida. A long and winding road had taken Jan to the Gulf Coast of Florida, where she was working as a certified nurse's assistant. As of this writing, she is the grandmother of twenty-two children and has eight great-grandchildren. Her husband is a retired stockbroker.

When Hanley phoned her, the first thing he did was swear her to secrecy.

"Sure, I won't say anything." Jan was curious about where this was going.

Hanley told her he was looking into the Maria Ridulph murder. Of course, Jan remembered the crime. To the people of Sycamore, it was like the assassination of President Kennedy, or 9/11 for another generation. For those alive in Sycamore in 1957, you never forgot where you were the night Maria was kidnapped.

Hanley dropped a bombshell, telling her that he was investigating her old boyfriend John Tessier for the kidnapping and murder.

Jan almost had to laugh. "I don't believe it," she said.

"Well, if you knew what I knew about him, you'd believe it," Hanley said.

Jan tried to fill Hanley in about what her life was like in small-town Sycamore in the fifties. "If my father for one second ever suspected John, he would have been so out of my life." She explained that her father was Sycamore's only professional photographer and consequently he was sometimes called upon to take pictures of accidents and crime scenes for the local police. As such, he had many friends among Sycamore cops who considered him a fellow officer in blue. Somebody in the department would surely have warned Mr. Edwards if John Tessier was trouble. She told Hanley that he must be targeting the wrong man. "It's totally against John's personality. It's not possible. He was a totally acceptable young man for me to date. And I only dated guys who were good to me. John was never sexually aggressive with me."

Hanley sounded unconvinced. He started probing. Why had she and Tessier broken up? Did it have anything to do with Maria Ridulph's kidnapping? Jan wondered whether Hanley was trying to browbeat her into cooperating. She explained that she was never in love with the guy, he was just someone she dated in high school, nothing more. In fact, she told Hanley, she was sort of relieved when he enlisted in the U.S. Air Force because it saved her the ordeal of breaking up with him.

Hanley tried Jan again several months later. He was desperate for a photo of Tessier as he had looked in 1957 for identification purposes. Because he'd dropped out of high school, he wasn't in the Sycamore High School yearbook. The Tessiers had plenty of family photos of their brother when he was an adolescent, and in uniform in the air force, but 1957 was a big gap in the investigation.

Hanley asked Jan if she had any photos of John Tessier. "I'm pretty sure I have one," she told him. It was the photo of her and Tessier in the nightclub in Rockford six months before his induction into the air force, which would date it as having been taken in 1957—just what Hanley was looking for. Jan told him that she thought she kept it in her memory box because it had been a very special date for her, the first time she had ever gone to a nightclub, her first real grown-up date.

Bingo, Hanley thought. He said he would definitely be interested in seeing it.

Jan said she'd call him back after she'd had a chance to dig up the photo.

In a storage closet, she found the memory box with all her treasured memorabilia from so long ago inside it. Here was the time capsule of her life in Sycamore. There were the Brownie wings she'd received at the "fly-up" ceremony when she graduated to Girl Scout, and the first clipping from the hoof of her colt Pokey. There was a little wooden ladder—part of a bunk bed set from her doll collection. There were a few photos of guys she'd dated, one taken when a brazen young fellow took her to the Playboy Club in Chicago. It pleased her to see all the photos in pristine black-and-white condition. She had to smile. *After all, I am a photographer's daughter.* Then she found it, a cardboard picture frame that, when opened, contained the photo of her and John Tessier, from June 1957. Jan stared at it. It was John all right. She'd forgotten what he'd looked like. He wasn't a particularly handsome guy, she had to admit; then again, looks never really meant much to her when she was dating. Character meant everything. How could she have been so wrong about Tessier? Could he have really murdered a seven-year-old girl?

Then Jan saw something else tucked inside the picture frame. It was a one-way coach ticket to Chicago on the Illinois Central Railroad, with a U.S. government insignia, meaning it had been issued to the government rather than purchased by a civilian passenger. The date on the stamp was November 29, 1957. It was good until December 30, 1957. And it was in mint condition, having never been punched or stamped as used. A flood of memories came back. She remembered now how John had given her the ticket for safekeeping. Was it the night he came home from his air force physical—the night Maria Ridulph was kidnapped? Or was it the night after? Jan wracked her brain, but for the life of her could not remember. It was just too long ago.

When she called Brion Hanley back, it was Jan's turn to drop a bombshell. First she told him she had found the photo. Then she said, "And I have a train ticket that he gave me on the day he took his physical in Chicago."

"*What?*"

Jan told Hanley the story, and from his reaction, she could tell that the existence of an unused train ticket was not only a surprise, but potentially a very big deal. Hanley could not conceal his excitement. It meant that John Tessier may not have taken public transportation to Chicago or back to Rockford as he had long ago claimed. That meant he could have driven his car. In other words, he had the mobility to kidnap Maria and still make it to Rockford to establish an alibi. That ticket had the potential of demolishing Tessier's alibi. Hanley had to get his hands on it.

"Can you send it to me?" he asked.

Jan started to get a little worried. As she said at a later date, "I didn't know at that point whether he thought I had kept the train ticket as a sort of trophy, all kinds of nonsense like that. I didn't want there to be any kind of implication that I was involved or that I suspected John, because I didn't."

Jan saw it as her duty as a law-abiding citizen to cooperate. Her brother, Bill Edwards, was serving as city attorney of Sycamore. You could say that law enforcement ran in her blood. Hanley asked for the original ticket. On this he was unequivocal. Jan made several copies and mailed the original ticket to Hanley.

Then she started thinking things through. The timeline really bothered her. She had a clear recollection of sitting in a car with John in the driveway of her house on Somonauk Street in Sycamore at around 9:30 at night. What if it was December 3? What if he had just killed Maria Ridulph?

Oh, no, she thought. *Could Maria's body have been in the trunk of the car when he came to see me?*

Eleven months after their sister Janet Tessier had first gone to the state police, Brion Hanley met face-to-face with the other Tessier siblings, Jeanne, Katheran, and Bob. The gathering took place in Louisville, Kentucky, where Jeanne was living. Katheran flew in from Minnesota and Bob made the 190-mile drive from his home in the small town of Cadiz in southwestern Kentucky. They all rendezvoused at a hotel in downtown Louisville.

Hanley secured a conference room, and after swearing everyone to secrecy, he proceeded to outline the case that the state police were assembling against John Tessier for the murder of Maria Ridulph. Hanley told them things about John that they'd known nothing about. Even John's distinguished military record as an army captain was being called into question. According to Hanley, John had resigned for conduct unbecoming an officer; apparently, he'd been caught having an affair with a superior's wife. Then Hanley disclosed that John had been forced to resign from the Milton police department for sexually assaulting a fifteen-year-old runaway. It left them all slack-jawed. *Holy crap*, Bob thought. He'd always known John to be a womanizer and serial philanderer, but this was another level of perversion, and it hurt like hell to hear about it. He'd grown up idolizing his big brother, and he wanted to tell Hanley that John was nothing like this, but he also knew that Hanley was probably speaking the truth. His brother was really messed up.

The whole time the meeting had been going on, Bob observed that Jeanne was glaring at Hanley. She obviously didn't want to be there, and it wasn't only because she didn't have much trust in the cops. Hanley finally stopped talking and asked Bob and Katheran to step outside so he could speak with Jeanne privately. Something was going on.

Bob asked his sister, "Do you want me to stay in the room and be with you?"

Jeanne just shook her head. "No, I'll be OK."

"Well, I'll be right outside."

When they were alone, Hanley proceeded to question Jeanne. About the night of December 3, 1957, she told him how her parents had lied to the FBI when they'd said John was in Rockford when Maria was kidnapped. When the subject of John's history as a sexual predator came up,

Jeanne let slip some things she'd never told anyone but her therapist, not even her sisters. When she was a child growing up in Sycamore, a police affidavit would later allege, John had habitually molested her behind the tall bushes, and she knew that he was doing it to other girls in the neighborhood too, because he would take her along to serve as a lookout. She told Hanley how John had once invited a high school chum over and ordered her to pull down her pants and show him her genitals. And she revealed a horrifying story of what she claimed Tessier had done to her in 1962, when she was fourteen. He had pulled up to their house in a red convertible and driven her to a house on Carlson Street, where he'd invited the young men who were there to gang-rape her.

Outside the conference room, Bob and Katheran waited almost two hours until Jeanne and Hanley had finally finished, and they were invited back in. They found their sister sitting there, looking physically spent.

It was a difficult drive back to Cadiz. Bob was behind the wheel steering with his one good arm; the other, the consequence of a motorcycle wreck six years before, was a fitted hi-tech prosthetic device. Until this day, all Bob had known about Jeanne was that a dark cloud had hung over her when they'd lived in Sycamore. Now he knew why. He got to thinking about his parents and why they'd given false information to the FBI. What if John had been arrested for Maria Ridulph's murder back in 1957? Not to excuse his parents' actions, but he could just imagine the repercussions for the Tessier family. Ralph would never have been able to find work in Sycamore again; the Tessier children would have been ostracized. Family honor, their good name, would have been done for. They would have had to move. It also made Bob wonder whether the burden of living with this terrible secret could have accounted for Ralph's alcoholism. It must have been chewing him up inside. Now that Bob knew it, it explained a lot.

26

·········

JACK DANIEL MCCULLOUGH

John Tessier existed no more. On April 27, 1994, his name was officially changed to Jack Daniel McCullough.

The story of how John Tessier became Jack Daniel McCullough began when Tessier answered a help-wanted ad for drivers for O'Connor Transportation of Seattle. Daniel O'Connor was a six-foot-tall short-tempered Irish-American with red hair and blue eyes. Years earlier, in the 1980s, when he'd been an ordinary taxi driver, he'd noticed that airline pilots and flight attendants had to wait in line for taxis when they landed at Seattle-Tacoma International Airport, Sea-Tac for short. It gave him an idea: he could provide exclusive transportation services for airline crews to and from their hotel accommodations. He met with Sea-Tac's airline officials and a few of them bought into his plan. O'Connor sold his taxi and invested in a van. By the mid-1990s, he had struck deals with United, U.S. Airways,

Continental, and other major carriers. From a little business he'd built from scratch, he owned or leased nine vans. Now he needed to hire additional, reliable drivers.

On the surface, Tessier's job application was impressive: he'd achieved the rank of captain in the U.S. Army, plus years of service as a police officer in the towns of Lacey and Milton in Washington. He also knew his way around Seattle. Tessier told O'Connor that he was looking for a new line of work, and when Tessier told him he hailed from Illinois, they clicked. What a coincidence, O'Connor said; he'd grown up in Chicago. He'd also served in the military, the navy, and when his aircraft carrier had docked in Seattle and he liked what he saw of the city, he settled on the West Coast. So he and Tessier shared similar histories.

In some ways, O'Connor reminded Tessier of his late stepfather, Ralph, in that both men were strong, manly types but could also be surly and, on occasion, even menacing. Tessier told O'Connor he'd left police work after he'd suffered an accident on the job—a motorist he'd been issuing a ticket to had backed up and accidentally hit him in the knee. It was total bullshit, but O'Connor apparently didn't bother to call the Milton police for a background check. He was prepared to hire Tessier. Just one problem.

"I already have two guys named John working for me," he told Tessier. "I can't have a third. If you want this job your name is Jack." He didn't want any confusion when he communicated with his drivers over the radio. That was fine with John Tessier: just like that he became Jack.

O'Connor Transportation was a family business. Daniel O'Connor's son, Dan, ran operations, and his daughter,

Sue, the divorced mother of two girls, was in charge of schedules. But everything went through Daniel. He was the total hands-on boss.

When Sue O'Connor heard how her father had required that this new employee John call himself Jack, she had to laugh. "Yep, that's my dad all right." Over time, Sue came to appreciate John Tessier's work ethic. "He was an agreeable driver, very reliable. I could call him at any time, even in the middle of the night." The work was wearying: seven days on, twelve hours a day; then seven days off.

One day, O'Connor got on the radio and really laid into Tessier for some real or manufactured screwup. Sue overheard everything and just cringed. "My dad was very aggressive with the drivers. He intimidated people by fear. That's how I was raised, that's the way he was with the drivers. He'd yell at them on the radio, and all the other drivers would hear." And so would the airline crews, which was not good for business.

Tessier, probably figuring he was too old to listen to this crap, flicked off the radio. Not long thereafter, he gave O'Connor his notice.

Months passed, then a year.

One day, in 1994, Sue O'Connor answered the phone, and it was John Tessier calling to say hello. They chatted for a while, and a few weeks later, he called her again, said he was just checking in. He told her he'd always thought she had a sexy voice that he'd enjoyed listening to over the dispatch radio. He told her what pretty hair she had. "Do you want to go out sometime?" he asked.

Sue was a single mom raising two daughters. She was

very busy at work; plus, she hadn't hit the dating scene in a long time and wasn't eager to go out with a man, any man. She declined Tessier's invitation. But he was pretty persistent, and finally, Sue said OK.

Their first date was not what Tessier had had in mind. They, the three of them—Sue brought along her twelve-year-old daughter, Janey—went to a Chinese restaurant. Janey had seen Tessier around her grandfather's office on occasion when he'd worked for O'Connor Transportation, and at dinner, she got a kick out of seeing him squirm under her gaze. After the dinner, she and her mom giggled all the way home.

First impressions? "Nope, not good," recalled Sue. "I didn't care about him at all. Kind of a goofball. Not my type."

A few days later, Tessier called again. Just checking in. Said he'd had a great time the other night. And how about another date?

"No, thank you," Sue said.

More months passed. Tessier kept at it. Finally, recalls Sue, "He just wore me out."

Sue drove an hour and met Tessier at a movie theater to see *Jurassic Park*. This time she'd left Janey at home.

During the movie, Sue's purse slipped off her lap, and when she went to catch it, she accidentally grabbed John's thigh. She was embarrassed and didn't want her date to think she was coming on to him. "For some reason, I liked him better the second time," Sue recalled. "Don't ask me why. Maybe I was just in a different place."

They dated for the next two years. It was getting serious

enough for Tessier to tell his parents in Sycamore that he was getting married again. "She's the love of my life," Tessier said of Sue O'Connor. "She's my rock. But she's a little girl at the same time."

Within the extended Tessier family, the news spread, and Sally, John's ex, got wind of it. She wrote Sue O'Connor a letter that was chilling. It warned Sue that, before she married John Tessier, she must call his sister, Jeanne, and find out what he was really like. In her letter, Sally included Jeanne's phone number in Kentucky. Sue showed the letter to Janey and asked her to listen in on the extension when she made the call to Jeanne Tessier.

Jeanne told Sue a lot—not everything—but, in effect, she said that Sue needed to leave John. "He's evil. You need to be afraid for your daughters. They're in jeopardy."

Sue slammed the phone down. "I'm done with this!" she shouted. She was in tears, baffled. She didn't know what to do next. She was so alarmed that she thought about calling off the wedding. She confronted Tessier.

"She's your *sister*," Sue told him, "And she really hates you."

Tessier was embarrassed, but what upset him most was that Janey had heard everything on the extension. He told Sue he very much wanted Janey to feel safe in his company, and he asked her whether he should talk to her.

Around this time, Tessier got word that his mother was dying. Thanksgiving 1993 found him determined to see Eileen one last time, and when he told her he couldn't afford the airfare to Chicago, she put the ticket on her credit card. When Eileen died, in January 1994, Sue asked him whether he was going to attend her funeral.

"No," he told her, "I said my good-byes when she was alive."

Sue remembers Tessier occasionally mentioning a little girl who had been kidnapped in his hometown of Sycamore when he was a teenager. He didn't go into it in depth, just shared a brief recollection about the story now and then when they were passing the time. To Sue, it didn't sound very interesting.

Eileen's death triggered John Tessier's final break with his past: he decided that the time had come to change his name. His legal application for the name change was granted by a King County judge in Washington State. In this way, John Tessier, born John Samuel Cherry, became Jack Daniel McCullough.

"Jack" was easy—it was the name everyone started calling him after he went to work for O'Connor Transportation. "McCullough" was a tribute to his mother; it was her maiden name. When he'd told Sue he was changing his name, she was perplexed. What was the point? He tried to explain.

"Do you want to be the fourth Mrs. John Tessier? Or do you want to be the first Mrs. Jack McCullough?" There was a loopy but undeniable logic to it. To give Sue some input in the process, he left the selection of a middle name to replace *Samuel*, which he'd always hated, up to her. She picked *Daniel*, after her father, an arguably unfortunate selection as *Jack Daniel* McCullough conjured images of a bottle of whiskey.

Was he being a smart-ass when he went with such a name?

"No, no, no. It just happened to be Jack Daniel. That's why I don't call myself Jack Daniel very often," he told me.

Henceforth, in this book, John Tessier is called by his legal name, Jack McCullough.

Jack McCullough married Sue O'Connor on June 18, 1994, at a Catholic church in the Seattle suburb of Shoreline. He asked Janey to be his best "man." Her sister, Amy, was her mother's maid of honor.

It was a small wedding, just a "smattering" of people. "We had both done it before," Sue says. "I didn't wear a wedding dress. I wore a nice dress, though. Jack wore a suit. We were married by a priest."

McCullough piled all his goods into his pickup truck, and with Janey helping him with the heavy lifting, he moved into Sue's Spanish-style house, with its red-tile roof and stucco exterior. It was a spacious home with four bedrooms, a family room, a bricked-in patio, and, in the backyard, a waterfall and a pond filled with goldfish—all devoured one morning by a long-legged great blue heron.

Sue and Jack went into business together, starting a company that provided private transportation for airline crews at Sea-Tac, just like her father's. In the beginning, it was a struggle. They bought two full-size Ford Club Wagons; Sue drove one and McCullough the other. In time, they established a reputation for reliability, and Scandinavian Airlines signed on, then U.S. Airways, UPS, American Airlines. The business was growing. These were contented days.

McCullough's son, Sean, came out to Seattle to drive for them, but, according to his stepmother, it didn't work out, and he was let go. McCullough's daughter, Christine, had problems of her own, strung out on drugs and working as an exotic dancer at a strip club.

"She was very fragile because of all the drugs she was using," Sue said. "Jack would get very frustrated with her and hand me the phone. We offered to let her live with us. We tried to help her straighten out her life."

At least they still had their business. Then came the September 11, 2001, terrorist attacks on America. The airline industry was crippled. U.S. Airways filed for Chapter 11 bankruptcy in 2002, and again in 2004.

"We just couldn't keep it together after that. We were owed $200,000," Sue said. "We were paying for gas and repairs with our credit cards." Their company went bust, and the McCulloughs had to sell their house to pay back the loan on the Ford wagons they'd purchased. They moved into a 26-foot trailer in a small town in eastern Washington called Tonasket, population 994, about twenty miles south of the Canadian border. They stayed there for a year, until Janey, after she got married and gave birth to two babies, talked them into moving back to Seattle. She said she could use some help from the grandparents.

It was hard to believe that Jack McCullough was now a senior citizen approaching the age of seventy. He found a job working security at a swanky apartment building in the city, and he and Sue moved into a $600-a-month apartment at Four Freedoms, a retirement community on North 135th Street. When a position working security at the Four Freedoms came up, McCullough switched jobs, figuring all he had to do to get to work was take the elevator down six floors from his apartment to the lobby. It certainly saved on gas; plus, it was easy work: a little vacuuming, responding to smoke alarms, patrolling the floors and stairwells twice a night, keeping an eye on the front door.

Come the year 2011, McCullough had settled into a routine of quietude, working as a night watchman at Four Freedoms, babysitting Janey's children, surfing the Internet, and watching the Fox News Channel. He was seventy-two and had no idea that, for the past three years, he'd been under investigation by the Illinois state police for the murder of a little girl back in 1957.

27

....

POSITIVE ID

Back in 1957, Dennis Twadell stood six feet three and weighed 160 pounds. His mom was always urging him to eat more and put on weight. Now, more than fifty years later, at the age of seventy, he was physically a different man, weighing in at 328 pounds.

In March 2010, Brion Hanley appeared at Twadell's house in McHenry, Illinois, and asked the retired factory worker to accompany him to the Sycamore police department. Hanley didn't say much more, only that he wanted to ask him several questions regarding "something that happened in Sycamore" many years ago. Twadell figured he didn't have much of a choice. It was a long way to Sycamore, about forty-five miles, and when they got to police headquarters, Hanley, totally out of the blue, asked Twadell, "When did you and Jack McCullough become friends?"

Twadell didn't know who the hell he was talking about. "Who?"

"Jack McCullough."

"I don't know a Jack McCullough."

"Do you know a John Tessier?"

"Yes, we went to high school together."

Hanley picked up a black-and-white photo from 1957 and showed it to him. "Do you know who this is?"

Twadell blinked. "Well, that's John Tessier."

Hanley asked Twadell if he was still in contact with his old chum from high school.

Not at all, Twadell said. The last time he'd seen Tessier was in 1962, when Tessier had returned to Sycamore after his U.S. Air Force service. Over the years, they'd lost touch. A few years back, he'd Googled John Tessier, just for curiosity's sake, but nothing had come up in his search. Until this moment, he'd had no idea that Tessier had changed his name to McCullough.

Then Hanley asked him if he remembered anything significant that had happened on the night of December 3, 1957.

That was more than fifty years ago, for Chrissake, Twadell said. "I can't remember what I had two weeks ago for supper."

Hanley didn't crack much of a smile and, in police parlance, proceeded to "refresh" Twadell's memory.

What this was all about suddenly dawned on Twadell—Maria Ridulph.

"We think John Tessier was responsible for the disappearance of Maria Ridulph," Hanley said.

Twadell was stupefied. "I think you're barking up the wrong tree," he told Hanley. From time to time, he and

Tessier had double-dated, and he didn't recall a single occasion when Tessier had gotten out of line with a girl.

Hanley moved on. He wanted Twadell to think back to December 3, 1957. "Do you recall seeing John that day?" Hanley asked.

He sure did and proceeded to tell Hanley a remarkable story.

Around 4:00 P.M. he was walking west on State Street in downtown Sycamore, approaching Maple, when he saw Tessier's 1948 two-door Plymouth Coupe coming down the street.

"How could you be so sure?" Hanley asked.

"There wasn't anyone in town that had a car like it." Tessier had painted winged flames on the sides of the jalopy, and it was probably the best-known car in Sycamore. It was battleship gray, with hubcaps from a 1955 Buick that came with an inner-wheel ornament designed to spin when the car was in motion. But, Twadell said, the car was a block away at least. He wasn't sure who was behind the wheel. It could have been Tessier. Or somebody else.

"You didn't see who was driving?"

"No."

"Are you sure?"

"I was a block or so down the street. The windows were rolled up. I couldn't holler or flag it down."

Hanley kept pumping Twadell for something more definitive.

"I can't say for sure that it was John driving, but I saw the car in Sycamore. I didn't see the driver." Thinking about it, Twadell said, the driver could have been Ralph Tessier.

But it had to be one or the other because John Tessier never let *anyone* drive his set of wheels.

As Twadell told it, later that night of December 3, 1957, his buddy Dave Fredericks called to say that the Ridulph kid was missing, and everybody in town was out searching for her. Fredericks was rounding up the gang to see what they could do to pitch in. Twadell got off the phone and called John Tessier at home. Tessier's mother answered. She said John wasn't home.

"I figured he was on a date or something," Twadell told Hanley.

Hanley asked him whether he could recall if John Tessier/Jack McCullough wore sweaters in the winter. Sure did, Twadell said. John wore lots of sweaters. A green crewneck sweater was his favorite. Green for Ireland. His mother was an amazing knitter.

That was all for now. Twadell was driven back to McHenry.

Hanley kept a poker face, but he knew this was a milestone in the investigation. He now had a living witness who could place Tessier/McCullough in Sycamore around the time he claimed to be sightseeing and taking in a burlesque show in Chicago. In 1957, John Tessier had told the FBI that he had boarded the 5:15 train from Chicago to Rockford. *Baloney.* He had been driving around Sycamore since at least 4:00 P.M. Assuming, of course, Twadell remembered correctly.

Kathy Sigman Chapman and her husband, Mike, were home when they heard somebody at the door. They weren't expecting anyone, so they peeked out the window and saw a young man wearing a college football jersey and a baseball cap turned backward. His buddy was better dressed, in a white shirt and tie, no jacket. They looked like door-to-door salesmen, Kathy thought, or maybe they were running for a local political office. Whoever they were, she wasn't interested in speaking with them. The two men knocked several more times and got no response. Figuring nobody was home, they turned to walk back to their car. That's when Kathy saw that both of them had handcuffs clipped to the back of their belts.

Cops.

What were two plainclothes police officers doing here?

It was September 1, 2010, a Wednesday. The top news of the day was all about the economy. The Labor Department had announced that the national unemployment rate had risen to 9.6 percent. There was real fear that the United States was slipping into a double-dip recession. But America had come a long way. Who could have predicted, in 1957, that fifty years in the future an African American president would be sitting in the Oval Office?

Kathy Chapman opened the door and called out to the two men.

"Can I help you?"

They turned around and smiled. So she was home after all. Brion Hanley, the guy in the football jersey, showed Kathy his identification and said he was a special agent with the Illinois state police. The man with him was his partner, Todd Damasky.

When they were all settled in the living room, Hanley

told the Chapmans in strictest confidence that the Maria Ridulph case was being reexamined. More to the point, there was a serious suspect currently under investigation.

"We thought the case was closed," Kathy said.

Hanley shook his head. Not only was it not closed, but it was red-hot.

Kathy got up and dug around in a drawer. She showed Hanley a 1994 article from the *Sycamore News* that she had kept all these years. It was the statement from Lieutenant Patrick Solar that a truck driver from Nebraska had in all likelihood murdered Maria Ridulph.

Hanley knew the story and wished it would just go away. No, he informed Kathy, it wasn't the truck driver at all. The suspect they were looking at was somebody else entirely. Hanley pulled a document out of his briefcase, a memo from J. Edgar Hoover, dated 1957, that he'd found in the old FBI files. He started to read it out loud because he wanted to remind Kathy how important the case had once been to the nation.

Would she be willing to help? he asked.

"Of course I would be," she told him.

Then he asked her to tell him everything she remembered about December 3, 1957.

Her account was consistent with her previous statements to police and the FBI.

Now came the big moment. In his briefcase, Hanley said, he had with him several photos that he wanted Kathy to look at. He wanted to see if she could identify "Johnny." But before he showed them to her, he wanted her to "think about the case."

"Don't stress out. I want to give you time to think about it and get the memory of Johnny in your mind."

Labor Day was approaching. Hanley said he'd be back on September 9, after the holiday weekend. Kathy said she'd be ready.

When they'd left, Mike and Kathy could only stare at each other in disbelief. It was almost impossible to fathom, like hearing a fairy tale.

Nine days later, Hanley was back, and this time, he came with his supervisor, a state police sergeant named Dan Smith. It was 6:00 P.M., and Kathy and Mike were waiting for them. When they'd all made themselves at home in the living room, Hanley opened his briefcase. First he read Kathy the Illinois state police photo lineup advisory form, which he asked her to sign and date. Basically, it stated that she was not required to make an identification unless she could positively identify the perpetrator. Then Hanley and Smith countersigned the document.

It was time.

The array had been prepared by state police intelligence-analyst Larry Kot, and all the photos with the exception of one came from the 1957 Sycamore High School yearbook. They were black-and-white photos, and all the men were clean-shaven and wearing suits and ties.

Hanley placed the first photo on the coffee table in front of Kathy. It was marked number 1.

"Look at the photo," he told her. "Take your time. When you're ready for the next one, let me know."

Kathy studied the photo.

"That wasn't him." She indicated that she was ready for

the next one. Hanley took back number 1 and replaced it with the second photo, marked number 2. In this manner, he showed her six photos in total. Kathy eliminated numbers 3, 5, and 6. She asked to see numbers 1, 2, and 4 again. Then she told Hanley to take away number 2. Two were left. She studied number 4 for several more moments. Then she put her hands over her head and let out a deep breath. She was stunned.

"That is him. That was Johnny."

Hanley asked her if she was certain.

"That's him. That's the face I remember. To the best of my memory and recollection of that night, that's him."

Kathy was in a state of awe. Who was this young man who she had just identified as Johnny? In those intense days and weeks immediately following Maria's kidnapping, eight-year-old Kathy had been shown hundreds of mug shots, but she was certain she'd never seen this photo before. After all these decades, where had it come from? Who was this man? What was his name?

Hanley wasn't saying anything, but his body language told another story. Kathy and Mike knew right away that she had hit pay dirt. Hanley asked Kathy to sign the front of photo number 4 with her maiden name, Sigman. Then Sergeant Smith countersigned. Kathy kept at it with the questions. Finally, Hanley said he couldn't reveal much more except to say that the break in the case had come when a member of the suspected killer's own family had gone to the police to turn him in.

"How long is it going to take before you make an arrest?" Kathy asked.

Hanley wouldn't say. He and Smith, looking like they were eager to leave, gathered all the photos, thanked the Chapmans one more time, and headed out the door. Hanley's feet, Mike noticed, "barely touched the floor," he was so ecstatic; he was almost skipping. Now Mike understood why Hanley and Smith were in such a hurry to leave.

They wanted to celebrate.

28

....

SEATTLE

Detective Mike Ciesynski of the Seattle police department's cold-case squad saw the Post-it note fluttering on his desk. It was from his sergeant, Bob Vallor. The Illinois state police had called requesting assistance on a case that was right up Ciesynski's alley. Call Special Agent Brion Hanley, the note said. Ciesynski dialed the number.

"Well, there was this little girl . . ." Hanley began. He proceeded to brief Ciesynski on the Maria Ridulph case, and quite a yarn it was. In fact, Ciesynski had never heard of a cold case as ancient as this one, and he was an expert on cold cases. Hanley said the suspect, Jack Daniel McCullough, was believed to be living in the Seattle area. He and several other investigators from the Illinois state police and Sycamore police department were coming out to Seattle to continue their investigation, and they were wondering whether Ciesynski could confirm McCullough's Seattle address before they made the trip, at considerable taxpayers' expense.

"OK, no problem," Ciesynski said.

Ciesynski had a white mustache and combed-back hair flecked with gray. He had smooth skin and deep bags under his eyes from unsolved homicide cases that kept him up nights. This murder investigation, as outlined by Hanley, sounded truly compelling. Coincidently, Ciesynski had been born and raised in South Chicago, about ninety minutes from Sycamore, so he had an instantaneous affinity for the case and the people involved.

Ciesynski had gotten married at nineteen, and his first job had been driving a truck distributing Chicago's most popular beer, Old Style. But he'd always wanted to be a cop and applied for admission to the police academy of the city of Seattle, of all places. A funny thing had drawn Ciesynski to the Pacific Northwest. His favorite show growing up had been *Here Come the Brides*, a western comedy starring teen idol Bobby Sherman. It aired for two seasons on ABC, from 1968 to 1970, and was based—very loosely based—on the historic, nineteenth-century campaign to bring marriageable young women to Seattle. The show had a catchy theme song, "Seattle."

The bluest skies you've ever seen are in Seattle
And the hills the greenest green, in Seattle!

Ciesynski found *Here Come the Brides* so enchanting that he took out a road atlas, calculated the route from

Chicago to Seattle, and told his bride, "This is where we'll live."

"*Here Come the Brides*—that's how I got to Seattle," Ciesynski says with a laugh. He was sworn in on December 21, 1983. After working street patrol, he took the detective's test on a whim, passed, and was assigned to narcotics for five years, then four years in the robbery unit, and, finally, ten years in homicide.

Now he was working the Seattle cold-case squad, an elite division that consisted of a single detective—Mike Ciesynski.

Cold-case detectives never say a case is reopened because, strictly speaking, no unsolved murder or missing-person case is ever closed. The preferred terminology is *reexamined*. It takes a special kind of detective to work cold cases. Persistence is a necessity. You can't let disappointment get to you because cold cases are so time-consuming. Organizational skills are a big asset because a cold case is a major administrative undertaking that requires the gathering of old files from storage and the collection of forensics from the medical examiner. A gift for communication is another plus because you don't want the original case detective to think he's being second-guessed. One other trait is essential—having a keen internal antenna to scope out bullshit.

"There's a reason why a case is cold," Ciesynski liked to say. "You have to broaden your horizons. Think outside the box. Reinterview people. Don't go down the same path the case detective had taken. You're not here to critique somebody's work, but a lot of times you see a glaring problem in the investigation. You're here to solve the case."

After his telephone conversation with Brion Hanley, Ciesynski strode out of his office—he was the only detective other than the squad commanders to have an office, room 762—and found Detective Cloyd Steiger in his cubicle. The hulking Steiger was one of Ciesynski's closest friends in homicide.

"Hey, I've got these guys coming in from Illinois. They've got a cold case from 1957, and the guy they think did it lives here."

Steiger whistled. "Nineteen fifty-seven. Wow."

Ciesynski and Steiger had a lot in common, even a birthday, October 3, although Steiger was three years younger. They were street-savvy but also book-smart. They liked to kid each other. "Mike Ciesynski's a typical Chicago guy," Steiger would say. "He's a good Catholic boy in every sense except he doesn't do anything a Catholic should." They had mutual regard for each other's aptitude as investigators. They also both enjoyed American history. Ciesynski read presidential biographies, books on World War II, and military history. Lincoln was a specialty. Steiger was another big reader, mainly the Civil War era and World War II, in which his father fought as a combat marine. A dream vacation for Steiger was touring the sacred grounds of Arlington National Cemetery or the Civil War battlegrounds of Gettysburg, Antietam, or Vicksburg. He's been to all of them.

Their first task was locating Jack McCullough. Motor-vehicle records quickly established that his last known address was the Four Freedoms retirement community on the

700 block of North 135th Street. The state records also showed that he'd worked in private security at Metropolitan Tower Apartments, on Westlake Avenue. This seemed like a good place to start. Ciesynski took a ride over. Metropolitan Towers was quite the swanky place. Tenants paid some of the highest rents in Seattle, and for it, they got hardwood floors, granite countertops in the kitchen, and impressive views overlooking Seattle's central business district. Ciesynski spoke to the assistant manager. It turned out that Jack McCullough had retired about a year before. The manager didn't remember much about him except that, technically, McCullough didn't work for the building but for a private security company, Star Protection Agency.

The date was June 17, 2011. Ciesynski had an idea, which came to him after a round of golf on his day off. *What the hell*, Ciesynski thought. If Illinois state police wanted him to verify McCullough's presence, he'd have to eyeball the guy up close. He drove from the golf course to the Four Freedoms and pulled into the parking lot. He found Jack and Sue McCullough's names and apartment number listed on the directory in the lobby entrance.

Four Freedoms was in the Bitter Lake neighborhood of Seattle. It had three hundred units, all rent-subsidized at reasonable rates strictly for senior citizens. Most of the apartments were studios renting for $400 a month. A one-bedroom apartment like the one Jack and Sue McCullough lived in cost closer to $600 a month. No one rich lived at the Four Freedoms, but the place was clean and secure from crime.

Ciesynski flashed his badge at the front desk and took

the elevator up to the sixth floor. He knocked on McCullough's door, number 616. Ciesynski was still in his golf shorts but carried his service revolver in a fanny pack along with extra ammo and a set of handcuffs. He deliberately wanted to keep the encounter low-key and not set off any alarm bells with McCullough. Go in real casual.

When the door opened, there was Jack McCullough. He was a perfect match with the photo Ciesynski had obtained from the Department of Licensing. He had a full head of snow-white hair and a thick white mustache. He stood just under six feet; had a pasty, blotched complexion; and weighed about 200 pounds; but he appeared to be in decent-enough shape for a man born in 1939. He wore a white T-shirt and khaki Dockers pants. Detectives make spot assessments of people all the time, and for no reason other than pure instinct, Ciesynski thought, *This is a bad guy.*

Ciesynski introduced himself and showed McCullough his Seattle police department ID. McCullough just stood there at the door, not inviting the detective into the apartment—not being rude but not unduly friendly either. Ciesynski would have expected more courtesy from an ex-cop. *Another reason not to like him*, he thought. From his position in the hallway, Ciesynski could hear the TV on in the apartment.

Ciesynski had the story all worked out in his head. He told McCullough he was investigating an assault that had taken place about a year ago at a bar near the Metropolitan Towers high-rise apartment building. Didn't McCullough used to work there in security?

"Yeah, I remember that," McCullough said.

Ciesynski suppressed a snicker. The story was a figment of his imagination, but it was a story that also had a foundation of authenticity because Metropolitan Towers was in a neighborhood packed with hip bars, and cops were always being summoned to break up fights. Ciesynski started hammering McCullough with questions about what he recalled of his experiences at the Metropolitan Towers and the assault that never was. Ciesynski found it amusing to be playing head games with a presumed scumbag like McCullough, to throw him off balance. The questioning got around to what McCullough was doing now.

Working security at the Four Freedoms, McCullough said. Mostly the night shift.

Did he come from around Seattle?

Illinois.

"No kidding," Ciesynski said. "I'm from Chicago."

"What a small world," McCullough said. He grew up in a place called Sycamore.

Ciesynski took a peek inside the apartment. There was a little girl who looked to be about ten on her stomach reading a book, nibbling on a snack, and watching TV at the same time. *Who could that be?* Ciesynski wondered. He knew McCullough was a suspect in the kidnapping and murder of a seven-year-old girl. To see a child in McCullough's apartment was unnerving.

He looked at McCullough. "You babysitting?"

"Yeah."

"That your daughter?"

"My granddaughter."

Ciesynski nodded, then handed McCullough his business card and asked him to call if he remembered anything more about that bar fight.

"Sure, no problem," McCullough said.

Ciesynski walked back to his car and drove to Seattle police headquarters, at the corner of Fifth and Cherry, directly east of City Hall. As soon as he was in his office, he called Brion Hanley to let him know that he had positively identified Jack McCullough as living in a sixth-floor apartment at the Four Freedoms retirement community of Seattle. He recounted his encounter with McCullough.

"Oh, man, I got a bad vibe as soon as he opened the door," Ciesynski said. "You just get that feeling."

He told Hanley about the girl he'd seen in the apartment. McCullough had identified her as his granddaughter, but who knew?

"I'm worried about the girl on the couch."

Hanley considered everything the Seattle detective had to say and announced, "We're going to get going and head out to Seattle." He said he'd be flying with three other detectives, plus an outside consultant who had been hired by the state police to advise them on the case.

Whoa, Ciesynski thought. Four detectives *plus* a consultant? When he flew out of town on a case, he'd sometimes travel with one detective, if that. What gives here? And why hire a consultant? He had never heard of such a thing in a homicide investigation. He wondered who was calling the shots. So be it. This was Illinois's baby; he was just here to help out.

· · · · · · · · · ·

The Illinois task force flew out on Southwest Airlines and checked into the Crowne Plaza Hotel, in downtown Seattle. Hanley and special agent Todd Damasky arrived first to work the case in the field. They were followed two days later by two detectives from the Sycamore police department, Sergeant Steven Cook and Tiffany Ziegler, and then came the outside consultant, Dave Zulawski.

When Cloyd Steiger saw all these out-of-town detectives assembled in the conference room of the homicide squad, he had the same reaction as Ciesynski. This investigation must be big. He knew it was a cold case dating back to 1957, but he didn't know much more. For the first time, Steiger heard the name Maria Ridulph. He excused himself for a moment, went to his desk, and ran a quick Google search on Maria Ridulph. There wasn't much. He found a photograph for sale on eBay depicting the 1958 search in Sportsmans Lake for Maria's body. There was also an article about the crime from a *Los Angeles Times* blog, dated 2007.

Steiger was a thirty-three-year veteran of the Seattle police department and had served in the homicide squad since 1994. He had worked or assisted in the investigation of hundreds of murders. He knew right then that the Maria Ridulph case would rank right up at the top. *This is why I became a detective.* "A great case. A great story," he would say later, "but a tragic story." Steiger also realized that an arrest and conviction in this case would make criminal-justice history as the oldest cold case ever to be adjudicated.

Now he understood why the state of Illinois had invested so much money and resources. It really was a big deal.

Steiger returned to the conference room, where the investigators from Illinois had laid out the files. Sergeant Cook was a gray-haired six-footer and a nineteen-year veteran of the Sycamore police who kept a pen tucked inside his shirt pocket always at the ready. Detective Tiffany Ziegler had been hired in 2005 after studying criminology at Northern Illinois University. She had long brown hair with blonde highlights.

Going through the material, the strengths and weaknesses of the case were plain to see. One big hurdle was the FBI polygraph examination that John Tessier/Jack McCullough had passed back in 1957. Steiger wasn't particularly distressed by this fact. Polygraphs were not admissible at trial because of reservations about reliability. Gary Ridgway, the Green River serial killer linked to the murders of seventy-one women in Washington State, had passed a polygraph test in 1984 after he had been taken into custody for soliciting prostitutes, but he wasn't arrested until 2001, when he was finally nailed by DNA evidence. Aldrich Ames, the CIA counterintelligence officer convicted in 1994 of spying for the Soviet Union and Russia for nearly a decade, had passed two CIA lie-detector tests after his KGB handlers advised him to get a good night's sleep, remain calm during the test, and develop a rapport with the examiner. In Steiger's experience, a psychopath believing his own set of lies or coldly detached from emotional stresses could pass a polygraph with flying colors. He put Jack McCullough in this category.

Reviewing the files, Steiger came to believe that Jack Tessier had lied to the FBI when he claimed he took the train to Chicago for his U.S. Air Force physical. He must have driven his car, which would have given him plenty of time to drive back to Sycamore and kidnap Maria. It also explained why his car had been spotted in Sycamore the afternoon of Maria's disappearance, according to witness Dennis Twadell.

When Steiger looked at the FBI files spread out before him, the amount of pointless paperwork the FBI had amassed in its investigation disgusted him. Business as usual for the FBI. *Federal Bureaucracy of Investigation*. In Steiger's experience, a rookie cop in a small-town police department had more flexibility in his decision making than a twenty-year veteran of the FBI.

He was shown a copy of the unpunched train ticket that had been turned over to the state police by Tessier/McCullough's ex-girlfriend Jan Edwards. Steiger's reaction? It wasn't as compelling as DNA, but it was still a pretty cool piece of evidence that would undoubtedly impress a jury.

Hanley made a good impression on Steiger. The young agent was operating on a shoestring budget and feeling guilty about every penny he spent in Seattle, making a point of getting the cheapest rental-car deal he could find. Hanley had been working the Maria Ridulph case on and off for three years now, and in a job that turned too many detectives into burned-out cynics, his dedication was refreshing.

Later that night, Steiger drove with Hanley to the Four

Freedoms building, which he was quite familiar with because just a month before, a routine dead-body call about an elderly woman found in her apartment there was now suspected of possibly involving foul play. When they drove into the parking lot, it was a relief to see that Jack McCullough's truck was still there.

The next morning, Hanley, Damasky, and Steiger drove out to Tukwila to pay a visit to the third ex–Mrs. Jack McCullough. They had obtained her name and address from McCullough's sisters, who thought she potentially could be a source of information and was definitely worth talking to. She has requested, for privacy reasons, that she be called D in this book. They found D in her office, where she worked as an industrial engineer and product designer. Dying of curiosity, she invited the detectives in and was taken aback when they told her why they were there.

D was thirty years old when she got married to Jack McCullough, or John Tessier as she knew him, in 1983. Back then she had brown hair and wore glasses, and considered herself average looking. Now she was gray-haired and happily remarried.

She told the detectives that when she met Tessier he was working as a staff photographer, shooting head shots and portfolios at a "fashion college" in downtown Seattle. Her roommate, who had been a model there, had a crush on Tessier and invited him for dinner one evening. D did the cooking—lasagna and garlic bread and a salad. First impressions of John Tessier?

"I didn't like him," D said.

At some point, her roommate's infatuation with Tessier came to an end after she "got to know him better," D says and, forswearing a career in modeling, she left Seattle.

Then Tessier invited D out on a date, and another Tessier whirlwind romance was launched. Tessier asked D if he could move in with her. She gave it a lot of thought before she said it would be all right with her. In truth, romantically, she had very little interest in him.

"I felt trapped, and I wasn't sure how to get out of it. I got caught up in events that you're not in control of, and off you go," she recalled.

They got married in Coeur D'Alene, Idaho, his idea. The drive from Washington State took about eight hours, and as the mileage mounted, so did the sinking feeling D had, but she went through the ceremony and returned to Seattle the third Mrs. John Tessier.

It was a bizarre marriage. D paid all of the $400 monthly rent, plus the utilities, grocery bills, and taxes. About the only expense Tessier covered was the chemicals he bought for the darkroom he'd built in the basement. He did all the cooking—one of the terms they'd informally reached to keep the marriage going. Mornings, when D woke up, he'd already be in the kitchen, ready to pour coffee. Then he'd fry some eggs and home fries, and she'd hustle off to work while he stayed home doing who knows what. When she got home, she'd find a nice home-cooked meal of chicken or spaghetti.

"I didn't starve," D recalls.

Every now and then, photography work came Tessier's

way. He shot an album cover and had an exhibition of his photographs at a gallery in the artsy Capitol Hill District of Seattle. D was impressed, but it frustrated her that he didn't seem to mind not having a steady income. He claimed he couldn't function in a regular work environment because he was suffering from post-traumatic stress, which to D sounded like a lot of bullshit.

D knew nothing about Tessier having pled guilty to communicating with a minor for indecent purposes. All he'd told her about his service as a police officer in Milton, Washington, was that he had quit the department after his partner had been shot in the line of duty.

The detectives from Seattle and Illinois listened with keen interest as D told them that Tessier's parents came out twice to visit, and D thought Eileen was a lovely woman and Ralph a "sweetheart," who really poured on the charm.

Tessier's daughter, Christine, was a teenager when her mother, Sonja, was diagnosed with lupus, and Christine came to live with him and D. It was an uneasy state of affairs. Christine was pretty, blonde, and very sweet, but she was dealing with a lot, being shuttled from a mother fighting a serious disease to a father she barely knew who was living with a new wife. She had "anger management issues," D says, and in her opinion, Christine also dressed too provocatively for her age.

D had never seen anything like the father-daughter dysfunction she witnessed between Tessier and Christine, the inappropriate body language and off-color jokes they exchanged, including one sexually suggestive crack Tessier made about a banana that just shocked her. Sometimes, Christine would walk around the house in baby-doll pajamas.

"I called him out on that," D says, "and it went away. John didn't want to lose his meal ticket, and so he did whatever was required to retain that. He knew I would always pay the bills, and he'd have a roof over his head while I made the money."

D tried to get along with Christine. She urged her to wear "age-appropriate" clothes and believe in herself and understand that a happy life awaited her if she worked at it. To build a kinship, she drove Christine to and from school. A bond was developing. Then D found something in the house that disturbed her. She had emptied out the desk drawers and come upon four 8-by-10-inch photos taped to the bottom. They were of Christine in various stages of undress. The clothes she did have on were very provocative. In one photo she was nude—not graphic enough to be deemed pornographic if she had been an adult but certainly out of line for a teenager.

D had no doubt that the photographer was John Tessier. She recognized his work. She showed the photos to her husband.

"What about these?" she asked.

He looked at them and shrugged and simply walked away. The subject never came up again.

Christine lived with her father and D for a full school year and then went back to Illinois to be with her mother.

D and Tessier found themselves living independent lives

in the same house. It wasn't a marriage so much as a peculiar arrangement of mutual convenience and indifference. Tessier never seemed to sleep; he existed on power naps instead. He spent many hours in the finished basement monitoring a police scanner, and God help D if she disturbed his concentration. John would lose it and tell her to shut up. He told her he was doing important freelance police work. Knowing that he was an ex-lawman, D, in the early days of the marriage, bought into this implausible story, but she came to realize that it too was complete nonsense.

A new twist: John told D to start calling home when she was leaving work every day; that way, he explained, he'd know when to start preparing dinner. He was so insistent on this point that a friend she mentioned it to put a bug in her ear. Why not head home without calling, just to see what was really going on.

"And I did," D noted. D drove home and, sure enough, there was a car she didn't recognize parked in front of the house. She pulled into the driveway and went in the front door. From the dining room window, what she saw was startling: "A young woman ran out the side of the house with her clothes in her arms, got into her car, and drove off. John ran up the basement stairs all flushed. So much for that. I'm not sure who she was. I didn't care."

D was merely going through the motions of a marriage. Her mother, the day before she died, knowing the end was near, asked her, "Are you going to be OK?"

"I'm going to be OK, Mom, but this isn't working out." She meant her marriage. She was fed up with the manipulation and mind games. Tessier was never physically abusive, D says, but he unnerved her.

"He was just . . ." She searched for the right word. "Creepy."

In December 1989, D served Tessier with divorce papers on grounds that the marriage was "irretrievably broken." They had been for married six years. D worried that John would give her a hard time, but much to her surprise, he was a gentleman about everything. He moved out four weeks later.

Hanley, Steiger, and Damasky thanked D for her cooperation. Confidentially, they informed her, her ex-husband was under investigation for kidnapping and murdering a seven-year-old girl.

D could hardly believe it. She knew John Tessier was a terrible human being, but kidnapping and murder? Then she thought about it some more.

"Wouldn't surprise me," she finally said.

When they were in the car and could speak freely, the detectives thought it had been a revealing interview. They found D to be credible but couldn't figure out how a mature and successful professional woman who wasn't even romantically interested in McCullough could have been manipulated into marrying him. They were developing insight into McCullough the man: D's story about the photos of the teenage Christine Tessier that, in her opinion, skirted the edge of child erotica was freaky and unsettling, and it could characterize McCullough as a potential pedophile.

"She's a Jack hater," Steiger said of D. "Nothing better than an ex-wife who's willing to pass on nasty information."

After they ran the name Michelle Weinman through LexisNexis, they found her working at a bar in Tacoma. It had been twenty-nine years since her encounter with Police Officer John Tessier, and a lot had happened to her since she'd been run out of the town of Milton and taken to a crisis clinic for wayward teens. A long hard road had brought her to this place. Michelle was now forty-four years old and had three sons, the oldest being twenty-seven, the youngest twelve. She had gotten pregnant with her first son when she was seventeen. She hadn't seen her family in Milton in two decades, and she didn't even know where they lived anymore. Nor did she ever attend another day of school after the day she reported John Tessier's sexual assault to the Fife police, though she had earned her GED high school equivalency when she was twenty-three. She'd always worked in the food and beverage industry and didn't mind serving beer for a living, though the tips kind of sucked, but the flexible hours suited her lifestyle. She was divorced and had commitment issues about marriage but was currently seeing a bad-boy biker dude named Jeff who drove a Harley and had long hair and tattoos.

When Brion Hanley walked into the bar with the detectives from Seattle, Michelle wanted to hide in the corner, disappear. They knew everything that had happened to her in Milton. They showed her all the court records on her case, which she read with complete astonishment for the

Left: Maria, the Little Lady.
Courtesy of the Ridulph family

Below: The Tessiers (left to right): Johnny, Jeanne, Eileen, Ralph, Katheran, and Bob.
Courtesy of the Tessier family

The Ridulphs (left to right): Frances, Chuck, Kay, Pat, and the baby of the family, Maria.

Courtesy of the Ridulph family

1957 photo of John Tessier at a nightclub. Janice Edwards, his then girlfriend, gave the photo to police.

Courtesy of Janice Edwards

Courtesy of Chicago Sun-Times

OG 7-806

of the unknown subject and was further suspected because
of his eagerness to assist in the search for the missing
girl on the night of December 3, 1957. SA DAVID L. BURTON
assisted in this interview.

The recorded reactions on the polygraph charts
did not reflect evidence of guilty knowledge or implication
by TESSIER in this matter. It is believed that he was a
~~bient for such a test and would have reacted~~

The recorded reactions on the polygraph charts
did not reflect evidence of guilty knowledge or implication
by TESSIER in this matter. It is believed that he was a
proper subject for such a test and would have reacted
significantly if he had been involved.

Sycamore, Illinois, at approximately 6:57 p.m. on that
date. This latter number is listed to one RALPH E. TESSIER
and according to his records, the call was made by one JOHN
S. TASSIER. Mr. SCHAEFER was of the opinion that the
spelling of the name TASSIER was merely a spelling error
on the part of the operator who handled the call. He also
stated that this call lasted until 6:59 p.m. and that it
was accepted by the TESSIER family in Sycamore.

LEADS

CG will complete and report investigation conducted
re the additional suspects.

REFERENCE

Reports of SA SOL E. DENNIS at Chicago dated 12/11/57
and 12/17/57;
Report of SA RAYMOND A. DRISCOLL at Chicago dated 12/13/57.

1957 FBI report clearing John Tessier.

RE SUSPECT JOHN SAMUEL TESSIER,
aka John Samuel Cherry

      Mr. DAN SCHAEFER, general manager, Sycamore-Ogle
Telephone Company, Sycamore, Illinois, on December 9, 1957,
informed SA DAVID L. BURTON that his company records reflected
a collect call was placed on telephone number 2-9297,
Rockford, Illinois, on December 3, 1957, to number 3257,
Sycamore, Illinois, at approximately 6:57 p.m. on that
date. This latter number is listed to one RALPH E. TESSIER
and according to his records, the call was made by one JOHN
S. TASSIER. Mr. SCHAEFER was of the opinion that the
spelling of the name TASSIER was merely a spelling error
on the part of the operator who handled the call. He also
stated that this call lasted until 6:59 p.m. and that it
was accepted by the TESSIER family in Sycamore.

REFERENCE

Reports of SA SOL E. DENNIS at Chicago dated 12/11/57
and 12/17/57;
Report of SA RAYMOND A. DRISCOLL at Chicago dated 12/13/57.

1957 FBI report confirming the collect call made by John
Tessier the night Maria was kidnapped.

Maria's body was discovered under the tree by mushroom hunters
in 1958.   *Courtesy of* Chicago Sun-Times

Maria's checkered shirt, worn the night she was kidnapped.

Courtesy of Chicago Sun-Times

To: Lt. E. Toffant

From: Troopers D. Fraher & R. Bales

Subject: Summary of ~~week~~ Investigation on Maria Ridulph Case

At this point of the investigation we returned to the Sycamore-DeKalb area. We feel certain facts might have been overlooked.

Following this line we first interviewed Tom Braddy, the Standard Oil Bulk dealer in Sycamore who figured prominently in the case because he had delivered oil in the immediate area of the crime on the evening of December 3rd. Braddy appears to be reliable and sincere and stated he was most anxious to see the case come to a successful end. He stated further that he was delivering oil to Mrs. Cliff's _____ corner of _____ that _____ left the area at 6:15

**We feel certain facts might have been overlooked...
a man was with Maria at a much earlier time than
was indicated by previous reports.**

where they noticed footprints. One set of footprints were of adult size and the footprints to the right of the adult's were those of a child. He compared the adult footprints with his own size. Believes it was a size 9. The footprints lead up to the Johnson garage. The last adult print showed a sharp movement to the right, such as one would make when using body-english, to either throw a doll or pick up the girl. They noticed that the snow was undisturbed except for these prints. They attached so much importance to finding these prints that Braddy instructed Bud Sigman and his son to go around the garage quickly, "and then we'll have him". (It should be pointed out that these prints went up and did not return back down the drive.) When they didn't find the offender at this point, Braddy walked over through the back yards and garden area and between a small tractor shed and a plowed area found two more adult footprints in the snow. He searched the tractor shed, went west, searched another barn, continued west out onto Fairplace and by a utility pole at the edge of the street noticed fresh tire tracks in the snow, indicating someone had pulled in sharply and pulled out sharply, going north on Fairplace to Rt. 64. The tracks indicated regular tread and not snow tires.

The above information indicates to us:

1. That it was known a man was with Maria at a much earlier time than was indicated by previous reports.

2. That the man went west and across the back lots and got into an auto on Fairplace and did not walk south on Centercross towards DeKalb Ave. and then got into an auto.

Excerpts from a July 27, 1958, Illinois state police report that reevaluated the timeline, moving up Maria's kidnapping a critical 15 minutes or so.

The so-called smoking gun: The train ticket from Rockford, Illinois, to Chicago, issued to John Tessier by the U.S. military. It was never used.

Courtesy of Janice Edwards

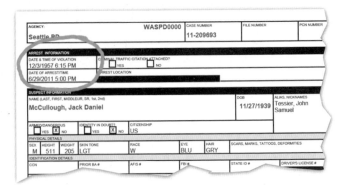

Jack McCullough's charging papers from the night of his arrest in Seattle. Note the date of violation: 1957. Note the date of arrest: 2011. A span of 54 years, making it the longest cold case in U.S. history ever to be brought to trial.

John Tessier in his days as a professional photographer in Washington State. One of his specialties was nudes.

Courtesy of Jon (Doc) Herrick

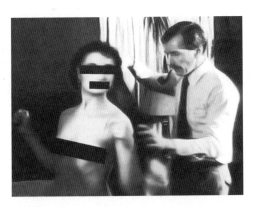

Janet Tessier and Jeanne Tessier. *Photo © by Shaw Media*

DeKalb County State's Attorney Clay Campbell. Behind him are members of the Tessier family. *Photo © by Shaw Media*

Jack McCullough at Pontiac Correctional Center, where he is serving a life-prison term.
Courtesy of Chicago Sun-Times

The disputed timeline. Every second counts. The defense maintains Maria was kidnapped at 7 PM, which makes it impossible for Jack McCullough to have committed the crime. The prosecution says she was taken before 6:20, crushing McCullough's alibi.

HOW THE DEFENSE SEES IT:

3:30 PM
Maria Ridulph and Kathy Sigman walk home from school and play at Maria's house.

5:00
Kathy goes home for dinner.

5:30
Maria has dinner with her family.

6:30
Maria and Kathy go out to play Duck the Cars in the snow.

6:40
Johnny gives Maria a piggyback ride. Maria runs home to fetch her doll.

7:00
Kathy asks Johnny the time. She heads home for a pair of mittens. Two neighbors hear a child's shriek. They look out their windows but see no one.

8:10
Maria is officially reported missing to Sycamore police.

HOW THE PROSECUTION SEES IT:

3:30 PM
Maria Ridulph and Kathy Sigman walk home from school and play at Maria's house.

5:00
Kathy goes home for dinner.

5:00
Maria has dinner with her family.

6:02
Maria calls Kathy and they meet outside and play Duck the Cars in the snow.

6:02
Oil deliveryman Tom Braddy unloads his shipment at a house at the corner of Archie Place and Center Cross Street. He sees Maria and Kathy playing. Johnny is not with them.

6:05
Maria's mother pulls out of the driveway and takes her daughter Kay to a music lesson. She sees Maria and Kathy playing. When she returns Maria and Kathy are still outside playing.

6:20
Tom Braddy drives back to his office. He does not see the girls on the corner.

6:30
A Sycamore bus driver passes the corner of Center Cross Street and Archie place. He does not see the two children.

7:00
Two neighbors hear a child's shriek. Investigators believe it is Kathy Sigman looking for Maria, or perhaps Maria's brother or parents calling out her name.

first time in her life. Only now did she come to understand that Tessier had been arrested for statutory rape and dismissed from the Milton police department because of what he had admitted doing to her. She also saw that, in 1983, he had pled guilty to a lesser charge, but the sentence was suspended and the fine reduced to just $350. *Suspended sentence.* She couldn't believe he had gotten off that easy. What infuriated her more than anything was the failure of the prosecutor's office in Pierce County to ever reach out to her, to inform her of the charges or the plea deal. Until now, she hadn't even known that Tessier had been fired. Brion Hanley told her that John Tessier had changed his name to Jack Daniel McCullough and was a suspect in the kidnapping and murder of a seven-year-old girl from Illinois named Maria Ridulph.

Had she ever heard of Maria Ridulph?

Michelle shook her head. "How did he get away with it after all these years?" she asked Hanley.

It was complicated, Hanley answered, but justice was about to catch up with him.

Michelle told the detectives that she had never returned to Milton in the intervening years. Not once.

"I'm scared to death to go back to that town," she said, because she assumed that John Tessier still lived there. Even when she became an adult and was hired to work at a bar in Fife, she quit after a few weeks because Fife adjoined Milton, and she was afraid she'd run into somebody who'd recognize her.

Hanley asked for Michelle's driver's license and all her personal information. She retrieved her purse from under the bar and handed Hanley the license. She watched him take down her date of birth, home address, and ID number. Then she excused herself. She went to a far corner of the bar and hid there for a long time, trying to regroup and absorb all of what was happening. She felt like throwing up. Finally, she got herself together. Her customers were getting antsy.

The detectives said they'd be in touch.

When Michelle got off work that night, she had an overpowering hunger to learn everything she could about Maria Ridulph. Unfortunately, she didn't have a computer, but she had a friend who had one and was computer-savvy. They looked up Maria Ridulph. Later that week, Michelle bought her first smart phone; Jack McCullough's arrest was expected any day, and she wanted Internet access to follow any breaking developments.

29

....

ARREST

On the morning of June 29, 2011, the task force gathered in the conference room at police headquarters in Seattle for one more strategy session. Clay Campbell, the state's attorney in DeKalb County, Illinois, told Hanley over the phone that there was probable cause and signed off on the plan to bring McCullough in for questioning.

It was agreed that the shrewdest move would be to lure McCullough to police headquarters on his own volition. That way they wouldn't have to worry about things getting out of hand at his apartment if he resisted arrest— they'd have complete physical control over him.

At noon, Ciesynski put in a call to McCullough. His wife, Sue, answered the phone.

"He's sleeping now," Sue told Ciesynski. Her husband had gotten off work at 7:00 A.M. "What do you want to talk to him about?"

Ciesynski kept up the ruse that he was investigating an assault that Jack McCullough had witnessed when he was working security at Metropolitan Towers. Sue told him to hang on; she'd wake him up.

The next voice Ciesynski heard was Jack McCullough's, still groggy from having worked the night shift. Ciesynski reminded him that they'd spoken thirteen days ago regarding an assault probe. He told McCullough he was wondering whether he could come by in a couple of hours to pick him up and take him to police headquarters, where they could continue their interview.

Ciesynski could tell that McCullough smelled a rat, but he said OK, so long as the detective could drive him back home in time to start the graveyard shift at 11:00 P.M. No problem, Ciesynski said.

Jack McCullough looked at his wife. Something was very wrong. *Lying sack of shit*, he thought. He told Sue, "I think it's some kind of cock-and-bull story."

"Tell him you're not coming down; you work the graveyard shift," Sue said.

McCullough called Ciesynski back, but the detective had stepped away from his desk. McCullough listened to his answering-machine announcement, and what he was hearing was truly unsettling. "This is Detective Mike Ciesynski from the cold-case unit. I'm not at my desk now but . . ."

McCullough left a message saying he'd changed his mind, he was too busy, and Ciesynski shouldn't bother picking him up. "People need to respect me, and I need to get to work," McCullough added. Then he hung up. But it nagged at him. *Cold-case unit*. What the hell?

When Ciesynski saw the red message light on his phone lit up, he had a funny feeling it was McCullough. He listened to McCullough's annoyed voice say it was a no-go. Then he strode back to the conference room, where everybody was waiting.

"He doesn't want to participate. He's not coming."

Dave Zulawski, the civilian consultant, said, "Here we are all dressed for the dance and our date doesn't show up." He wasn't surprised. "This is a guy who has done so many, many bad things in his life. He doesn't know what this is about, but he doesn't want any part of it."

Steiger spoke up. "Let's get a warrant. Let's go get him." Everyone agreed this was the only sensible course of action. Steiger banged out an affidavit on his computer, and he, Hanley, and Todd Damasky headed over to the county courthouse, where they got a judge to sign the arrest warrant. The time was now 3:00 P.M. Rush-hour traffic was already building. It would take at least forty-five minutes to get to McCullough's place.

A convoy of police vehicles weaved its way to Four Freedoms. Remaining behind at Seattle police headquarters were Hanley and Dave Zulawski, while Clay Campbell, the state's attorney, sweated it out in his office in Sycamore.

Ciesynski, Steiger, Hanley, Damasky, Steve Cook, and Tiffany Ziegler were joined by a Seattle homicide detective, Al Cruise, and Sergeant Bob Vallor, who were recruited just in case the arrest went bad and extra muscle was required. They all piled into the elevator to the sixth floor and headed down the hallway to Jack and Sue McCullough's apartment. One more look around to see that everyone was in position. Then Ciesynski and Steiger drew their service pistols. Ciesynski knocked on the door.

"Hey, Jack, Seattle police."

Silence, then McCullough's voice from behind the door.

"You're not free to come in here."

Steiger wasn't surprised. He'd picked up intelligence that McCullough was into survivalism and apocalyptic visions of the country going to hell. To deny the police entry fit the profile. Finally, McCullough opened the door. He was wearing a white T-shirt and blue jeans. He had shoes on but no socks.

"What's this about?"

"Jack, you're under arrest," Ciesynski told him.

Ciesynski told McCullough that he could make it easy for himself and come downtown with them, and if he cooperated they wouldn't put him in handcuffs. The team didn't want to come across as badasses, embarrassing him in front of his neighbors. All that would do was spoil any prospect of his agreeing to sit for an interview at headquarters. Neither did they want to frighten the elderly folks at Four Freedoms. The lobby was already buzzing with people wondering what drama was taking place on the sixth floor. McCullough agreed to go quietly and found himself being escorted down the hallway and into the elevator. He was silent during the ride down.

When they placed him in the backseat of the unmarked

Chevy Impala, he didn't utter a word. Todd Damasky got in the back with the suspect, while Steiger took the driver's wheel. On the drive downtown, McCullough stared straight ahead. Steiger waited for him to say something, *anything*. *How odd is that*, the detective thought as he glanced at McCullough in the rearview mirror. A normal reaction would have been for the suspect to ask what the fuck this was about; what did I do, and why are you taking me in?—but not McCullough. It made Steiger wonder what other evil deeds McCullough might have committed that police had no knowledge of. It was just a hunch, but Steiger thought that McCullough didn't have a clue that this was about Maria Ridulph.

Sue McCullough had been in the bedroom watching TV when she heard her husband say, "There's somebody at the door." Jack had been at the computer monitoring his favorite websites and half-listening to cable news. The next thing she heard was a commotion. She got out of bed and found a stranger standing in her apartment, and no Jack. Jack was gone.

"Where's Jack? What's going on?"

Suddenly, people were swarming all over the apartment, uniformed Seattle police officers, two Seattle detectives, and Sergeant Steve Cook and Detective Tiffany Ziegler, who told Sue they were from Jack's hometown of Sycamore, Illinois. They sat her down on the couch in the living room and showed her the search warrant a Seattle judge had signed that morning. Then they gave her the news.

"Jack's been arrested for killing a little girl."

Sue burst into tears.

"We know he did it," Cook said.

The detectives looked around. There was a little balcony in the bedroom that gave the place some decent natural light. Hanging on the wall was McCullough's Bronze Star for bravery in Vietnam. Three agitated cats scrambled over and under the furniture. Seattle police were all over the apartment, looking in the refrigerator, all the drawers and the desk, flipping over cushions. Sue couldn't imagine what they were looking for.

"Is there any part of the apartment you're not allowed to go in?" Cook asked.

Between sobs, Sue said, "Look at this place. It's small." She didn't want to say anything more until she could speak with her husband.

A cop came over and showed Cook and Ziegler a plastic bag they had found in the refrigerator. Inside was about an ounce of marijuana. Cook held the bag in front of her.

"You're going to have to cooperate with us, or we're going to have to talk about what was in the refrigerator."

Another cop came over and showed them a box of ammo they had found in a grab bag that McCullough kept for emergencies.

"Does Jack have any guns?"

Sue shook her head no.

"Then why does he have so many bullets?"

Sue then admitted that her husband kept several rifles in the apartment. She took the detectives to a large safe, opened the combination lock, and stepped aside. Inside, the police found the rifles, none of which were registered. Sue tried to explain that Jack sometimes took the rifles for target practice to a remote piece of property they owned in Tonasket, near the Canadian border, where they taught her daughters how to shoot. But she was really worried now and terrified she'd be busted for pot and firearms possession.

The police asked Sue if there was anyplace else where Jack kept stuff, and she told them about a storage unit in the basement. She led the way as they all followed her down. There wasn't much there: cages for transporting their cats to the vet, an old tire jack for changing flats, some candles they kept in the event of a power blackout. When the police said they wanted to search the McCullough's blue Ford F-150 truck, which was now parked in the lot, Sue took them to it and unlocked it. She still couldn't fully comprehend what Jack was under arrest for and thought that by being cooperative she was helping her husband. She knew he must be in the worst jam of his life. They told her again that it was for the murder of a seven-year-old girl named Maria Ridulph.

The name drew a complete blank with Sue.

"We have hard proof. We know he did it. There is not a shadow of a doubt he did it."

They asked her why Jack had quit being a cop in Milton. She said he'd been injured on the job. A truck had backed up while he had been issuing a ticket, and it hit him in the knee.

Cook laughed. He wanted to know why, if that story

was true, McCullough didn't receive a pension or disability. He set her straight; the truth was that he had sexually assaulted a fifteen-year-old runaway.

"I don't believe it. None of this is anything like Jack. We've been married nineteen years." She said she and her daughters had known about the accusations in Milton for more than twenty years.

"We know he beats you; just tell us he beats you."

"He never laid a hand on me. The worst he did was yell at me."

Finally, after two hours, they left. Sue was alone in the apartment with the cats.

30

....

Q&A

Dave Zulawski's involvement in the Maria Ridulph investigation had begun in March 2011, when he got a call asking him if he'd be willing to consult with the state police on an interesting cold case. Brion Hanley and Larry Kot drove over to his office, at Wicklander-Zulawski in Downers Grove, west of Chicago, to brief him on the case. Zulawski was acquainted with Kot from a previous investigation. Hanley he didn't know, but Zulawski could see that they made a good team. Hanley would be doing the legwork in the field, while Kot fixated on establishing the timeline of Maria's death, so critical in blowing up McCullough's alibi that put him in Rockford, Illinois, forty miles from the scene of the kidnapping. That timeline could make or break the case.

Zulawski was regarded as one of the country's premier experts on police interrogations and polygraph tests. Most of his business was in the private sector and dealt with loss prevention and employee thievery. His approach, known as the Zulawski Method, was to entice a bad guy into making a full "you've-got-me" confession through flattery, collaboration, and rationalizations for their crimes, rather than the in-your-face style of the traditional police third-degree that worked only in the movies.

Zulawski went over the case file with Hanley and Kot, and at the end of a long day, he said, "This is the right guy by everything I'm seeing here. He's local, he matches the description, his alibi is falling apart." Zulawski said that in his experience, grilling a man like Jack McCullough in an interrogation room wouldn't work because "you might as well be talking to a shoe." He assured Hanley and Kot that the Zulawski Method was definitely the only approach that had a prayer of working with somebody as manipulative and smart as McCullough.

"They don't have the emotions or feelings of guilt that the rest of us have. It doesn't work. Jack's not an emotional offender. If he's not a psychopath, he's pretty darn close."

Hanley and Kot wanted to know if Zulawski would be interested in leading the interrogation of Jack McCullough. Just one problem: they didn't have the funds to pay for his time and effort. Not a problem, Zulawski said. "I'm in." He said he was prepared to offer his services pro bono. Being a key player in solving the coldest case in American history? You bet he was interested—he was practically jumping out of his skin to get started.

....

Now it was June 29, 2011. Zulawski had invested four months in learning everything he could about Maria Ridulph and laying out the evidence that Hanley and the other detectives had assembled against McCullough. The stakes could not be higher. The time was finally at hand. McCullough was under arrest and en route to police headquarters.

It was five o'clock when McCullough arrived and was taken to the interview room.

"Everything in here is recorded," a uniformed cop told him. "Just to let you know."

"I understand."

(A copy of the tape recording was made available to the author. Everything that follows is as it happened.)

McCullough's cuffs were removed.

"I need you to empty anything that's in your pockets," the cop told him. The belt had to go, too.

"I'm going to have to go to the bathroom soon," McCullough said.

"Let's do that right now."

McCullough took a leak, and when he returned to the interview room, he slumped into his chair, folded his hands, and considered his surroundings. The camera was positioned on the ceiling in the corner, not hidden exactly, but you had to look for it to know it was there. Behind the two-way mirror, all the detectives—from Seattle and Sycamore and the Illinois state police, and Dave Zulawski— were watching. Live-streaming video was also being fed into the conference room.

They let McCullough stew a little, to get a measure of what made him tick.

Behind the mirror, Zulawski broke the silence: "I'll bet you a thousand to one he doesn't have a clue what he's here for. A fifty-four-year-old murder case isn't on his radar."

They sent Mike Ciesynski in to make contact.

"Do you take medication or anything like that?" he asked.

McCullough looked at Ciesynski. "I take a lot of medication. I'm a heart patient. But I took them just before we left so I'm good until tomorrow." Three years earlier McCullough had had quadruple bypass surgery. He took medication for high blood pressure and had a supply of nitroglycerin at home in the event of an emergency. He also suffered from diabetes, which he kept under control by diet and exercise.

"OK, so you're squared away with that?" Ciesynski asked, just to make sure. McCullough nodded. Ciesynski stood there for a moment. "You know who I am, right?"

McCullough glared at him. "Yeah, you're Ciesynski."

"OK, sit tight."

"I'm good."

When Ciesynski left the room, McCullough crossed his legs and closed his eyes for some shut-eye. He squirmed a little, trying to find a comfortable position on the hard steel chair. He actually dozed off. He's *sleeping*? What gives with this guy?

They let him snooze for an hour. All this time, the cops had been plotting strategy in the conference room. Now they were ready to make their grand entrance. The moment had come for Zulawski to take over.

He walked into the interrogation room carrying a load of files and reports. Right behind him was Brion Hanley.

McCullough woke up and sat up straight.

"We haven't been formally introduced. I'm Dave Zulawski."

"Dave, pleasure to meet you." McCullough couldn't have been more cordial. They shook hands.

"I'm an investigator, and Brion's with the Illinois state police." Hanley stepped forward so McCullough could get a good look at him. For Hanley, it had been three years of labor, all coming down to this.

McCullough snapped to attention. "With who?" He wondered whether he'd heard right.

"Illinois state police."

"Really?"

"You probably remember, a long time ago, back fifty years ago, a young girl was abducted . . . back in December 3, 1957. Maria."

"Maria."

"Maria."

"Yeah."

"We've been going back and doing some new investigations."

"Yeah, I'd be glad to help with that."

Zulawski nodded. "We value your insight with that. I know we've kind of inconvenienced you, but if we could count on your help, that would be great."

"Yeah, sure."

It was Brion Hanley's turn. He said he needed to take care of some administrative issues before they got underway. He asked McCullough about other names or aliases that he had lived under. John Cherry was his birth name, McCullough said. Then John Tessier, Tessier being his stepfather's name.

"That's it?" asked Hanley.

"That's it."

He was asked his height and weight. Five ten to five eleven, McCullough answered.

"I'll give you the half inch," Hanley said, and wrote *five eleven* on the information sheet.

McCullough said he weighed 210 pounds. His date of birth was November 27, 1939, in Belfast, Northern Ireland. He had blue eyes. He had two scars from a hernia operation.

"How many times have you been married?"

"Uh, four."

"You've been divorced three times?"

McCullough stopped him right there. It was suddenly dawning on him what this was about. "You're investigating a child? You're not investigating me?"

Hanley tried to calm him down. "This is a personal history form. We fill this out for everybody. I just do what I'm told." *I just do what I'm told.* As an ex-cop, McCullough knew all about that. His body language told Hanley to proceed. But he was definitely getting wound up.

"Are you a registered voter?"

"I am. Republican."

Asked about his military service, McCullough said ten years in the U.S. Army, and before that the U.S. Air Force.

"Type of discharge?"

"Honorable, of course."

"Addicted to drugs? Habitual user?"

McCullough laughed outright. "Yeah, right."

"It's here," Hanley said, pointing to the form he was filling out. "I'm not making this up," communicating the message that he was a low-level functionary just doing his job. At this point, Hanley read the suspect his Miranda rights, and McCullough listened with a bored expression as if he had heard this a thousand times when he was a cop.

"It's all good advice," McCullough said. "I'm on your side on this. I'm trying to help you. Are you going to get to the good part now?"

Zulawski took over. "Kind of take me back and give me a sense of what Sycamore was like." So far, it was textbook Zulawski methodology. Easy lay-up questions spoken like a conversation, nothing confrontational, keep the guy talking.

McCullough was happy to oblige.

"Sycamore was like *Mayberry R.F.D.* It was a wonderful place to grow up. Still is. If I was going to raise kids, that's where I'd do it."

Zulawski asked McCullough how he got around town when he lived in Sycamore. First he rode a bike, McCullough recalled. Then he got his first car, a 1948 Plymouth Coupe, a real "clinker." He said he paid for it from his paper route.

"So that was a family car?"

"No, it was my car."

"So you didn't loan it out to buddies or anything?"

"No, it was my car."

He'd come back to that later. For now, Zulawski had just nailed a key component of the evidence against Mc-Cullough.

"What was your family like?"

"Five sisters and one brother."

"What were they like to grow up with?"

"Great!"

"So no conflicts?"

"No! It was Mayberry, like I told you."

"*Leave It to Beaver* kind of thing?"

"Exactly."

"So you would find them to be honest, kind people?"

"Exactly." McCullough grinned and added, "None of them brighter than me."

"Then they must be pretty smart." More of the Zulawski Method at play. Flatter, seduce, keep it friendly, and above all else, keep the subject talking. Clearly, McCullough had no idea his siblings had turned on him.

"We all remember when President Kennedy was shot. Or 9/11. This was kind of the 9/11 of Sycamore."

McCullough exhaled deeply. "The day Maria was kidnapped I was in the induction center in Chicago joining the air force. I spent the entire day there, and they have the entire record there, minute by minute. It was a nightmare. Spread your cheeks and all that stuff all day long. At the end of it, you're sworn in." He admitted he had come under suspicion in 1957. "I was really pissed. The FBI talked to me back then as a suspect, and they even interrogated me because the suspect that took Maria had a green coat, and I had a favorite green jacket at the time."

"So how did you wind up at the induction center?"

"I don't know how I got there. I may have taken the train. I was there most of the day. And you can check with the FBI. They gave me a lie-detector test. And I was disappointed in them, I was really disappointed, because I had an ironclad alibi of where I was, and they didn't even check. Didn't even make a phone call."

"You had to stay downtown [Chicago] overnight?"

"I don't remember that."

"At some YMCA or something?"

"I don't remember that."

"What do you remember? How did you get downtown?"

"See, I don't remember. We're talking about many years ago. I know no family member was with me so I don't think anybody drove me there so I must have taken the train."

"Did you have to purchase your own ticket? Did they give you a ticket?"

"Don't know. Just don't remember at all. Is it important?"

"Yeah, as much as you can remember is important."

"You're treating me like a suspect now, and I don't like this."

Zulawski said, "Well, as I told you, there have been some discrepancies in interviews that we're having, and that's why I'm trying to find these things out, to try to see what happened, what went on, whatever, and I'm looking for you to be as candid as you can and remember as best you can."

"I'm trying, but you're barking up the wrong tree. There's nothing there."

"I may be barking up the wrong tree, but I'm trying to find out what happened on the day and where you were on the day she disappeared."

"I already told you. I spent the entire day in Chicago that day."

"OK, what time did you get home? Because she wasn't abducted at noon so that doesn't mean anything to me."

"I don't know what time she was abducted. I assumed it was daytime."

"So nobody ever told you?"

"Nobody ever told me."

"OK, so let's start at the beginning. So you went into the induction center. What time did you get there?"

"I don't know."

"Well, here's the thing. That story that you gave the FBI just doesn't match up."

"Match up to what?"

"To what people say."

McCullough snapped, "What people say about what?"

"What people said what you were doing and where you were."

"Nobody knows what I was doing that day. Because I was in Chicago!"

"Well, you do. When you got back in the evening, what did you do? This was a big day."

"I probably crashed, because it was a hard day."

Zulawski shot McCullough a skeptical gaze. "So you think you were home asleep?"

"I'm assuming. I didn't have anyplace else to go."

"So why would people say you weren't there?"

"Who? What people?"

The moment had come to let him know where he stood in this investigation. "Your sisters."

McCullough answered with unconcealed distaste. "They don't know."

"They say they do."

"They don't know where I was back then."

"Yeah, they do."

McCullough shook his head. "No."

"Uh-huh."

"All right, we're done."

It was a critical point. If McCullough wanted to, he had the legal right to shut down the Q&A. Instead, Zulawski kept on talking—and so did McCullough.

"Actually," Zulawski said, "I am disappointed, because here's the thing—"

"You're disappointed I don't have any memory of it?"

"Actually, I am disappointed that—"

"My sisters say I had anything to do with her abduction?"

"They just said you weren't home. How about if I told you what you told the FBI?"

"All right."

"See if this helps you at all." Zulawski pulled a report from his paperwork.

"The story that you told the FBI was that on December 3 you went to some burlesque shows after you left the green machine [McCullough's nickname for the induction center] or whatever you called it and took the train back to Rockford at five o'clock and it got you in about 6:30. You go to the post office to drop some papers off."

"I don't know."

"You told them that. They said you made a call home to get a ride."

"I don't know if I had my car then. I think I probably sold it. So Dad would have probably came and got me."

"So then they say that you went and had coffee and a piece of pie."

"Why would I tell them shit like that? That doesn't mean anything."

"I don't know. I obviously wasn't there. I was probably still in diapers. Then they said your dad came and got you."

"Probably."

"And then they said that you were going to go out with your girlfriend."

"So?"

"I'm just asking if you remember."

"I don't remember."

"That's what they say anyway, and that you had a date with her."

"I had a girlfriend back when I was going to go into the service, yeah."

"And what was her name?"

"Jan Edwards."

"When we start to look at the story that you tell here . . . there are things that just aren't right. OK. First of all, you had the nickname 'Johnny.'"

"Yeah."

"OK, so the person who introduced himself to the girls said his name was Johnny. The description of the person matches you down to the gap in the teeth."

"Yeah, that really was surprising."

"Well, I'm sure. The height, the weight."

"But see, that was my neighborhood; everybody knew me. Maria's parents knew me. I used to play with their daughters in the backyard."

"The description isn't coming from Maria at all."

"No, she was kidnapped."

"Right, it's coming from Kathy, the other girl that was there. She described somebody who looked remarkably like you and had the gap in the teeth."

"The only thing I heard was that he had a green jacket."

"Well, actually it was a sweater."

"OK, I don't have a green sweater. I had a jacket."

"It wasn't a green sweater, it was a multicolored sweater."

"See, it's not me."

"Your family says that you had a multicolored sweater that was the same description and that after Maria disappears, that sweater disappears."

"This is bullshit! No! I don't remember a multicolored sweater. My favorite jacket was a fuzzy green jacket that I bought myself."

"Here are the other issues. Let me just go through it. I'm going to tell you what you said and what everybody else says, just to be fair to you. OK?"

"Yeah."

"You call your house in a collect call and you're on the phone for about two minutes."

"I did that a lot. Go ahead."

"Well, you did that the evening of her disappearance." McCullough shrugged, and Zulawski continued. "OK, now, it's supposed to be for somebody to go pick you up. Now, the family says that nobody can go pick you up because Ralph's not at home. He's taking Kathy to a 4-H club meeting in DeKalb someplace, OK, and by the time he gets back it's like 8:30, twenty to 9:00, because the police have already been contacted. There are squad cars all over the place. Everybody's looking for Maria, who's gone. OK? But you tell the FBI that your dad picks you up at eight o'clock, but he can't, because he's running your sister back and forth—"

"This is all so what. Because who knows about what time exactly you do anything. I was a kid."

"Well, we know for sure. We know what time the police were contacted, we know what time they arrived, so for [Katheran] to see all these cars and ask what happened, it already has to be done. At this point it's 8:30, twenty to nine. Now you, in your statement to the FBI, you claim that you're back in town at 9:20."

"So? It's a half an hour drive to Rockford."

"Let's review. Your name is Johnny. The guy who took her says his name is Johnny."

"Really?"

"Yeah, his description including the gap in the teeth, looks just like you. We've got a sweater that matches what she describes the guy was wearing, the sweater that disappears. You say your dad picks you up, but Ralph can't pick you up because he's taking care of your sister, running her back and forth. You said, 'I stayed the night.'"

"Where?"

"In your home."

"Probably."

"The girls say you weren't there. And they know you weren't there because Ralph and your mom went to help search and help feed the people and they put a lock on the front door so they couldn't get in and they put a 2-by-4 on the back door so they couldn't get in. And they told the girls one of them has to sleep on the couch and let us in. They come home at four or five o'clock in the morning to let them in, and you weren't there. So where are you?"

"I might be in Chicago."

"You couldn't be in Chicago because you said you were in Rockford. Your phone call comes from Rockford."

"This is all bullshit. I don't know anything about it. I can't remember any of this you're trying to tell me. You're trying to say there was a pattern, and there is no pattern."

Zulawski pulled out another FBI report from 1957 in which Tessier/McCullough detailed his whereabouts for December 4. Back then, he claimed that he had gone searching for Maria Ridulph with his high school chum Jack Manis and that they had come across a stash of pornographic magazines in a field, which they turned over to the Sycamore police. Brion Hanley had done something the FBI neglected to do in 1957, which was to track down Manis. Manis's story was this: like everyone else in Sycamore, he had participated in the search for Maria on

December 4 but never with John Tessier. Manis told Hanley that if he found porno publications, he would have kept
them, like any red-blooded teenager under similar circumstances. Tessier was a "lying son of a bitch," Manis said. He
had other choice words for Tessier during his interview with
detectives in 2010: "loner," "a strange boy." Now Zulawski
pressed McCullough on his activities on December 4.

"Where did you go?"

"I went searching."

Zulawski said, "See, and that's the thing. To the FBI,
you say you're with Jack Manis and that you find sex magazines that you turn in to the police department. The
police department says we didn't get any magazines from
anybody. Jack Manis says, number 1, you weren't with him.
Number 2, he didn't find any sex magazines, and if he did
find them, he would have kept them."

"This is all bogus. I don't remember anything about any
magazines."

"I'm just telling you what you told the FBI."

"What *they* said I said. I'm not saying I said it. It sounds
to me like they're making shit up. I'm telling you already
how disappointed I am with the FBI."

"You also told the FBI that you had some sex play with
your sister."

"Oh my God! I took a lie-detector test! And [the FBI
agent] said when was this, and I said when we were little."

"OK, now your sister says that it just wasn't when you
were little."

"So?"

"What I'm pointing out here is if you say you told the

FBI the truth and you were little and at the same time you were having sex with your sister."

"I am not having sex with my sisters!"

"They said you are."

"I am not."

"Well, that's not what they said."

"Did not."

"That's not what they say."

"Doesn't matter."

"I'm just telling you not just one but multiple sisters are saying."

Zulawski collected his thoughts. It was time to bring in the specter of Eileen Tessier and her deathbed confession, which had set this entire investigation in motion.

"Your mother also says to Janet and Mary that you killed her—Maria."

McCullough exploded in anger. Zulawski had had a feeling the question would set him off, considering the intense affection he held for his late mother.

"That's a lie," McCullough said evenly. "That's a lie. *Not true*. My mother loved me to death. And she was crying when the FBI wanted to talk to me."

"I have no doubt because she also told them some lies, to the FBI."

"My mother doesn't lie."

"Well, she said you were home all night. Now, she may have been protecting you."

"Are you saying I murdered a girl? This is bullshit. It's all bullshit. My mother wouldn't say that."

"Your mother did say that."

"She didn't. Because my mother knew where I was that day."

"Forget about during the day at the air force, because that means nothing. The incident didn't happen until that night. Until after six at night."

"And where was I?"

"Well, you claim you were in Rockford."

"OK, if I'm in Rockford at seven o'clock—

"But nobody can come get you."

"So? I've got a thumb; I can hitchhike."

Zulawski dug into the case folder and pulled out the unpunched government-issued train ticket. "The other problem is when you're given a ticket by the military, that ticket didn't get used. Yeah. Here's your ticket to go to Rockford, to go to Rockford from Chicago, you never used it. You know where this comes from? Jan Edwards. You know how women are sentimental; they keep everything. She's got pictures of you, and she said yeah, John gave me this."

"That's really funny."

"Well, I think it's not funny. I think it questions whether or not you were involved in this."

McCullough leaned forward in his chair and looked Zulawski in the eye. "OK, I'm going to tell you. *I'm not involved*. You give me a lie-detector test, and I'll pass it."

Zulawski nodded. "OK, why don't we do that now."

"OK."

Zulawski stood up. As friendly as could be, he asked, "You want coffee?"

McCullough nodded his head yes. Zulawski said, "Back in just a second." With that, he walked out of the interview room. McCullough was now alone with Brion Hanley. He stared at the young detective.

"I want to talk to you."

Hanley shrugged. "You want to talk to me? About what?"

"About who I think did it."

"OK."

He proceeded to tell Hanley that the guy they should be fingering for Maria's murder was a libertine who lived near his house on Center Cross Street, who was always "talking about sex" and lurking around the grounds of West Elementary School. That's who police should be investigating. McCullough couldn't remember the name of this dreg of society. "Nobody seems interested in what I'm saying."

Hanley steered the interrogation back to the fundamentals. He brought up all the inconsistencies in McCullough's account.

"You can find anything from anything," McCullough said dismissively. "I was devastated that that little girl was taken."

"Would there be a reason why your mom would say something like that?"

"There is no reason—I don't believe it was said. My mother loved me; we were very close. I adored her."

"She loved you?"

"I adored her."

"Why do you think she would say something like that?"

"She didn't say anything like that. She wouldn't say something like that. This is a lie."

"Who do you think is lying?"

"Whoever's talking."

"Do you talk to your family members now?"

"No."

"Why? I mean you guys are brothers and sisters, grew up together."

"We've all just grown apart."

"Let me ask you this: you said when you were younger you had a sexual encounter with your sister. Accidentally, on purpose, whatever, doesn't matter. That was the only time that that happened? Jack, just be honest with me."

"I don't know."

"You don't know if that was the only time?"

"No."

"So there could have been other times?"

"Yeah."

"As you got older, there could have been other times?"

"Yeah."

"OK."

McCullough seemed to physically shrink under the weight of his admissions about the taboo of incest. "But this doesn't make me a suspect in a murder case."

"Did I say that?"

"No."

"I didn't say that. When Dave asked you, you said only once. Well, that's a lie."

"I never had sex."

"Well, what did you have?"

"Just playing around."

"Playing around with your sisters?"

"Yeah."

"We just want you to be honest. When Dave asked you that—"

"He said sex."

"Well, you know what we mean."

"No, I don't. I'm not going to assume anything, and you guys shouldn't assume anything either. What does that have to do with this little girl?"

"It's just a background of your childhood and your life. We've talked to people. The questions that we've asked you—we know the answers."

"You *think* you know the answers." McCullough leaned forward in his chair. "Let me tell you something. I did not kidnap that little girl. Look at my eyes. I did not have anything to do with that little girl. She was loved in the neighborhood. She was a little girl with big brown eyes, and she was as sweet as could be. Hardly said a word to anybody, and everybody loved her. This was crushing to the entire Sycamore community, and it was crushing for me as well because I knew the family."

Hanley stood. "Do you need to use the restroom or anything?"

"Yes."

"Because I do, too."

They laughed. McCullough asked for Hanley's business

card and promised to call once he came up with the name of that suspect the cops should really be going after. "This is the guy you should be looking at."

In the conference room, watching the video feed, Dave Zulawski and the others stared at each other in utter disbelief. Who was playing who? Did McCullough really believe he was going to walk out of there? Then Hanley came in. They pondered what to do next.

Two minutes later, McCullough returned from the bathroom break. He was now alone in the interrogation room. They watched him on the monitor taking a sip of water, tapping his thumbs on the plastic cup like a drum. Suddenly he clapped his hands as if he remembered something important. "Brooks!" He looked straight at the camera. "OK. You're recording. Brooks is the name!" This was the villain who was loitering around Maria's school in 1957. Then McCullough released a loud belch. It was two hours and twenty-seven minutes into the interrogation. Zulawski returned to give McCullough an update on the polygraph test, which was in the works.

"They should be ready for you in just a couple of minutes. You need a coffee, or are you OK?"

"You follow up on Brooks?"

"Absolutely. Absolutely."

They let McCullough simmer a little longer. Then a cop came in. "Jack, we're ready to go."

McCullough was escorted to the polygraph office down the hall, where Seattle detective Irene Lau was prepared to administer the test. But it came to an abrupt end before it could really get going because McCullough absolutely refused to be hooked up to the machine. He objected to the pretest list of questions the examiner was putting forward, which, from McCullough's point of view, focused on his relationship with his sisters and the incest allegations and not the murder of Maria Ridulph.

"I don't want to take this test anymore. You're outside the bounds I've set."

He was brought back to the interrogation room.

In the conference room, the detectives huddled. It came as no surprise to anyone that McCullough had bailed out of the polygraph. The examiner happened to be a petite Asian woman, and it was thought that McCullough would never allow himself to be put in a deferential position because it would offend his self-esteem and even his masculinity.

So far, Cloyd Steiger thought the interrogation was going well. He found the suspect to be incredibly narcissistic, a man who thought he was smarter than anybody else in the room. No one had really expected McCullough to make a full confession after five decades of suppressing the truth; he just wasn't the type to break down in tears, but if the goal had been to lock him into a story that was filled with holes and absurdity, everyone thought that had been achieved.

"A ridiculous story or a lie is just as good as a confession," Steiger reminded them.

Dave Zulawski agreed that the taped interview would be a major asset at trial, but something was worrying him. The questions about the incest allegations and Eileen Tessier's confession had sent McCullough into a fit of anger.

"Boy, that didn't go so good. It really set him off." Zulawski was taken aback by McCullough's outburst. What concerned him was McCullough giving him the cold shoulder in the next round of questioning. Would he shut up and demand a lawyer if Zulawski went back in the room and carried on with the interrogation where he had left off? It could happen. They had to keep McCullough talking. Zulawski decided a fresh face was needed. Brion Hanley was deemed a good candidate. He and McCullough seemed to have an affinity going; plus, no one knew the case better than Hanley. But then Zulawski said, "I think Mike Ciesynski should go in."

At first, Hanley seemed cool to the proposal. After all, this was his case. Then he thought some more. "If that's what you think, I'm with you."

Ciesynski had been sporadically in and out of the conference room watching the video feed of the interrogation while he worked on his own Seattle investigations. As far as he was concerned, his involvement in the Maria Ridulph investigation was over when he'd placed McCullough under arrest. He came in just to see how things were going.

"Hey, what's up?"

"He won't want to talk to any of these guys anymore," said Steiger. "They want you to do the rest of the interview."

Ciesynski looked startled. "Me?"

Zulawski explained, "I was the one who instigated the polygraph. I'm going to be his target. It'll be counterproductive if I go in again. I'll just be in the way. We need a fresh face. You already have a relationship with him."

There was also tacit acknowledgment that Ciesynski had more experience than Brion Hanley in interviewing homicide suspects. Not that anyone wanted to be critical of Hanley; it was just a fact.

Ciesynski didn't appreciate being put on the spot and pointed out that he didn't have a great command of the facts on the case, certainly not like Hanley. Finally, he saw the wisdom in Zulawski's analysis and agreed to go in with the one key piece of evidence that had been taken off the table. He couldn't wait to hit McCullough with this one.

Five hours and nine minutes into the interrogation, the door to the interrogation room slid open, and Mike Ciesynski walked in. He handed McCullough a cup of coffee.

"That might be real hot," he said.

McCullough took a sip. "Yeah, it's battery acid. Cop coffee."

"I gather the polygraph was underwhelming." He took a swig from a bottle of water.

McCullough nodded agreeably. "She was fishing, and I'm anxious for this case to be solved. We're talking about the murder of a little girl. But if she's fishing into my personal life, I'm not going to answer any questions about my personal life."

"Well, your personal life is at issue right now."

"No, that little girl is the issue. Does anything make me a murderer? I am not."

"That's a good point. And that's the point I was going

to bring up with you. You do any personal research on me after you found out who I was?"

"I don't know who you are."

"You know who I am."

"I know you're Mike Ciesynski."

"You know I'm a cold-case detective, right? For the Seattle police department."

"Yeah, you answered that on your telephone. You made me really uncomfortable. I knew something was up."

"I'm assisting the Illinois state police and Sycamore police department. All I do is I just work cold-case homicide. That's all I ever do. I'm in this room all the time dealing with guys from your age, to midfifties. So I know what this is all about. I can usually tell when a guy is lying to me and when they're not lying. When they've got something to hide. Like I know some of the issues that are embarrassing to you and your family. I don't give a shit about that. Because it has nothing really to do with this case. I'm not going to ask you about you and your sisters. I'm going to tell you exactly how I feel about it. I feel that you're hiding something, that you're holding something back, and that you did something that's embarrassing to you. You've got to realize that you're kinda in a world of shit right now, and you're going to have to give up the truth. OK? To save your own ass. To be smart." McCullough tried to say something but Ciesynski shot him down. "Just listen to me. I'm not saying here from reviewing this file that you killed that girl. I'm not saying that you did."

"I did not. That's what I'm being investigated for, right?"

"That's exactly what you're being investigated for. But you're holding back on some things here—"

"Which has nothing to do with anything."

"Well, that's the part that you're going to have to get out and let me decide that, all right?"

"If we veer away from the little girl's murder, I'm clamming up."

"I don't want to go away from the little girl's murder. You're missing my point. I'm talking about the little girl's murder here. You're holding something back on that."

McCullough shook his head. "I'm not holding anything back on that."

The moment was here. Ciesynski said, "I really think that one of the problems that happened here, from reading all the reports and the interview with the other little girl who was there—"

McCullough looked at him with a blank expression. "What other girl?"

"There were two girls there."

"I don't know anything about that."

"Well, there were two girls out there. I believe you came out there—"

"What!"

"I'm not saying you killed anybody, you understand me?"

All McCullough could utter was a feeble, "Oh, man."

"There was another little girl out there, too."

"Was she kidnapped, too?"

"No, she wasn't."

"How old was she?"

"She was the same age. They were best friends."

"Oh, really?"

"She's still alive today, actually." In fact, Ciesynski said, the police had recently interviewed her. "This is where I believe you're hiding something."

"I'm going to tell you you're wrong."

"I believe you did go out there."

McCullough shook his head vigorously. "Did not."

"And I believe that person was you and you did give her a piggyback ride."

"Oh my God. All right—I'm lawyering up."

"That's fine. Just listen to what I'm saying."

McCullough talked right over the detective, desperate to lay out the alibi that had gotten him off the hook in 1957. "There is no way. I couldn't have been in the area. OK? I was in the induction center all day long. I found out when I got home, and Mom says, 'Maria's been kidnapped.' That's all I know. But if I made a phone call from Rockford at seven o'clock after I got off the train, Sycamore is thirty miles away from Rockford. This is an hour after she was kidnapped. I was on a train. I spent the whole damn day there [in Chicago]. They've got records—they had records—from every goddamn minute I arrive. I mean they were looking up my butt and everything all day long. And when I was done with it, I don't remember perfectly, but I'm assuming I took the train because I wouldn't have—I wouldn't have driven my car to Chicago." McCullough said he had sold his "piece of crap" 1948 Plymouth prior to December 3 because he knew he was entering the service.

Ciesynski considered all this. He knew that two witnesses, Dennis Twadell and another Tessier buddy from the old days, Dave Frederick, had told the state police that they saw Tessier's vehicle in town on the afternoon of Maria's kidnapping, although neither man could make out who was driving. For the moment, he decided not to spring this on McCullough. "I'm going to grab a picture. I'll be right back."

He went back to the conference room and asked everyone how they thought he was doing. So far, so good, he was told. Keep it up. Hanley handed Ciesynski a folder with an array of photos, and Ciesynski returned to the interview room. He thought he had started out cold and maybe a little unsure of the facts, but he was warming up for the big climax. It was definitely a challenging interview, and he was wielding all the tradecraft of his job. He was also thinking, *There is no doubt in my mind that this is the guy who did it.*

When he sat down again, McCullough was eager to say something.

"I took a lie detector, and I passed it."

Ciesynski thought he had an opening now to throw McCullough off balance. "Actually, I looked at that lie detector also. Did they tell you you passed it?"

"They freed me!"

"Did they tell you that you passed it? Do you recall?"

"I don't recall. But they just said you're free to go, and the FBI agent that was taking care of me took me, he took me home. They played Mutt and Jeff. One guy was mean to me, and the other guy was nice, like you. The good-cop, bad-cop. And the bad cop said, 'I know you did it, you bastard,' blah, blah, blah."

A little defensively, Ciesynski said, "I don't think anyone's been playing bad cop here. That's kinda old school; we don't really use that too much. We're trying to get to the truth." He asked about his mother, Eileen. "You were real tight with her." He knew the question would keep the conversation going because McCullough couldn't stop talking about his mother.

"Oh, oh, absolutely. I called my mom every month of my life. I loved my mom. My mom was brilliant. When she died, my dad was asked how many people do you think are going to come to the funeral, and dad says maybe thirty, forty." McCullough paused for dramatic effect. "Three hundred fifty showed up."

Ciesynski knew the answer, but he just had to ask, "Did you show up?"

"No, I was in the service."

Incredulous at the answer, Ciesynski said, "They wouldn't let you come home from military leave for your mom's funeral?"

"In Vietnam, '69, '70."

"When did your mom die?" Ciesynski very well knew the answer: 1974.

"I don't remember the year." Suddenly, McCullough did an about-face. "Oh, I was here, I did go home to see her one last time, but I didn't go to the funeral."

"Was there a falling out or something?"

"No, it was just how things worked out."

Another little white lie to add to the toll. That's what Ciesynski was thinking.

Ciesynski opened the folder. It was time to display all his cards. "I'm going to lay out a couple of things for you." They were six yearbook-style photos from the 1950s. "I just want to show you something. Remember about the second girl?" McCullough nodded. "She signed her name at the bottom of the photograph."

McCullough examined the photos. "Don't know any of these guys. Don't know any of them. And I don't think any of these guys are from Sycamore."

"Take a look at every picture."

He did and discounted each one. "No. No. No."

Is this guy for real, Ciesynski was wondering. He pointed to one photo. "Who does this guy look like?"

McCullough studied it again. "I don't know."

"You don't know who that guy looks like?"

He looked at it even longer. "Dunno."

It was almost comical. McCullough won't even concede that was him in the photo? Ciesynski found himself asking one more time, "You don't know who that guy looks like?"

At last, McCullough conceded, "He might look like me—but he's too feminine looking."

Ciesynski's eyes blazed. What a weird thing to utter. Did McCullough construe himself as oddly soft and effeminate? The detective wasn't a fan of armchair psychology, but it made him think maybe there was something psychologically meaningful in what McCullough was seeing in the photo.

"That's you. Obviously, that's a Xerox. It's a little whited out, but that's you from a wedding picture that was put into this montage that the girl said was Johnny and gave the piggyback ride. Number two. Listen to this part. Jack, look at me." Bleakly, McCullough obeyed. "Number two," said Ciesynski, "know who told us that you did this? Someone who I think is a very smart person, a very intelligent person. And someone who had lived with a bunch of guilt for a long time before she passed away."

McCullough glared at him. "If you're going to say my mom, that's bullshit."

"Why do you say that's bullshit?"

"Because she wouldn't suspect me of a murder, and she knew where I was."

"There's no doubt in our minds that you were the guy who was there."

"You're full of shit. I don't remember anything like this."

"Do you remember giving any little girl a piggyback?"

"No."

"You never gave neighbors or your sisters or anybody piggyback rides?"

"Well, uh, yeah. But she was seven. She was tiny."

"How tiny was she?"

He extended his arms a few feet to demonstrate the height of Maria Ridulph as he remembered it. "This tall. The last time I saw her was probably months before this happened. She was just walking down the street, and I just passed her and that was the last I saw of her."

"Did she say, 'Hi, Johnny?'"

"She didn't know me. She wouldn't walk more than two or three houses away from her house. She was just little."

"How would you know that? Or are you just surmising?"

"I lived in the neighborhood."

"Did you know her family?"

"Knew her family—knew her sisters. I had seen them. I had been over to their house a couple of times. Her sisters were aspiring actresses. They would always create a play. I went one time."

"To watch the play?"

"Which I didn't think much of." Yet another dig at the Ridulph sisters.

It was almost six hours into the interrogation. As Ciesynski stepped out to take a break, McCullough stretched his legs. He had a cramp from sitting all this time. Sitting alone in the interrogation room, he couldn't stop staring at the photo. Then he muttered, "It's not a very good picture." He pushed it aside in a gesture of dismissal.

When Ciesynski returned, he tossed another photo on the desk. It was the shot that Jan Edwards had turned over to the state police, the one taken on her first "grown-up" date, when John Tessier took her to a nightclub in Rockford. Ciesynski also displayed for McCullough the government-issued train ticket from to Chicago that had never been stamped as used.

"Who's that?"

"Oh, that's me."

"Remember that night?"

A flood of fond memories made McCullough's tense mouth spread into a slight thin smile. Of course he recognized his ex-girlfriend. All at once, Sycamore was the land of Opie and *Leave It to Beaver* and Mayberry again. "That's interesting. I was in love with that woman for so many years. She didn't even know it."

"What's the date on that?"

McCullough squinted at the tiny lettering with his reading glasses. "June 22, 1957." He sighed, remembering. "Jan Edwards." He spoke the name with great care. "Thank you for showing me this; this brings back wonderful memories. They had a mansion on Main Street or something like that. I went back a few years ago, and the house was on display. People had renovated it and fixed it up. It was a huge house." He looked at the photo of the two of them again. "But that's great."

Ciesynski decided to bring McCullough out of his dream state. "Remember a couple of times you said that you took the FBI test? The polygraph at the FBI? You told your mother that you passed it."

"Yeah."

"Actually you failed that test. Did the FBI tell you you passed that test?"

McCullough shook his head in objection. "I watched the test. I was hooked up to it. I watched the test."

"There was a part of that polygraph when they were interviewing you they said, 'Did you know anything about the homicide or the disappearance of this girl?' And you said no. And had you ever seen her before? Were you in contact with these two girls that day? The thing said you were deceptive."

McCullough had had enough—again. He wanted to end this now. "You remember me asking for a lawyer?"

"No."

"When we were walking out of the [Four Freedoms], I said I want a lawyer. And you were standing right beside me."

Ciesynski played along. "Uh-huh. And who did you say that to?"

"You."

"*Me*? No, I don't recall that."

"Interesting, because you said don't worry about it."

"Is that what I said to you? What is it you're saying to me now?"

"What I'm saying to you now is you think I had something to do with it."

"You were deceptive in your polygraph with the FBI. Your mother on her deathbed believes that you were involved in this. On her deathbed she said this."

"Don't know about that."

"You don't believe that? I'll go and find the documentation on that and bring it to you."

"Doesn't matter. There's a whole bunch you're making up here."

"Why would your mother say that?"

"This didn't happen. My mother knew I didn't do it."

"So she's just making this up?"

"Somebody's making it up. There's a whole bunch of making up here. There's no way my mother would say that. Unless she was out of her mind."

A uniformed cop came in. As friendly as could be, he asked, "Hey, Jack, we've got some pizza here. You hungry?"

"OK. Great. Thanks."

Ciesynski suppressed a smile. The pizza had been sent in by Zulawski and the others in the monitoring room to keep McCullough content by filling his stomach and keeping him talking. In police parlance, suspects like McCullough were called Chatty Cathys: they demand a lawyer and then they can't stop talking.

The cop came back with two slices on a paper napkin. Anything to keep McCullough happy. He was asked what he wanted to drink.

"Water good?"

"Water's good," McCullough said.

Ciesynski disappeared. McCullough consumed one slice with a couple of gulps and left the other one uneaten. He was full. He let out a deep and prolonged sigh. Thirty minutes later, Ciesynski returned and noticed the single slice laying there on the desk.

"Didn't eat your pizza?"

Dismissing the pleasantries, McCullough said, "OK, now that I know that you think I'm involved, I really do want a lawyer."

That remark elicited an unconcerned gesture from Ciesynski, as if to say he could not be bothered with this case from so long ago. "OK. Sounds like a winner to me. Sounds like a winner to me. I'll end our conversations then. You do not want to talk to me anymore, is that what you're saying?"

"Yeah, we're done."

"That's fine with me. That's fine with me. You'll be booked."

McCullough looked at him defiantly. He had been thinking things through during the meal break. "You've heard of the fruit of the poisonous tree, right?"

Ciesynski repeated the words as if they were the ravings of a blockhead trying to sound like a big-shot lawyer. "Fruit of the poisonous tree?" The phrase was legal terminology for evidence illegally obtained and therefore inadmissible in court. McCullough would have knowledge of its meaning from his years as a police officer.

"Right," McCullough said triumphantly. "So everything you've asked me since we left the building is no good when I asked for a lawyer." He sounded cocky, certain he had outwitted everyone.

Ciesynski asked, "You asked me for a lawyer?"

"Yes, I said I want a lawyer."

"And I said no?"

"Well, you didn't say no, but you blew me off."

"I blew you off?"

"Yeah."

Ciesynski had had enough. "You're going to be arrested. You're under arrest for murder." It was 12:45 in the morning.

"OK. I need a phone call."

"Hang on; I'll get to that. Phone-call stuff all comes from over in the jail. They'll give you a phone call as they see fit. You'll have a first appearance, probably tonight. They'll ask you if you want to waive extradition or not. It doesn't make any difference. You're going to be extradited to Chicago and placed in the DeKalb County Jail. There'll probably be a little media on this thing, too."

"You're making a really big mistake. I am innocent."

"Prove it to me."

"You've made up your mind already."

Ciesynski wasn't through yet. He pulled out another photo and showed it to McCullough. It was his final Hail Mary. It was a crime-scene photo of Maria's body after it had been discovered by the mushroom hunters, in 1958, in Jo Daviess County, Illinois.

"Who's that?"

McCullough forced himself to look at it. "I don't know if it's Maria or not."

"Yeah, it's Maria. Jack, this is between you and me. I want the person who did that to be strung up. What do you want to happen?"

McCullough agreed. "Electric chair," he said.

"They don't have the death penalty in Illinois anymore." Ciesynski slammed down the photo of McCullough that Kathy Sigman had identified as Johnny. "She signed her name right there."

"I didn't even recognize that picture as myself."

Pounding his fist on the table, Ciesynski said, "So you go tell that to the grand jury investigating this and you tell them, 'Nah, it wasn't me,' and you tell why, when your mom was on her deathbed, why the family didn't want you to come to her funeral—*insisted you didn't come to her funeral*. And what was your other little sister's name? What is her name?" Ciesynski dug for the report. "It's Janet Tessier." He showed the report to McCullough. It was Janet's statements to police, quoting her mother Eileen as saying on her deathbed, "Remember those two little girls? John did it." McCullough read the document.

"Who's saying this?"

"Your sister."

"Janet?"

"You'd better start doing some selling yourself. You'd better start selling me why you didn't do this or who did this."

"I have no idea. And why wouldn't I be cooperative? I've been cooperative. Normally, I wouldn't have said a goddamn word."

"I'll be honest with you. I haven't seen those autopsy reports so I don't even know if they have allegations that this girl was raped or not. I don't know about that—if she was sexually assaulted." He learned forward and got right in McCullough's face. "But I do know there's allegations about you sexually assaulting other people, and you're pretty defensive about that. And I believe those other little people you were sexually assaulting were your relatives. And I'm sure when they get on the stand there and they talk about how you sexually assaulted all those little girls and how many years this shit went on. And I think there's something else here about when you were a policeman, some allegations about some young girl. When this all goes to the grand jury, give me a holler. Maybe you're going to think back and say, 'You know that Detective Ciesynski, that guy from Seattle who's done all these cases, maybe he's not all that bad, maybe I should have come clean to him.'"

"I already have come clean to you."

"Oh, bullshit! You contradicted yourself twenty-five times. Oh, you're telling me you weren't there, you didn't give that girl a piggyback ride? Of all the people in the world, this girl [Kathy Sigman] says you're the one who gave the piggyback ride."

"I have no idea."

Ciesynski spewed forth a torrent of mockery. "Oh, that's going to be your defense? 'I have no idea why that girl picked me. I have no idea why my mother said I did it. I have no idea why I lied and failed the FBI polygraph test. I said I took the train even though here's the ticket that you gave to your girlfriend, that she kept for fifty years.' Kinda a good stroke of luck on our part. Not so lucky on your part. You agree?"

"I didn't do it."

"Well, who did then?"

"I have no idea."

"'*No idea*,'" Ciesynski scoffed. "Do you know how many times I've been in this room I have to listen to this kind of bullshit from people like you saying, 'Oh, I didn't do this, I didn't do that,' and then it comes down to court time and all of a sudden, 'Uh, I'd better start thinking about what really happened here,' and it's usually a little bit too late. You do realize you're under arrest. You're going right next door here to the King County Jail and then you're going to be taking the big airplane back to your hometown of Sycamore. When was the last time you were in Sycamore? You weren't there for the funeral."

"I was there two weeks before the funeral."

"He didn't make it for the funeral." Again, the mockery. "Why didn't they want you there?"

There was dead silence from McCullough, and Ciesynski let the question soak in. Then he let him have it. "It wasn't that bullshit you told me earlier that you were in the army because actually you weren't in the army back then."

"We're done."

"What happened?"

"We're done. Where's my lawyer?"

Ciesynski got up from his chair. "Gimme a holler some-time."

"You think you're right, but you're wrong."

Ciesynski shook his head with vexation. He didn't know what to make of this guy. Every time he thought Mc-Cullough wanted to exercise his right to remain silent, he kept on talking. Of course, that was fine with Ciesynski. "You want to talk to me or not talk to me? I can't keep going back and forth here with you. I've got shit I've got to do, too." He started clearing the desk of his files and the uneaten slice of pizza. As if on cue, the door to the interview room slid open and a uniformed cop appeared.

"Arrest this guy," Ciesynski told the officer. Then he turned to McCullough. "I'm going to need your watch. Stand and empty your pockets." McCullough did as he was told. Ciesynski had one more sucker punch to deliver. "You want any more coffee? Because they don't give you coffee in prison."

When McCullough shook his head, Ciesynski left the room with the uniformed cop. McCullough sat there all alone again. It was seven hours and thirty minutes into the interrogation. He played with a rubber band to pass the time.

Then he let out a great big belch.

BOOK IV

31

·········

"ISN'T THAT A STRANGE COINCIDENCE"

It was past two in the morning Seattle time when Brion Hanley finally called Clay Campbell at his office in Sycamore. The state's attorney of DeKalb County, Illinois, had dozed off waiting to hear from his people in Seattle. He sprang off the couch and answered the phone.

"I was wondering what was going on," he said.

Campbell's voice came through the speakerphone in the conference room at Seattle homicide. They were all there. The Jack McCullough interrogation had just wrapped up, and the suspect was about to be transported to King County Jail for booking.

Hanley looked at Detective Cloyd Steiger. He wanted an outsider to speak out, an independent thinker not from Illinois who hadn't been engrossed in this case for these last three years. "Cloyd, tell Clay what you think."

Steiger spoke directly into the speaker. "This is your fucking guy. *That's* what I think. If you watch this video, you will know this is the right guy."

True, McCullough hadn't broken down, nor had he blurted out a confession, but no one had really expected that to happen. What he did do was run off at the mouth and entangle himself in a web of half-truths that could prove very useful at trial. Campbell said he wanted to see the video right away. They tried to upload the tape to him, but the file was too large, and they had to wait until daylight for the tech guy to come in and figure out how to send it to him over an FTP site.

Campbell thanked everyone for their hard work and said he was going to make the announcement of McCullough's arrest at daylight, in just a few hours.

In Seattle, it was time for a postmortem over drinks. It was a tradition in the homicide squad to celebrate when a big job wrapped up. A large bottle of bourbon was pulled out of a desk drawer for the occasion, and shots were poured all around. As they sat and talked about the case, Steiger said he was beginning to understand what made McCullough tick.

"It was Johnny and his mother during the war. He was everything to her. It was, 'You and me against the world.' Then she met Ralph." McCullough was a momma's boy, went Steiger's dissection of McCullough's head, and who knew how that messed him up when Eileen came to America and started having babies who, from Johnny's perspective, replaced him in his mother's eyes. But Eileen always had a special relationship with her firstborn, knitting him sweaters, protecting him from Ralph's physical abuse, even covering up for him when he became a suspect in the abduction of a seven-year-old girl.

Mike Ciesynski looked at Dave Zulawski and knocked back a shot. "You know, when they told me you were coming, I didn't like it. But you did OK."

Zulawski grinned. "Thanks for the compliment," he said, and he really meant it. He also thought that the interrogation had gone as well as could be expected. He'd been worried because an ex-cop like Jack McCullough would be expected to have knowledge of the tradecraft of interrogation, but Zulawski was surprised by how little McCullough seemed to know about it, though he did seem to be well-versed in his Miranda rights.

"Jack had a real need to communicate and manipulate, so he decided he had to continue talking," which he did for more than seven hours.

It was time to walk McCullough across the street and turn him over to the county jail. Steiger handed the officer on duty the charging paperwork that he'd filled out to process the prisoner into the system. When the duty officer looked at it his eyes widened.

"Holy shit," he said

It was mind-boggling. For date of arrest, Steiger had typed: *6/29/2011*.

For date and time of violation: *12/3/1957. 6:15 P.M.*

A span of fifty-three years, five months, and four days. It was a historic first in the annals of criminal justice.

Another officer took a look at the charging papers, then studied the senior citizen standing in front of them in handcuffs.

"Is this right?"

Steiger nodded yes.

"Wow."

All this time, McCullough took it like a man, trying to just deal with it and get through his first night of incarceration. Steiger wondered what he was thinking about, and the veteran homicide detective reckoned he knew the answer. *How do I get out of this mess?*

Chuck Ridulph pulled into his driveway in Sycamore at 6:00 P.M. He wasn't even out of his car when he saw his wife, Diane, running out of the house.

"You have to call the state's attorney right away," Diane told him. "*Right away.*"

"What happened?"

"They found the guy who killed your sister Maria."

Chuck reached Clay Campbell, but the prosecutor said he couldn't really say anything over the phone. He'd come right over. Ten minutes later, Campbell, accompanied by Sycamore detective Dan Hoffman, was at Chuck's front door. Chuck didn't know Campbell except to say hello to him on the street. Until this moment, they had never exchanged a word about the Maria Ridulph investigation, which Chuck had assumed was not only dormant, but dead.

"We know who killed Maria," Campbell announced.

The news took Chuck's breath away. Campbell explained that the state police had received information about three years before that had led to a full-scale reopening of the investigation. A man had been taken into custody for Maria's murder a few hours earlier in Seattle. Campbell told Chuck that, as they spoke, he was being interrogated by lawmen in Seattle.

The suspect was Jack McCullough, but in another life, he had grown up in Sycamore. In fact, he had been a neighbor. His name was John Tessier.

Chuck could scarcely believe what he was hearing. Of course, he knew the family. The Tessiers had lived about two blocks from the Ridulph house on Archie Place. All this time, Chuck had assumed the kidnapper was a stranger, ten to one a truck driver passing through town, and either dead or in jail for another crime.

Chuck had never known John Tessier, but he did know his sisters, and best of all, he knew their father, Ralph Tessier. As a recovering alcoholic, Chuck would encounter Ralph at the regular Tuesday night Alcoholics Anonymous meeting at St. Mary's Church, in Sycamore. Ralph had been active in AA, and on several occasions, in the 1990s, when Ralph was an old man, Chuck had even visited him at his home, at 227 Center Cross Street, as part of their continuing 12-step program. Chuck also knew Ralph through his business dealings. When he'd owned the bar Beak's Place, before he was ordained in the Lutheran ministry, Chuck had hired Ralph to paint signs for the establishment and had found him artistically gifted and perfectly likable.

Campbell didn't want to give away too much information but told Chuck he didn't have any doubt that Jack McCullough murdered Maria. Proving it in court was going to be another matter.

"Do you want me to call you when we issue the arrest warrant?" Campbell asked.

"Yes. Absolutely."

At 10:30 P.M., the telephone rang. It was Campbell, informing Chuck that it was really happening.

The first two calls Chuck made were to his sisters, Pat and Kay.

When Kay learned about McCullough's arrest, she had only three months left to live. She'd been battling stage-four breast and liver cancer for seven years. Being a generous Christian soul, her first instinct on hearing the news was to express sympathy for the Tessiers. What made it so inconceivable to Kay was that when she was a little girl, she'd been close to Johnny Tessier's sister Jeanne and had been invited to the Tessier house many times for tea parties and games with Jeanne and her sister Katheran. Kay didn't really know their big brother Johnny at all. But in those final weeks, as her life ebbed away, she was certain that Ralph must have known what Johnny had done.

"The father must be involved," she told Chuck. "Johnny could not have acted alone."

Chuck had to disagree. He told Kay that he had gotten to know Ralph very well at the AA meetings and had heard him speak from the heart on several occasions about the challenges of abstinence. "I just cannot believe that he knew anything about Maria's murder," Chuck told his sister. "I cannot bring myself to believe that this person, who I knew in his sobriety, could have lived with the knowledge of such a terrible, evil act."

Kay just shook her head. Nothing Chuck said could convince her that Ralph didn't know. He *must* have known.

How ironic, said Kay's son, Lawrence "Larry" Hickey Jr., that his own father had stood in a police lineup back in 1957 because he was dating Kay, and the police wanted to eliminate him as a suspect. So had dozens of other innocent Sycamore youths. It seemed that at one time or another, every young man in town had been hauled in for a once-over from little Kathy Sigman.

"How could my dad be in a lineup and Jack McCullough not be?" Larry wondered. It was a legitimate question that said plenty about the ineptitude of the 1957 investigation.

Pat Ridulph Quinn got very upset for similar reasons. "If they had shown Kathy Sigman a picture of Johnny Tessier or put him in a lineup in 1957 it would have been over immediately."

When Pat learned that the apartment unit where McCullough lived at the Four Freedoms in Seattle was 616, she got another shock. It was the same number on Archie Place, where the Ridulphs had lived in 1957—616.

"How spooky is that?" Pat exclaimed.

Kathy Sigman Chapman got home from work and listened to a message on her answering machine. It was Clay Campbell, asking her to give him a call ASAP. She punched in the number.

"Are you sitting down?" Campbell asked.

"Yes."

"We've made an arrest in the case."

Ten months earlier, Kathy had positively identified a photo of John Tessier as Johnny the kidnapper, but until his arrest in 2011, she had never been told his name.

With the hindsight of half a century, the arrest of Jack McCullough was starting to make a lot of sense to Kathy. After Maria's kidnapping, she'd had the funny feeling that the Tessier house on Center Cross Street was off-limits to her. For some reason, Eileen and Ralph Tessier had always made her feel unwelcome. Now she knew why.

"I'm sure the issue was if I ever saw a photo of Johnny in their house, I'd know who he was," Kathy said.

She also had some tough questions about the original 1957 investigation. Why, she wanted to know, had she never been shown the photo of John Tessier in 1957 when it was fresh in her mind?

"I was never shown that picture. Had I, he would not have gone free. The police back then were so naive they couldn't conceive it was somebody from the neighborhood. We all bought into the idea that it couldn't have been somebody local."

Kathy and her husband, Mike, drove over to Sycamore and paid their respects at Maria Ridulph's grave in Elmwood Cemetery. They thought it was the decent thing to do. Somebody must have gotten there just a few hours before them because they found a handwritten note taped to Maria's headstone.

"They got him," it said.

·········

On July 1, all of Sycamore exploded with the news of Mc-Cullough's arrest.

Sycamore's mayor, Ken Mundy, had been eleven when Maria was kidnapped. He reached out to Chuck and told him, "Hopefully this is the right suspect so you and your family will never have to reopen these wounds again."

Everyone wanted to know what had prompted the police to reopen the case and how it had gotten solved. Clay Campbell refused to disclose any of that information, limiting his public comments to a press release in which he declared, "This crime has haunted Sycamore for half a century."

The only thing Sycamore police chief Donald Thomas would say on the subject was that police had received "new information several years ago" that led them to focus on Jack McCullough. For the time being, Janet Tessier's role was being kept under wraps. In the newspapers, a big deal was made of the unpunched train ticket from Rockford to Chicago on the Illinois Central Railroad that had been kept tucked inside a picture frame for these five decades by McCullough's ex-girlfriend. Jan Edwards's name, like Janet Tessier's, was yet to be revealed. It made for an irresistible headline in the local newspaper, the *Daily Chronicle*:

UNUSED TRAIN TICKET CRACKS
ALIBI OF SEATTLE MAN ACCUSED
OF KILLING MARIA RIDULPH

It was as if the key piece of evidence had literally floated into the laps of the police.

Reporters were calling Kathy Sigman Chapman for interviews. Then a sharp *Daily Chronicle* writer who was combing through the old newspaper archives came across something striking: it seemed that Kathy's family had crossed paths with Jack McCullough once before, when he was known as John Tessier. According to an April 1, 1947, article in the *Sycamore True Republican*, an eight-year-old boy named Johnny Tessier, newly arrived from England, son of Ralph Tessier and his war bride, Eileen Tessier, had been struck down by a taxi driven by Henry "Bud" Sigman. Bud Sigman was Kathy's father.

Johnny had been walking home from school when Sigman's cab had hit him, at the intersection of State and California in Sycamore. Johnny had landed on his head with a "sickening blow," according to the 1947 article, and had to be hospitalized for shock and "serious bruising." This was the head injury that John Tessier's aunt Mary believed had forever altered his personality. He was "never the same" after that, which may or may not be true, but family lore has it that Ralph Tessier ran to the scene of the accident and really got into it with Bud Sigman. He grabbed the cab driver by his lapels and swore he'd bust him up if little Johnny didn't recover.

Kathy's father went on to own the Phillips 66 gas station on Main Street. He died in December 2010, at age eighty-four, and Kathy does not recall ever hearing the family discuss that taxi accident. When she read about the connection, she shook her head, baffled.

"Isn't that a strange coincidence."

But some who remembered a theory that had been briefly contemplated and then rejected back in 1957 now wondered if it had some validity after all. Could little Kathy Sigman, not Maria Ridulph, have been Johnny's intended victim all along?

32

·········

PIECES OF THE PUZZLE

The night Jack McCullough was arrested, his stepdaughter Janey O'Connor received several voice messages from her mother on her cell phone. Sue McCullough said, "Call me!" sounding distressed, but she was always calling with one crisis or another. Janey didn't get around to calling her back until she was at a shopping mall running errands.

"Jack's been arrested," Sue said.

"For what?"

"For murder."

Janey froze. It could not be possible. Her beloved stepfather, Jack, who babysat for her daughter, Emily, and son, Andrew. *A murderer?* She tried to get more information out of her mother, but Sue was sobbing hysterically, and Janey couldn't follow what she was saying. Was he accused of the slaying of a seven-year-old girl or a fifteen-year-old runaway? She couldn't figure it out. In Sue's understandably befuddled state, she was confusing Maria Ridulph with Michelle Weinman.

Janey got in her car to drive home, but on the way she had to pull over; when she did, she burst into tears. She'd seen Jack earlier that day when she'd dropped Emily and Andrew off at his apartment so he could take them to school later. She'd been in such a hurry to get to her job, she gave Jack a "half-assed" hug, and she regretted it because it now seemed so dismissive.

Janey was an attractive thirty-four-year-old with tawny, wavy hair. Her live-in boyfriend, Casey Porter, forty-three, was a good-looking tax accountant who had red hair—plus a red goatee—and stood six feet seven. They had met on an online dating site. Between them, they had six children from previous marriages. They'd been together for about a year and a half in what was a lively household, to say the least. When Janey got home, she broke the news to Casey, saying, "Let's see what we can find online."

Casey went to his computer and started digging while Janey looked over his shoulder. Casey had said hello to Jack a few times, but they hadn't really gotten to know each other. Three days earlier, Jack had taken little Emily to Costco and, to Casey's irritation, bought her a three-foot-tall teddy bear that was taking up too much space in her bedroom.

Casey searched Sycamore and the murder of a fifteen-year-old girl. Nothing came up.

"All I'm finding are these stories about this little girl." Her name was Maria Ridulph.

"No, no, the girl was fifteen," Janey insisted. It was the

tangled information she'd gotten from her mother. "It probably wasn't big news."

Momentarily, they were completely in the dark. Then it hit them: it had to be about Maria Ridulph. Janey got sick to her stomach. Oh, no, she thought; a seven-year-old girl—so close to her nine-year-old daughter's age.

Casey, being an accountant, lived by the edicts of tax regulations and the IRS tax code, and he liked to think that he conducted his personal life the same way—"by the book." People needed to be held accountable, he believed.

He looked in his girlfriend's eyes. "Maybe he did do it." It was a hard thing for him to say, but he thought Janey should brace herself for more disturbing revelations to come.

Less than a month later, Casey became convinced that the police had busted the wrong man.

McCullough was having a rough time of it in the county lockup. His reading glasses were nowhere to be found, and three days after his arrest, he was transported to Harborview Medical Center, in Seattle, after experiencing chest pains. It looked like a serious medical crisis, but once he got back on his heart meds, he was returned to jail. A bail hearing was held, and a district judge found probable cause to hold him, pending extradition to Illinois.

Sue McCullough had terrible problems navigating her way through the jail's bureaucracy and figuring out the process of visiting her husband behind bars. For that first visit, Janey went with her, having drummed into her mother how important it was to try to be upbeat and forward thinking.

"It's really important that he see us as a ray of sunshine," Janey told Sue. "We are his only source of sunshine." She also warned Sue that all their conversations were potentially being recorded. Above all else, Janey begged her mother, "Don't ask him if he's guilty."

Sue and Jack looked at each other through a glass partition and picked up the phones they'd have to talk on. Sue was shocked to see her husband in a bright-red jail jumpsuit. Of course, the first thing she asked him was, "Did you do this?"

McCullough faced her squarely through the glass and, as resolutely as he could, said, "No, I did not."

Seven days after his arrest, McCullough got word that Gene Johnson, a reporter for the Associated Press, wanted to interview him. He said that was fine with him. Why not? He wanted his story out there; plus, he figured he didn't have much to lose. A lawyer would have advised him to keep his mouth shut and let *him* do the talking. But McCullough did not have legal representation, and talk he would.

When Johnson sat down across from McCullough, he was startled to see the inmate press a crinkled piece of paper against the glass partition. On it he'd scrawled letters and words in several exotic languages, including Urdu and what looked like ancient Egyptian hieroglyphs. According to the reporter, McCullough wanted to prove that "he wasn't an idiot." Before his arrest, he told Johnson, he'd been studying cuneiform script, an ancient system of writing on clay tablets, and had been praying to Ahura Mazda, the ancient god of the Persians. As to the charges that he killed Maria Ridulph, McCullough told Johnson, "I have an ironclad alibi. I did not commit a murder."

During the interview, he kept trying to finger this guy "Brooks" for the crime, insisting that it was he, Mc-Cullough, who had prompted the reopening of the cold case. After he'd had a dream about Brooks "a few years ago," he'd notified the FBI in New York City about him.

"I called the FBI. They said thank you. And here I am." The FBI maintains it has no record of a call from Jack McCullough regarding the Maria Ridulph case.

Doing his time in jail had apparently refreshed Mc-Cullough's memory as to his whereabouts on December 2, 3, and 4, 1957. He told Johnson there was a plausible explanation for the train ticket being unpunched; he'd never used it. His stepfather, Ralph, he told the AP reporter, had driven him to Chicago, and after his physical, he'd hitched a ride to Rockford with a fellow inductee he had met at the Chicago armed-forces recruitment center. Pointing to the collect call he had made from Rockford at 6:57 P.M., he said: "How am I involved in a kidnapping at 6:00 P.M. in Sycamore? A fifth-grader can figure this out."

Even in the face of murder charges, McCullough's quirky sense of humor—or was it his colossal ego?—came through when he reminisced about his high school sweetheart and the photo and the train ticket that she had kept for all those years.

"She doesn't know it, but I loved her for decades. She got married, and I put it aside and said, 'Eh, give up.' But she keeps a picture of me and her for fifty years. Imagine that."

When Jan Edwards was asked about this, she had a big laugh and said, "*Whatever.* I didn't keep it because I was in love with him. I kept it because it was a picture of *me.* Sorry, John."

McCullough's siblings may have turned on him, but he was lucky to have the vocal support of the O'Connors, Sue and Janey, and his stepniece, Jenn Howton, who came to court when he appeared before the judge.

The man she knew could not have murdered a child, Jenn insisted.

"Other people have said crazy things about his past, but I never saw it. I was alone with him umpteen-million times. Never ever was he inappropriate in any way. Never—not a look on his face, not the tone of his voice. Nothing." And she lived with him for a year.

Janey O'Connor expressed sympathy for the Ridulphs and "the little life that was lost." But as she dug into the case, deep within her, skepticism took hold, and the more she learned, the more it grew. The timeline made no sense to her. Contemporary newspaper reports from 1957 and the FBI's own files stated that Maria had been kidnapped close to around 7:00 P.M., making it impossible for McCullough to get to Rockford in time to place the collect phone call at 6:57 P.M. Now, suddenly, the kidnapping was supposed to have taken place at 6:15 or thereabouts.

"They moved the timeline," Janey said. "Somebody decided to cut their own pieces of the puzzle to make it fit." Whatever the truth of it, she wondered how the charges against McCullough could stick. "Really, the only documentation is the phone call. You actually had a woman who sat in front of a switchboard and plugged in the phone call. It's a record."

On July 20, 2011, in prison scrubs, McCullough made a brief appearance before a King County judge in Seattle. Janey sat in the front row, straining to hear over the din in the courtroom. Through his legal-aid lawyer, McCullough waived his right to an extradition hearing.

In the hallway outside court, Janey was surrounded by reporters. The beautiful stepdaughter defending the accused killer of a seven-year-old girl made for an interesting take on the story that was already picking up national attention.

"The sooner he gets to Illinois, the sooner he can come home," Janey told them. "He's a strong person. His main focus is my mom and how this is affecting the family." Some tough but legitimate questions followed. What about those sexual-assault charges that McCullough had faced when he was a cop in Milton? Janey acknowledged his "checkered" past. She said she'd known about McCullough's transgressions in Milton since she was sixteen.

"It wasn't a secret. It wasn't something he was proud of, but because you make a mistake does not mean that you're capable of murdering a little girl. That's a pretty big leap."

33

....

RETURN TO SYCAMORE

At the crack of dawn, on July 27, 2011, a black curtain was hung in front of Maria Ridulph's grave at Elmwood Cemetery in Sycamore in preparation for the exhumation of her mortal remains. State and local police vehicles blocked off all paths leading to the site, and a giant earth-moving backhoe was brought in to remove the dirt that covered her grave. When the operators dared not go deeper, two cemetery workers bearing shovels were called over to complete the digging. Finally, they reached the top of a concrete vault. Forensic anthropologist Krista Latham stepped up to the lip of the gravesite, looked down, and did a quick analysis. Then she ordered the workmen to remove the lid from the vault. There lay Maria's little wooden casket, built for the child buried on April 30, 1958.

There had been some water damage, but, overall, the coffin was in remarkably good condition. Next to the coffin, tucked into a corner of the vault, was something unexpected and gruesome: a jar in a paper sack. In it were Maria's upper and lower jaws. They had been removed during the autopsy in 1958 when her teeth had been needed to make a positive identification.

The workmen placed two straps around the casket, hefted it out of the vault, and carried it to a van, which transported it to the DeKalb County coroner's office. Dr. Latham remained at the site to examine the water inside the vault for any additional evidence. When she was certain that nothing had been left behind, she joined her colleagues at the coroner's. Just as she left, a heavy downpour burst over the cemetery.

Dr. Latham was in her midthirties. She had long brown hair and a serious demeanor befitting an assistant professor of biology and anthropology at the University of Indiana. She was a specialist in the extraction and analysis of skeletal remains and "transfer," or touch, DNA, meaning DNA that has been transferred from an individual to another person or item. She held a bachelor's degree in biology and chemistry plus two master's degrees and a doctorate in anthropology. Depending on the circumstances—say, if she were testifying as an expert witness, and a lawyer called her *Miss*—she'd admonish the individual: "The correct way to address me is Dr. Latham." She had been hired by the DeKalb County coroner, Dennis Miller, to serve as the principal forensic anthropologist on the Maria Ridulph case because of her expertise in examining bones for signs of trauma.

At the county morgue, Maria's coffin was placed on an autopsy table. In all, a team of fifteen pathologists and scientists from DeKalb County, Cook County, the FBI, and the state police had gathered to consult on the exhumation. The room was so packed with scientists and technicians that Clay Campbell had to climb on top of a table to get a decent line of sight. At last, the casket was opened. It was a heartbreaking sight. Maria's little feet protruded from a blanket that had covered her body before the casket had been closed. Her toenails and fingernails were still visible. Skin covered her right foot. There was the big toe. You could still make out her wavy brown hair. A one-and-a-half-inch section of skin on the ball of her left foot had been cut away; Maria had once cut herself while playing in the rain after a storm and, in 1958, the coroner had wanted to preserve the scar for identification purposes. A jar of embalming powder to inhibit mold and mildew was still present in the coffin. So were several leaves and a number of beetles. How they had gotten in there was a mystery. One of Maria's arms was folded across her little chest; the other was extended straight down. One leg was slightly bent; the other one extended straight down. Remarkably, Maria had been buried in the precise position that she had been found in when the mushroom hunters had come across her body in Jo Daviess County. The coroners knew this from comparing the crime-scene photos from 1958 to the body they were studying on the autopsy table in 2011. There was one additional macabre difference—the top of her cranium had been sectioned off, a remnant from the original 1958 autopsy, and had been placed between her legs.

The Ridulphs had known this was coming. A week earlier, after he'd obtained a court order, Clay Campbell had sat down with Chuck and explained why an exhumation was necessary. In 1958, no definitive cause of death had been established. Modern science might make it possible. It could prove critical to the investigation. He told Chuck that he was not taking Maria's exhumation lightly.

Chuck burst into tears. He knew the family's permission wasn't required, and he appreciated the gesture. Chuck gave Campbell his blessing.

Now Dr. Krista Latham was using all her training and years of education to determine how Maria had been killed fifty-four years before. It was a challenging mission.

They all watched as Dr. Latham took a scalpel and manually removed any existing soft tissue from the skeletal remains. Then the soft tissue was returned to the casket and would stay behind in the coroner's office in DeKalb County while the skeletal remains were transported to the Archeology and Forensics Laboratory at the University of Indianapolis.

The lab at the University of Indianapolis is a limited-access facility. Only authorized personnel are allowed entry. A perimeter alarm surrounds the entire 2,600 square feet of floor space. Maria's remains were stored in a secure evidence room.

Dr. Latham's first task was to simmer the bones in a water, bleach, and Borax solution. Next, the bones were thoroughly dried. The process took several days. When she was ready to conduct her examination, she started by measuring the size of the bones and reconstructing the various components into a complete skeleton. Then she examined the skeleton for any signs of trauma, both with her naked eyes and under the microscope. Assisting her was a team of advanced graduate students and the director of the lab, Dr. Stephen Nawrocki.

Surgical cut marks from the original autopsy were all over the skeleton. Dr. Latham saw them on the left collarbone, or clavicle, where the chest plate had been removed. There were cuts along the sternum, or breastbone, and there were cuts along the ribcage. She could tell these were the product of an autopsy because the cuts were sharp and horizontal and very shallow, less than a millimeter deep into the bone, and obviously performed with a surgical scalpel or surgical saw.

Then she saw something unexpected, something that the coroner must have missed in 1958. There were multiple sharp-force trauma cuts located just below the throat and deep inside the body, within the chest cavity. These cuts were deeper and much wider and were in stark contrast to those produced by the scalpel. They were consistent with the markings of a large blade or knife. Dr. Latham observed three distinct "cutting events," presumably by a knife, going through the throat and down into the chest cavity.

Maria Ridulph had been stabbed to death.

· · · · · · · · ·

On the morning of the exhumation in Sycamore, at 6:08 A.M. West Coast time, Jack McCullough was being escorted out of King County Jail, in Seattle, in the company of the two men he probably despised most, Detectives Mike Ciesynski and Cloyd Steiger of Seattle homicide.

McCullough was put in a waist chain, his hands cuffed to his sides. He turned his head and spat, "Mike Ciesynski, I'm not going to say a word to you."

Ciesynski glanced at Steiger and rolled his eyes, as if to say, *Yeah, right.*

Until this moment, McCullough had had no idea that Ciesynski and Steiger would be the detectives assigned to escort him back to Sycamore. *Did it have to be these two guys?* he thought. It was somebody's idea of a cruel joke, and he had a funny feeling this was a setup.

Under ordinary circumstances, the state of Illinois would have been responsible for picking up the prisoner, but Brion Hanley had talked things over with Clay Campbell, and they'd asked Ciesynski and Steiger to do the job, the thinking being that McCullough might get so stirred up, who knows what he'd say.

McCullough was taken to police headquarters, where he changed out of his prison jumpsuit into civilian clothes. After all, nobody wanted to unduly terrify the other passengers on the plane. Then they all climbed into an unmarked police car requisitioned from the transport detail for the ride to Sea-Tac Airport. A driver was assigned to them.

No surprise, McCullough was "chitty-chatty" the entire way, and once they got to the airport, he really let loose. The three of them were standing in line at the United ticket counter, handing in the required forms and notifying the airline that they were armed and transporting a prisoner, when McCullough craned his neck and scanned the terminal. *Who was he looking for?* Ciesynski asked him what was up.

"Greg Fisher from CBS is supposed to meet me here." Fisher was a highly regarded producer for the program *48 Hours*, and he had started researching a story about the Maria Ridulph case. "This is going to be a big deal."

Ciesynski gave off an expression of complete indifference, and that's all McCullough needed to lay it on thick with his usual swagger.

"Remember Casey Anthony," he said. He held up one finger. "I only have to convince one juror." Casey Anthony was the young mother from Orlando, Florida, accused of murdering her two-year-old daughter, Caylee, so she could return to a swinging lifestyle. It had seemed like an open-and-shut case, but three weeks earlier, following a nationally televised trial, a jury had found Casey Anthony not guilty of first-degree murder, and there had been a public outcry.

Steiger grinned and said, "Well, Jack, let me remind you of an important fact you seem to be forgetting. That one juror is going to get you a hung jury. You need twelve to get you acquitted."

Steiger and Ciesynski really got a kick out of busting McCullough's chops.

Two officers from the Port of Seattle police department came over to escort the trio to the security gate, and, following airline protocol, they were the first to board the plane. They sat in the last row. Steiger had the bigger frame and needed the aisle seat to give him some legroom. McCullough sat in the middle. Ciesynski got stuck with the window seat. Just to be decent, they unlocked one of McCullough's waist chains to give him a free hand to hold a drink.

Passengers standing in line to use the restroom stared at McCullough—and his chains. One woman asked, "Is he a prisoner?"

"Yep," said Steiger.

"What did he do?"

"Murder."

About forty-five minutes into the flight, McCullough let slip something that Steiger found worth noting in a police report he wrote up when they landed. Maria Ridulph's name had come up in conversation. No surprise there, but what really jolted the detectives was the language that they say McCullough used when he talked about her.

"She was like a beautiful little Barbie doll," he said. According to Steiger, the prisoner was "glowing" and using his arms as if to form a figurine in the shape of Maria Ridulph.

Then McCullough brought up the night of December 3, 1957. He told the two detectives that he now remembered hitching a ride from Chicago to Rockford and then hitching yet another ride from a fellow he met in Rockford, who drove him to Sycamore. In this way, McCullough was trying to explain away the lie that his parents had told the FBI when they claimed Ralph had picked him up after receiving the collect phone call at 6:57 P.M.

According to McCullough's new account, when he got home and found the door at 227 Center Cross Street locked, he told the detectives, he had "crawled in a window" to gain entry into his house. His story, as implausible and full of holes as it sounded, was his way of explaining the statements of his sisters Katheran and Jeanne that he had not come home the night Maria was kidnapped.

"The next day I got up. My family was really surprised to see me there in the morning," McCullough said.

Steiger was taking it all down in his head.

There was one minor annoyance on the flight, when the attendants wheeling the food cart ran out of meals just before they got to the last row.

"You've got to be kidding me," Ciesynski complained.

All the flight attendant could offer was an apologetic "Sorry."

Ciesynski had been up since 4:00 A.M. and had had no breakfast. "Oh, man, I'm starving." All McCullough had had was a cup of coffee. Ciesynski turned to McCullough and told him not to worry. "We're going to feed you."

Other than that, it was a smooth landing at O'Hare International Airport. The trip in the air took in total about four hours. As the plane taxied to the gate, Steiger stared out the window and saw a fleet of state police vehicles and a prisoner van parked on the tarmac outside the United terminal.

"I think that's our ride," he said.

"Make sure you remember how long it takes to get from Chicago to Sycamore," McCullough said enthusiastically. "That's going to be a big part of my alibi."

"You'd better have more than that, Jack," Ciesynski quipped.

They waited for the other passengers to disembark. Then, with the aircraft emptied out, they exited. Ciesynski and Steiger walked their prisoner to the van. The FBI was also there. They all hopped inside. First stop was the Chicago police station at O'Hare because McCullough really had to take a leak. Then they climbed back in the van, and the state police trooper at the wheel steered it onto I-90 for the drive to Sycamore. McCullough sat in the middle row, between Ciesynski and Steiger. Two state troopers sat behind them. Up front were two other troopers, including the driver.

McCullough seemed to be in an upbeat mood. Even under these circumstance, it was exciting for him to be heading to his hometown, where he hadn't been since 1993, just before his mother died.

Ciesynski looked up the highway.

"That looks like a good place."

It was a Steak 'n Shake. No surprise there. The Steak 'n Shake chain had been founded in Illinois back in 1934. They were everywhere in the state.

It was close to noon when the van pulled into the parking lot. The restaurant was jammed. McCullough took baby steps to a booth, still cuffed to the belly chains, but none of the patrons seemed to take notice. Ciesynski sat opposite him, and the prisoner ordered a double cheeseburger, fries, and a large milk.

"You know, I've got the body of a thirty-five-year-old," McCullough boasted.

"No kidding."

McCullough was pretty buff. When he worked as a night watchman, he'd sometimes pass the time doing curls with a set of barbells he kept under the front desk. Then he told Ciesynski, "But if I don't take my medication, I'm dead tomorrow."

Meanwhile, Steiger had taken a table directly behind McCullough. His back could almost touch McCullough's. In a quiet aside, Steiger asked a state trooper, "Hey, got a pen I can borrow?" In front of him on the table there was a Steak 'n Shake placemat, pushing the restaurant's latest promotions. Steiger turned it over to the blank side and started taking down verbatim whatever McCullough had to say. The prisoner just would not stop talking about the case.

McCullough said he believed the man who had murdered Maria had to be a serial killer. He said the mushroom hunters who discovered her body had come under early suspicion because "who would be looking for mushrooms in the middle of the winter?" (The body was actually discovered in late April.) He also said that if he killed anyone, he wouldn't dump the body all the way up in Jo Daviess County; he'd dump it in the Kishwaukee River because he knew the site from target shooting.

When Ciesynski pressed him about the location of the

body, McCullough snapped, "I don't know where she was found. If you told me, I wouldn't know."

Then Ciesynski put forward a theory. What if, he suggested, McCullough had given Maria a piggyback ride and then wandered off and somebody else had come along and kidnapped her. Wasn't that possible? Was he covering up for somebody?

McCullough didn't bite. "That didn't occur."

Forty minutes later, with their check paid, they got back on the road to Sycamore. Steiger hadn't eaten a morsel; he'd been too busy writing everything down. Just about every inch of the placemat was covered with his notes. He folded it and put it in his jacket's side pocket, wondering whether for the first time in legal history a Steak 'n Shake placemat would be entered into evidence in a murder trial. He was sure it would be useful once he turned it over to the state's attorney. On the way back to the police van, he and Ciesynski exchanged knowing looks. Ciesynski had known exactly what his partner had been up to. They'd worked together for so long, their communication was almost telepathic. In this case, they were both thinking the same thing: *Keep McCullough talking because he might say something incriminating*.

The closer McCullough got to Sycamore, the giddier he got with excitement. When their police van entered the city limits, it stirred up a lot of memories, and even under these circumstances, for McCullough, it was good to be back in "Mayberry." They drove past a vacant lot that had once been a used-car dealership where he'd bought his first car, the Plymouth Coupe, with money he'd made from his paper route. That same Plymouth Coupe, the police suspected, that he was driving when he kidnapped Maria.

"I loved that car," he said, adding that he wouldn't allow anyone else to drive it.

On Somonauk Street, they drove past a lovely Victorian mansion. That's where his ex-girlfriend Jan Edwards once lived.

"It's a landmark in Sycamore. It has something like ten fireplaces." He was still bragging that one of the richest girls in town—and so pretty, too—had dated him.

They passed the Jane Fargo Hotel, on State Street. Originally a mansion built in 1882, it was still there. So was his old hangout, the Uptown Bar, and fried catfish fillet remained the specialty on the menu.

When Ciesynski asked McCullough whether he'd like to see his old house again, he jumped at the chance. The detectives had worked all this out beforehand, wanting to see if McCullough would have anything incriminating to say when he was back at the scene of the crime.

McCullough gave directions to the state trooper at the wheel and truly seemed thrilled to be seeing the old neighborhood again. In no time, he found himself at the intersection of Archie Place and Center Cross Street, where Maria Ridulph had been kidnapped more than five decades ago. Ciesynski and Steiger looked at him. If they were expecting to see a double-take from McCullough, they didn't. He just took it all in. But he really perked up when he saw his old house on Center Cross Street. The van pulled up and came to a halt. The landscaping was in better shape than when the Tessiers had lived there, less of a jungle of vegetation. Everything looked spruced up a bit, more middle class. He pointed to a ground-floor window on the south side of the house.

"That's the window I crawled in that night. Right there." He said he climbed on top of a garbage can and then raised the window and climbed in.

Steiger asked him a reasonable question: why didn't he just knock on the front door? "Weren't you afraid of somebody seeing you crawling through the window?"

"Oh, no, there was nobody around. This is like Mayberry, or *Happy Days*. Small town."

(Steiger told me, "He had already read the affidavit. He was trying to figure out how to get around his sisters' testimony that he wasn't home on December 3. He was saying he was home, they just didn't see him.")

Steiger asked McCullough whether he remembered where Maria lived.

"Oh, sure. Turn around and I'll show you."

The driver made a U-turn and then took a right onto Archie Place. A few houses down, McCullough pointed to a little cottage on the left.

"She lived right there."

Steiger looked at the house. He turned to McCullough. "It was very cold and snowing on December 3, 1957. You went hitchhiking after dark in the snow and the cold?" It was hard to believe.

McCullough nodded. "I'm acclimated to the weather, and I was dressed for it."

It was time to take McCullough to the county lockup. The whole town was waiting for his arrival.

As the state police van headed in the direction of the jail, the prisoner settled back in his seat.

"Thanks for bringing me here, guys. It hasn't changed much." He was caught up in the nostalgia of the moment.

It was a short drive to the DeKalb County Jail, on North Main Street, and, once more, McCullough had to give them directions. There was quite a scene out front as they pulled into the facility, maybe a dozen TV camera crews, still photographers, and reporters from Sycamore, Chicago, and the Associated Press. Inside the van, McCullough beamed.

"Is that for me?"

"Yeah, Jack, that's all for you," said Steiger. *Enjoy your fifteen minutes*, the detective thought ruefully. He watched in amusement as McCullough waved at the cameras, or as much as he could; the belt cuffs restricted physical movement. Steiger had to laugh. The police van had tinted windows, meaning McCullough could see out, but nobody could see in.

Once they were inside and the paperwork was signed, McCullough was officially no longer their problem. Custody had been transferred to the DeKalb County sheriff.

Steiger and Ciesynski were not done yet, however. They headed over to the county office building to meet Clay Campbell in person.

It had been an eventful day for the state's attorney. First the exhumation of Maria Ridulph's remains, now the return of Jack McCullough to Sycamore to face murder charges.

Clay Campbell was lean and diminutive, with fine-boned facial features, a square chin, and thinning hair. Folks in DeKalb County considered him a maverick, and he rubbed the power brokers the wrong way with an in-your-face personality that on occasion could be grating. Sometimes, he did not play well with others in the legal establishment. Campbell was a Republican who had unsuccessfully run twice for state's attorney. Third time was the charm. After the incumbent state's attorney was appointed to a judgeship, Campbell finally won the office with 53 percent of the vote in a tightly contested special election. He was sworn in on December 1, 2010, and only then was the Maria Ridulph investigation dropped in his lap. It was the first he'd heard that an arrest was imminent for the most famous crime in Sycamore's history.

Until he screened the videotape of McCullough's interrogation in Seattle, Campbell had had concerns about moving the charges forward. Several veteran prosecutors on his staff were reportedly making a compelling argument that it was an impossible case to bring to trial.

"There's no way you can possibly prosecute a fifty-five-year-old murder," one senior prosecutor on his staff told him.

As they watched the video of McCullough's interview, Campbell kept wondering, *Do we have enough to charge him?*

Assistant state's attorney Julie Trevarthen was really

pushing for a prosecution. Campbell had assigned her to the case with another young assistant state's attorney, Victor Escarcida, and Trevarthen was chomping at the bit. At age thirty-eight, she had intense green eyes and an effortless midwestern appeal. What struck Trevarthen was McCullough's demeanor whenever Maria's name came up. *How creepy*, she thought, that he had spoken about her as an exquisite Barbie doll with big brown eyes.

"This isn't just a guy where things broke bad one night while he was hammered and otherwise he's a decent guy," she said. "He is inherently evil." She told her boss, "You need to do the right thing for Maria, and whatever comes of it, comes of it."

With Campbell up for reelection, everyone in the office understood they'd be facing accusations of grandstanding in a small county with a highly charged local political scene. The fallout could be serious, or superbly effective, depending on the outcome. A lot was riding on this for Campbell: glory, should there be a conviction in the coldest case in U.S. history ever to be brought to trial; or a blemish on his record, in the event of an acquittal. There was already buzz about the diversion of resources and money to a cold case when the state's attorney should be focusing on drug arrests, burglaries, and street crime. Wasn't that what he was there for? At least that was the position of some taxpayers in DeKalb County.

Maria's murder really got to Campbell, the father of two young daughters. Chuck Ridulph had given him access to Maria's homework assignments and family album, and

Campbell genuinely felt for the family. He wanted to bring them closure. There was something else that motivated him: he was certain that Jack McCullough had killed Maria.

The challenges were daunting. Kathy Sigman Chapman's identification of Johnny from the photo lineup more than a half century after her brief encounter with him the night of December 3, 1957, was certain to be challenged by the defense. Could she really recall with certainty, so many decades later, what Johnny had looked like? The train ticket was an amazing piece of evidence, but was it really the smoking gun? What did an unpunched train ticket really prove? Eileen Tessier had made her deathbed confession while morphine was coursing through her veins. Was it even admissible in court? And no confession or DNA. Campbell doubted the exhumation would find any physical evidence that tied McCullough to the murder. DNA degrades in a matter of days. More than fifty years later? Not likely at all. The case against McCullough would have to be built entirely on circumstantial evidence.

"Proving guilt beyond a reasonable doubt in court, that'll be very hard," said Patrick Solar, the former Sycamore police lieutenant who had devoted so many years of his career to cracking the mystery. He had been left with egg on his face because he'd pushed the discredited theory that a truck driver from Nebraska had killed Maria. "I don't envy them having to do it." Solar knew whereof he spoke. When he first looked into the case, in the 1980s, he wanted to pull all existing physical evidence out of storage. There was nothing. Maria's rubber doll? Gone. The clothes she wore the night she was taken? Also gone. Also gone were the fibers removed from Maria's body. Nothing was left. The evidence box could not be found, and they looked everywhere: at state police archives, the FBI, and the local Sycamore police department.

Just thinking about it was daunting.

But Campbell had an ace up his sleeve that only a few of his most trusted advisors knew about.

If they couldn't nail McCullough for murder, well, maybe they could convict him of something else having nothing to do with Maria Ridulph.

34

....

THE DEFENSE

Janey O'Connor was asking some tough questions. Her stepfather's life was on the line, and she wanted to know whether Regina Harris, the DeKalb County public defender, had the resources to mount a full-scale defense. Janey's mother, Sue, had already reached out to a private lawyer in Sycamore who was interested in taking on Jack McCullough's defense pro bono, but he required a $500 monthly retainer just to cover expenses. Janey asked Sue how she'd gotten the lawyer's name. By looking online, Sue told her. Janey just rolled her eyes. Sue meant well, her heart was in the right place, and she loved Jack, but since his arrest she'd been helpless, drowning in raw emotion. Janey tried to bring her mother down to earth. "No matter what happens, you'll never be able to pay off the legal bill."

Now Janey was on the phone with Regina Harris, trying to figure things out. Was Harris part of the old-boy's network in town? She wondered how an impartial jury could ever be found.

"In a town where there was such a heartache for fifty-four years, how would it be possible to find twelve people who are unbiased?" Janey asked. "Are you going to have the time to devote to it? From what I've read, it takes hundreds of thousands of dollars to do something like this. It doesn't seem like your budget is at all adequate for what he's up against."

Harris was aware of the case. By now, everyone in Sycamore knew about Jack McCullough. She had already taken a call from the public defender in Seattle who had represented McCullough at his bond hearing, and he had put Harris on notice that once McCullough got to Sycamore, he was going to need a public defender.

Harris tried to reassure Janey. "It's easy for people to think this is a small county with lawyers who never saw a murder case, but that's not the situation. I have an investigator on staff, attorneys on staff, and I have a good group of people working for me. I don't have any doubt of our ability to do it."

Janey said she wasn't questioning Harris's skill, but she admitted, "I just really wish we could afford to get him a lawyer. He's the only man who's earned the title of father in my life, and he's fighting for his life and I can't be there." Her mother couldn't help; she was facing hard times. Jack's Social Security benefits had been terminated upon his arrest, and Sue was trying to make ends meet by taking over his job as a night watchman at the Four Freedoms apartment complex in Seattle.

Janey wanted to get a few more things off her chest. All this nonsense about John Tessier having changed his name to Jack McCullough was drawing a lot of attention in the press, the implication being that no innocent man would change his name if not to disappear for nefarious reasons. Janey gave Harris the backstory.

"I knew him when he was John Tessier. I was in the house when my grandfather said if you want to work for him, he's going to have to change his name to Jack. It's so *frustrating*." She said Jack was heartbroken when his mother, Eileen, died, in 1994, and he took her maiden name of McCullough as a tribute to his Irish heritage.

Harris could hear how exasperated Janey was. By the end of the conversation, she'd assured McCullough's stepdaughter that this case would be a priority that would receive her full attention. From Janey's point of view, Regina Harris came across as a fighter who cared about due process. She also seemed patient in dealing with a family in crisis.

Regina Harris had grown up in St. Louis and had been studying for her master's in English lit at Illinois State University when she took a course in international law. It got her thinking about taking a different career path. She graduated Northern Illinois University law school, realized pretty quickly that working in a large private law firm would not be a good fit, and for the next eighteen years toiled in the public defender's office in Kane County, Illinois. In 2007, she'd been appointed chief public defender in DeKalb County. As to her credentials, Janey O'Connor need not have worried: Harris had twenty-five murder cases under her belt. There was no question about her credibility as a seasoned homicide litigator.

Harris walked over to the county jail with her chief investigator, Crystal Harrolle, to meet with McCullough for the first time.

Harris and Harrolle liked each other a lot and made a dynamic team, worthy adversaries of the prosecutor's office and with all the considerable resources available to the State. Harrolle was a statuesque blonde with big hair and a pretty dimple in her chin. She spoke in a fast clip, almost like a New Yorker, but she was all Midwest in upbringing. She held a master's degree in law enforcement and had worked in the public defender's office since 2003, following a career as a drug and alcohol counselor. She was the lone investigator for eight lawyers in the DeKalb County public defender's office, and they all fought for her attention and investigative skills. But the McCullough case was now her priority, too.

The two women who would be working together to free Jack McCullough sat down with the defendant on August 2, 2011, in the interview room at the county jail set aside for private conversations between inmates and lawyers.

What surprised Harris most was the frailty of the elderly defendant as he sat there looking forlorn and woebegone in his prison jumpsuit. He seemed bewildered by the set of circumstances he found himself in. He was a man who had "had his entire life come crashing down around him," Harris said later.

As Crystal Harrolle listened to McCullough's tale for the next two hours, she could only wonder how she would even begin to investigate a half-century-old kidnapping-murder.

McCullough made his first court appearance from the county jail via closed-circuit TV. Judge Robbin Stuckert set his bond at $3 million. She also laid out the grand jury's indictment and said the penalty, should he be found guilty, would be based on the statute that existed in 1957, the year the crime was committed. Except for one important difference: in 1957, the death penalty was the law of the state. That was no longer the situation. If convicted, McCullough would now face a maximum of life in prison and a minimum of fourteen years.

When the box containing the FBI and state police files was eventually delivered to their offices as part of the discovery process, Harris and Harrolle were overwhelmed by the sheer volume of material they had to go through. There were seventeen binders in all, and some of the printouts were so old and blurry or poorly scanned at the source that they were impossible to read, and everything was out of whack in terms of chronology or logical order. When Harrolle found a document she could read top to bottom without straining her eyes, she exclaimed in relief, "Oh, finally!"

A few things struck the defense team right away. The timeline was the big one. All over the FBI files, the timeline seemed to favor the defendant. Frances Ridulph told the FBI that she saw her daughter Maria and Kathy Sigman playing on the street at about 6:15 P.M. the night of the kidnapping when she pulled into her driveway after dropping off her daughter Kay for a music lesson. Then, at about

6:40 P.M., Maria had come into Mrs. Ridulph's bedroom asking permission to take her doll outside to play.

Two neighbors from Archie Place, Kenneth Davy and Mrs. Stanley Wells, were quoted by the FBI as seeing Maria and Kathy playing on the street between 6:30 and 7:00 P.M. This could be enormously important. How could Jack McCullough make it to Rockford—a half-hour to forty-minute drive from Sycamore in the snow—in time to place the collect call home at 6:57 P.M.? It just didn't make sense, at least according to the defense team. On the other hand, there was also that pivotal state police report from July 27, 1958, that concluded the kidnapping had taken place closer to 6:15 P.M.—"a much earlier time than was indicated" by the FBI.

Then there was Kathy Sigman Chapman. She had come face-to-face with Johnny for a few fleeting moments in 1957. How could she be expected to positively identify a suspect more than fifty years later? It made for an interesting argument. Kathy was saying she could never forget the face of the man who kidnapped her best friend and the indelible impression it had made on her. But Harris and Harrolle were noticing something peculiar about the photo array that had been displayed to Kathy by special agent Brion Hanley. The photos of five of the six young men laid out before Kathy Chapman were taken from the 1957 Sycamore High School yearbook. They were all shot in front of white backdrops, the kind you typically see in high school yearbook photos. Because McCullough had dropped out before graduation, his photo from 1957 had been taken on the evening he took his girlfriend Jan Edwards to a nightclub in Rockford. This photo of McCullough had a somewhat darker background. Had this been a subtle way of coaching Kathy that she should pick photo number 4—the photo of McCullough?

Then there was the interesting matter of a police lineup in Wisconsin, on December 22, 1957, when little Kathy Sigman, according to the FBI files, identified a thirty-six-year-old farmhand as Johnny.

"That's him," she exclaimed.

The suspect had a ruddy complexion, blue eyes, and dirty blond hair. He had a small gap in his front teeth and stood just five feet four. He was in custody for passing a bad check. There was lots of excitement after Kathy's identification, but it all fizzled after the farmhand's boss and the other farmhands swore he was with them the night of December 3. The alibi was airtight. If Kathy was wrong about this guy, could she not also be wrong about McCullough?

Something else struck Regina Harris as she read through the material: the sheer number of "freaks and perverts" living in Sycamore and the surrounding towns in the 1950s who had come under suspicion in those early days of the investigation. It was also a time of endemic homophobia. All known homosexuals in the county were viewed as potential suspects.

"The perception was gay men went after children," Harris said. "It was just astounding to see the mind-set that existed at the time."

One disreputable character in particular drew her attention. Johnny Clay "Bud" Hillburn was a twenty-eight-year-old truck driver and factory worker who was arrested for molesting his five-year-old daughter in Rockford. Interrogated in jail, Hillburn at first admitted he was driving from Rockford to the city of Rochelle, in Ogle County, on December 3, 1957, when he somehow got lost in Sycamore, maybe twenty-eight miles out of his way, and asked two little girls for directions. He also said he'd "swear on a stack of Bibles I never touched that girl," meaning Maria Ridulph. Later, he denied ever having been in Sycamore on that night. Just the same, the FBI wanted to administer a lie-detector test, but Hillburn lawyered up, and that was the end of that. Interest in Hillburn as a suspect waned after his photo was shown to Kathy Sigman and it simply didn't register with her. Hillburn was sent to serve a two- to seven-year prison term at the Stateville maximum-security penitentiary on the molestation charge and then fell off the radar screen.

Regina Harris was sitting at her desk trolling for anything remotely helpful to the defense when she came across the information on Hillburn, and it almost made her jump out of her chair. *Are you kidding me?* she thought. *How did this guy not get arrested?* She was so excited that she almost wanted to dance around her desk.

Harris became convinced that McCullough had been unjustly accused. "He is genuinely innocent of Maria's murder," she would say. "There is not one doubt in my mind. If you read those reports, you have no doubt."

Harris showed Crystal Harrolle the material, and the

investigator spent a lot of time in Rockford trying to track down Hillburn, but to no avail. It would later be established that Hillburn died in 1978.

There were more frustrations because all the witnesses who could buttress McCullough's alibi were dead or couldn't be located. After making a collect call home at 6:57 P.M. the night of Maria's kidnapping, McCullough stopped by a diner near the post office in Rockford and ordered pie. He wolfed it down and paid the check but hurried back because he'd left his shaving kit behind. Harrolle tried to track down the waitress who served McCullough, thinking she might make a good witness for the defense if she could recall the occasion. Unfortunately, it proved impossible to discover her identify or whether she was even alive. Such was the case with all the U.S. Air Force personnel referenced in the FBI files who had encountered McCullough at the third-floor recruitment office in Rockford the night of December 3. Staff Sergeant Jon Oswald had told the FBI that John Tessier had pulled out a "little black book" containing the names and addresses of several young women in Sycamore, along with their bust and hip measurements. Regrettably, Oswald was now dead. Also dead: Technical Sergeant John Froom, who told the FBI that he thought young John Tessier looked "bewildered" and "acted like a 'lost sheep.'" The only witness found to be alive was Theodore Liebovich, the lieutenant colonel who said Tessier made such an awful impression that he thought he was a "narcotic." Unfortunately, Liebovich was living in a nursing home and in no shape to sit for an interview.

· · · · · · · · ·

Kay Ridulph Hickey was the pretty fifteen-year-old middle daughter with a lovely voice when her sister Maria was kidnapped. Now she was a sixty-nine-year-old widow, absolutely bewildered by the arrest of her neighbor from long ago, John Tessier. Kay had been riveted by the coverage of the murder of JonBenét Ramsey, the six-year-old child beauty queen found strangled in the basement of her parents' home in Boulder, Colorado, on Christmas Day 1996. In July 2011, she got hooked on the trial of Casey Anthony. Now, as she lay in her bed, terminally ill, having spent the last seven years battling breast and liver cancer, she found her own family in the center of an equally fascinating criminal case. Even as she faced mortality, Kay followed the steps of McCullough's progress through the criminal-justice system.

"She would have been fascinated by the process," her son Larry told me. "Bless her heart."

Kay died in September 2011, sharp as a tack until the end. After her death, her three sons, Larry, Lee, and Lynn, had to clear out their mother's house and sort all her belongings. That's when they came upon the diaries she'd kept as a teenager. They'd been stored all these years in a box in the attic. Two of them were written during those terrible days in 1957 and 1958, in Kay's hand, with a fountain pen, and with extra pages clipped to the back because Kay had so much to say. Her three sons, now grown men, were awed by what they read. It was a time capsule into a family calamity. Here were the expressions of their beloved mother as they never knew her, a fifteen-year-old girl of great religious faith. Kay's boys talked it over and made the difficult decision to turn the diaries over to Clay Campbell's office, just in case they might help the prosecution of Jack McCullough.

"We knew that Mom would not be pleased if she knew that people were reading those diaries," Larry said, "but we felt it was important for her to have a voice in this."

All of Kay's old friends came to the visitation, and the funeral home was filled with beautiful floral wreaths. People were ushered to the receiving line to offer their condolences to Kay's sons and her sister Pat and brother, Chuck. It was three months to the day since Jack McCullough's arrest. Pat was first in line when a middle-aged woman she didn't recognize appeared. She knew everybody at the services but not this woman, so she asked her who she was.

"I'm Maria."

Pat failed to process what she was hearing. Then the woman explained, "I'm Maria—Chuck's daughter."

Pat turned to her brother. "Do you know who this is?"

He shook his head no. Chuck was introduced to his daughter Maria Annette, the daughter he had named after his slain sister. Standing before him was a forty-five-year-old woman he hadn't seen since she was five.

35

....

"YOU HAVE TO DO THIS"

Something was up. Jeanne Tessier received a call from Clay Campbell saying he wanted to meet with her in person to discuss "this case." Jeanne said fine, no problem. Naturally, she assumed it concerned Maria Ridulph. She took the conversation at face value.

Jeanne had been cooperating with the probe into her brother's life since her sister Janet Tessier had first gone to the state police. In 2009, special agent Brion Hanley had flown to Louisville, Kentucky, to meet face-to-face with Jeanne in a hotel conference room, and she had told him everything she could remember about McCullough's history as a sexual predator, and how, in 1962, when she was fourteen, she said McCullough had pulled up in a red convertible and driven her to 751 Carlson Street in Sycamore, where she was gang-raped.

Now the authorities were calling on her once again.

Jeanne lived in a rustic cabin in Kentucky with Spirit, her border collie. Her brother Robert lived next door with his wife, Kathy, his sweetheart from Sycamore High who he had married when he was twenty, and he was a comforting presence and reliable helper when Jeanne's kitchen needed repairs. She was a snow-haired woman of sixty-five, coauthor of the college textbook *Interviewing Art and Skill*, retired now after a distinguished career as a tenured professor in the department of communication at the jointly managed campus of Indiana University and Purdue University in Fort Wayne. Jeanne had a bachelor's degree from prestigious Northwestern University and a master's in communication studies from Northern Illinois University. In 2003, she'd switched careers and earned another master's from St. Mary-of-the-Woods College, the nation's oldest Roman Catholic college for women, in Terre Haute. For seven years, she'd served as a chaplain in the intensive-care units at Kosair Children's Hospital, in Louisville.

Jeanne had raised three children. Shelly was her husband's daughter from his first marriage. She was forty. Steven was adopted when he was six weeks old. He was now a cop in Louisville. Her biological son, Ben, was twenty-eight. Jeanne was thirty-six when she gave birth to Ben, and her hair had turned gray during the pregnancy. It was a medical puzzle. When he was growing up, Jeanne used to point to her head of prematurely silver hair and kiddingly say to Ben, "You did this to me."

On September 8, 2011, Clay Campbell flew to Kentucky with Hanley, Sycamore police detective Tiffany Ziegler, and prosecutor Julie Trevarthen. Campbell and Trevarthen asked to meet with Jeanne alone and sent the others over to Bob Tessier's cabin next door. Jeanne showed Campbell to her couch and he filled her in on where things stood in the investigation. All the while Jeanne was thinking, *Why are you here?* She had no idea that she was about to get hit right between the eyes. According to her recollection of the conversation, Campbell conceded that the murder case against McCullough was weak. There was no DNA. No confession. No physical evidence of any kind. It was entirely built on circumstantial evidence. Finally, Campbell came out with it.

"We're going to charge Jack McCullough with raping you when you were fourteen."

"*What?*"

Campbell continued. "We think there's a good chance we can get a conviction. We want to charge him with that first before we go ahead with the murder trial." Jeanne knew exactly what Campbell was getting at: if they couldn't nail McCullough for murder, at least they could get him for raping his sister. She didn't think such a criminal charge could even be possible. How could a man be put on trial for raping a woman fifty years after the event when there was no physical evidence or prior police report? Even the date of the rape was murky in Jeanne's mind. It was 1962, she was certain of that, and in the spring but maybe the summer. But what month? She couldn't remember.

Jeanne sat there dumbfounded. Campbell explained that the statute of limitations had not expired because the law permitted the tolling, or suspension, of the statute if the defendant lived out of state. In McCullough's situation, he had not been a resident of Illinois from the time of his enlistment in the army in 1962 until his arrest in 2011.

Was this really happening? All Jeanne kept repeating was, "What? What?"

Campbell tried to reassure her. "Jeanne, I won't do this unless you give it your blessing."

With those assurances, Jeanne breathed a little easier.

"Brion would like to talk with you now," Campbell said. He left to find Hanley and Detective Ziegler at Bob Tessier's cabin and sent them over to Jeanne's place. When they were all seated, and Spirit had curled into his usual place under the kitchen table, Hanley pulled out a series of black-and-white photographs. He wanted to know whether Jeanne could identify any of the men who had participated in the 1962 gang rape. A defiant Jeanne folded her hands across her arms and just stared at the array of photos. She had *No way in hell* written all over her face.

"You have to do this," Hanley scolded.

Jeanne shook her head. She wanted to tell him that she regretted ever confiding in him. The thought of sitting on the witness stand and sharing the most terrible day of her life was inconceivable to her.

Hanley's voice rose in exasperation. "Jeanne, you have to do this because it's the right thing to do." All at once, Hanley felt something. It was Spirit, laying his head down on Hanley's lap.

"Oh, what's this?"

"I think my dog thinks you're yelling at me, Brion."

Hanley got the message. "OK, OK." He simmered down.

Two days later, Jeanne phoned Campbell, who was back in Sycamore. She told him she had thought it through, and there was no way she would consent to the rape charges being filed.

"I'm very disappointed to hear that, Jeanne."

"I'm sorry, but the answer is still no."

Seventeen days later, Jeanne's phone rang in her cabin. It was Clay Campbell.

"Well, I know I told you we wouldn't do it without your blessing, but we're going to do it anyway."

There was dead silence on the other end. Then Jeanne burst into tears. She felt used and betrayed.

Campbell told her, "I have an obligation to do this. It's my job as state's attorney to protect the people." He said it was impossible for him to turn away, knowing what McCullough had done to her.

"Clay, I don't even know what that means." Finally, she ended the conversation with these words: "Well, you do what you need to do, and I'll do what I need to do." She didn't tell Campbell, but she was seriously thinking of fleeing the country, anything to avoid taking the witness stand. She consulted with a retired judge she knew and weighed her legal options, but he told her that she had to cooperate unless she was willing to wage a long and costly legal campaign. When Campbell told her the grand jury would be taking her testimony, Jeanne insisted on being subpoenaed because she didn't want to be seen as a cooperating witness. "I've never been so alone in my life," she reflected. "And I was from the day Clay Campbell showed up here. What they wanted was just a nail for Jack McCullough's coffin. It wasn't about me at all. It wasn't about justice for me. It was using me for whatever it was they wanted."

On September 30, 2011, an indictment was handed down accusing McCullough of one count of child sexual assault and four counts of indecent liberties with a child. As is customary in sex crimes, the victim's name was not disclosed except to identify her as being fourteen years old when it had happened. The date of the assault was not revealed either. For now, Jeanne Tessier's name was being kept out of it.

Regina Harris was really burned up. She'd been working long hours preparing for the murder trial of Jack McCullough, and now she had to deal with an entirely new set of allegations having nothing to do with the Maria Ridulph case. From her point of view, it was a "bush-league thing" on the part of the state's attorney's office. When she went to the county jail and informed her client that he had been indicted for the rape of his sister Jeanne Tessier, he was, in Harris's words, "a complete wreck, completely devastated."

McCullough was brimming with confidence that he could beat the rap on the murder charges. About the rape, he wasn't so sure. "I'm scared to death of Jeanne. I'm telling you, she's a friggin' genius." The defense team saw a deterioration in his cognitive skills. Harris asked Crystal Harrolle, "Do we think he's going to be OK mentally?" She was worried that he might not live long enough to see the trial date.

Harris had the right to request an interview with Jeanne Tessier, which she did through Julie Trevarthen.

"Tell her I'm a nice person," Harris told the prosecutor. "I just want to ask her some questions and get a feel for her."

When Trevarthen got back to Harris, she said, "Jeanne doesn't want to talk to you."

It was up to the prosecution to determine which case to try first, rape or murder. Campbell went with the rape case. Evidently, he believed it was the more muscular of the two. He announced that he would personally prosecute, with Julie Trevarthen and Victor Escarcida.

"It's all hands on deck," he said.

36

·········

THE RAPE TRIAL

Michelle Weinman was now forty-five years old and had never flown on a plane. It was the thought of checking in at the Seattle airport that was stressing her the most. Michelle asked her live-in biker boyfriend, Jeff, a huge favor. "You know, I can't really do this without you."

Jeff agreed to go with her to Sycamore.

Easter Sunday 2012 fell on April 8, the date when Michelle and Jeff landed in Chicago. They made their way to Sycamore in a rental car and checked into the Jane Fargo Hotel, the hotel of choice, where the rooms were spacious and the history of Sycamore was chronicled in vintage black-and-white photographs in the lobby. Because it was Easter, downtown was deserted, and every restaurant was closed, with the exception of a bar across the street from the hotel. Michelle asked the bartender, "Is your kitchen open?"

"Sorry, no." The bartender looked at the two strangers. "Are you hungry?"

"Yeah," Michelle said.

"Let me see what I can do."

She disappeared into the kitchen and came back with two plates of chicken strips and French fries that she put in front of them. As Michelle ate, the thought came to her that Jack McCullough was right about one thing: Sycamore really was Mayberry. She slipped a shot glass in her purse as a memento, a reminder of how nicely she'd been treated there.

The next day, Monday, April 9, Michelle had an important duty to perform. She bought a bouquet of flowers; then she drove around Sycamore looking for Maria Ridulph's grave. She stopped at one cemetery and asked the custodian where Maria Ridulph was buried.

"You're at the wrong place. We get a lot of people trying to find it."

He gave her directions to Elmwood.

Elmwood Cemetery was very small, only about an acre. Local lore had it that ghostly disturbances took place there when it got dark. Michelle drove through Elmwood's magnificent cast-iron gate, which had been constructed in 1865 and was listed on the National Register of Historic Places as a structure deemed worthy of preservation. The groundskeeper pointed her in the direction of Maria Ridulph's grave. He told her she couldn't miss it; it was between two giant oak trees. There was another reason why it was easy to find: Maria's was the only grave at Elmwood that was not covered with a carpet of well-groomed sod. Because

Maria's body had been exhumed eight months earlier, in place of grass, the grave was now covered with freshly dug raw earth. Michelle looked down at a simple granite marker set flush to the ground with the inscription, *Maria E. Ridulph, Mar. 12, 1950–Dec. 3, 1957. The Lord Is My Shepherd*. The carving of a little lamb nestled into the corner completed the memorial to a child gone too soon. As she paid her respects at the gravesite, Michelle could not have known that Maria's body was in fact not even there; it remained in a freezer at the DeKalb County coroner's office, awaiting the final autopsy results.

She placed the bouquet of flowers on the grave, thinking how fitting it was that the little girl lay there between her parents, Frances and Mike Ridulph.

"We're connected and we didn't even know it," Michelle said softly, her head bowed as she ended her prayer: "Until we meet again."

Then she walked away. She was ready to take the stand.

Another woman was also making the journey to Sycamore in anticipation of testifying at Jack McCullough's trial. This was Jeanne Tessier. Jeanne, her brother Bob, and his wife, Kathy, piled into a rental car, the expenses defrayed by the DeKalb County state's attorney, and drove eight hours from their cabins in Kentucky to Sycamore. Jeanne wanted to go by car because she insisted on taking her dog, Spirit, with her, and they stayed in a hotel in Warrenville, about thirty miles outside Chicago, because it was the closest one to Sycamore that had a kitchenette and permitted large dogs.

"I wouldn't go without my dog, who was at that point in time the only one who wasn't telling me I had to buck up and do the right thing," Jeanne commented. She was very shaken up about testifying. All her siblings were exhorting her to play ball with Clay Campbell, Bob in particular. He wanted her to "go get" their big brother for what he'd done to her. Jeanne just wanted the case to go away. She dreaded taking the stand.

The Monday after Easter Sunday, as Michelle Weinman was driving around Sycamore searching for Maria Ridulph's grave, Jeanne called prosecutor Julie Trevarthen and asked a favor. She said she'd like to see the courtroom where the trial would take place the next day.

"I want to sit in the witness stand. I want to visually see where John would be sitting. Where I would be." Visualizing the physical surroundings was a technique she had taught her college students in speech class.

Jeanne and Bob met Julie and Clay Campbell at the county courthouse, where they were taken to the empty courtroom on the second floor that in less than twenty-four hours would be the setting for McCullough's rape trial. Campbell showed them around. He showed Jeanne where the prosecution team would be sitting, and the defendant, her brother. Jeanne breathed deeply and took it all in. A court advocate who worked with rape victims and survivors of abuse was also present to lend a hand.

Jeanne climbed into the witness stand and gazed out at

the courtroom. She asked Campbell to sit where Jack Mc-
Cullough would be sitting. Visually, it helped. Everyone
left soon afterward, advising Jeanne to try not to be nervous and to get a good night's sleep. She had a big day
ahead tomorrow. Just Jeanne and Bob remained in the
courtroom.

"I need you to sit where you can be the person I'm
looking at," Jeanne told him. "And I need you to not have
such a murderous rage toward John. I need you to sit
where I can see you and where you look only at me. Not
at John. I need to look at you, and I need you to somehow
keep letting me know that you're on my side."

"I will," Bob promised.

The next day, Bob Tessier had to take a deep gulp. At the
other end of the hallway in the county courthouse in Sycamore, he saw Chuck Ridulph. It was April 10, 2012, the
opening day in the trial of Jack McCullough for the 1962
rape of Jeanne Tessier.

Bob knew this was inevitable. He'd been worried about
running into the Ridulphs during the entire drive from
Kentucky. It was eating him up. He didn't know what to
expect, but he wouldn't have been surprised if he, as a
Tessier, was about to be shunned. He was, after all, the kid
brother of the man accused of murdering Maria.

Bob sucked it up and went over and introduced himself
to Chuck.

"I'm Bob Tessier. I just want you to know from the
Tessier family, I'm just so sorry."

Chuck gave Bob a warm embrace and said, "We're glad you're here. We're praying for you."

The greeting wasn't what Bob had expected, and it came as an enormous relief.

Court was declared in session.

Representing the People were Clay Campbell and his two young assistant prosecutors, Julie Trevarthen and Victor Escarcida.

For the defense: Regina Harris and an assistant public defender, Robert Carlson.

The presiding judge was Robbin Stuckert.

There was no jury. Harris had persuaded McCullough to opt for a bench trial, meaning Judge Stuckert would be the sole finder of fact, and she alone would determine the defendant's guilt or innocence. It was a thorny way to go, but Harris had met with McCullough and told him flat out, "Maria Ridulph is the elephant in the room." There was no getting around the pretrial publicity the murder arrest had generated. Who in Sycamore did not already view Jack McCullough with contempt and disgust?

"If it were me and I was in your shoes, this is what I would do," Harris had told McCullough.

McCullough had lots of questions about bench trials and what it all meant. Mostly, though, he just listened as Harris told him she didn't have much faith in finding twelve impartial jurors from DeKalb County who could focus on just the facts and the law, the way a judge presumably would. She had also defended many clients before Judge Stuckert, winning some, losing some, and had high regard for her judicial temperament. She considered Stuckert to be a straight shooter. In a case involving allegations of incest and the rape of a sister, a bench trial would, in theory at least, eliminate the shock factor and a jury bent on vengeance. McCullough considered everything. He had appeared before Stuckert several times for pretrial motions via video from the jail, and she had never singled him out for disdain; she'd always been courteous. He had "positive feelings" about her impartiality. He appreciated her evenhandedness.

"I trust you and your instincts," he had told Harris. "I trust this judge."

Harris had to feel good as she strode into court. The last-minute maneuver, waiving her client's right to a jury, had thrown the prosecutors for a loop.

As Jack McCullough was escorted into the courtroom to take his seat at the defendant's table, he gave a nod of encouragement to Regina Harris and Robert Carlson. Then he took a quick look around the courtroom; he could not have been pleased with what he saw. Sitting in the row directly behind him was his kid brother, Bob, who had once so idolized him but who now saw him as a monster who had disgraced the family name. The two brothers glared at each other with icy hostility. Also in the spectator's gallery were Maria Ridulph's siblings Chuck and Pat. They knew this was to be the opening act in the forthcoming trial of McCullough for the murder of their sister. They could not have stayed away. And there among the spectators, to McCullough's complete surprise, was none other than his nemesis from Seattle, Detective Mike Ciesynski. Raised in

Chicago, Ciesynski was there with his wife for a week's vacation to visit family. He had driven up to Sycamore to take in the trial, having gotten to befriend many of the key players in the Maria Ridulph case. When Regina Harris saw him, she had to laugh.

"This is what you do on your time off?" she said in an aside to the detective.

There was a grudging respect between the two professionals, even if they were on opposing sides.

Ciesynski shrugged. "The timing was right."

McCullough settled into the chair next to Harris. He wore a dark suit, a black dress shirt, and a maroon tie, an outfit that he had selected from a rack of clothes from the Goodwill Thrift Shop made available to needy defendants who wanted to look presentable at trial. It may have been an unfortunate choice of wardrobe because it gave McCullough a vaguely sinister look, like a retired gangster out for one last bank heist. All he needed was the black hat to complete the picture of a geriatric hoodlum from central casting.

Judge Stuckert entered the courtroom. She was a scholarly and attractive woman of fifty-nine, who, after a long career in private practice, had been appointed the first female judge in DeKalb County history, in 2001. She had three children. One daughter was a nurse, and her son had served in Iraq at the height of the war, in 2003.

Julie Trevarthen rose.

"Morning, Judge. Julie Trevarthen, Clay Campbell, and Victor Escarcida on behalf of the People."

"Good morning," Stuckert said.

Regina Harris stood. "Regina Harris and Rob Carlson on behalf of the defendant, who is present in court."

"This matter comes before the court today for a bench trial. Are the parties ready to proceed?"

All the lawyers said they were.

"Opening statements?"

Trevarthen stepped up to the well of the courtroom. Like a lot of good lawyers, she started by telling a story. "On a beautiful warm day in the spring of 1962, Jeanne Tessier was sitting by herself on the front stoop of her family home at 227 Center Cross Street in sleepy little Sycamore, Illinois, when her life changed forever. Jeanne was a fourteen-year-old high school freshman who lived in that family home with her mother and father and five siblings: Kathy, Bob, Janet, Mary, and Nancy. You will hear testimony that Jeanne has another sibling who did not live with the family in the spring of 1962 because he was older and he had already moved out and joined the military years before. That other sibling is the defendant.

"To Jeanne, the defendant is her brother John Tessier. He has since changed his name to Jack McCullough, but he is the biological brother of Jeanne." The young prosecutor laid out the case, and when she was done she called her first witness.

"The People will call Katheran Caulfield."

The little girl who had been born in England eight days after the surrender of Germany and sailed to America on-board the *Queen Mary* with her war-bride mother and seven-year-old brother, Johnny, was now a sixty-six-year-old grandmother who lived in Minnesota with her second husband, Joe, a psychologist. In 1962, she had been a sixteen-year-old junior at Sycamore High School. Trevarthen approached the witness stand and handed Katheran a family photo.

"That's my sister Jeanne and I," Katheran said. It was a photo of the two girls wearing the uniform of the Girls Athletic Association (GAA). In the photo, Jeanne was fourteen; it was taken the night of a big GAA dance.

Katheran testified that John Tessier had returned to Sycamore in November 1961, after four years of U.S. Air Force service.

"Was he living at home?" Trevarthen asked.

"For a brief period of time and then he was out."

"Do you recognize John Tessier in the courtroom here this morning?"

Katheran looked at her eldest sibling, and he glared back. It was the first time they had seen each other since Thanksgiving 1993.

"Yes, I do. He's at the end of the table there with a dark suit and a dark tie."

"You testified that he lived at home for a little while after he came back from the service."

"Yes."

"How long?"

"I'm really not quite sure. A short period of time."

"And then he left and moved out?"

"Right."

"Do you know where he was living?"

"I don't know, but I know he was living with a bunch of other people."

"And how do you know that?"

"Because he could walk from where he was to our place, and he talked about that he was living with somebody else."

"When he would come to the house, do you recall what, if anything, he would do when he'd come over?"

"Mainly come to have meals and do his laundry."

That was it. The defense had no questions for Katheran, and she stepped off the witness stand. The testimony was subtle but important. Katheran could not place McCullough at 751 Carlson Street, where the rape had allegedly occurred, but at least she had established the fact that McCullough had lived close by.

"You may call your next witness," Judge Stuckert said.

Clay Campbell rose from the prosecution table. The state's attorney would be personally handling this examination.

"Judge, the State would call Jeanne Tessier."

In the hallway outside the courtroom, as Jeanne waited to be summoned, she saw her sister Mary Hunt sitting on a bench with an attractive blonde.

"Jeanne, this is Michelle Weinman."

Michelle stood, and the two women embraced.

"Thank you for coming," Jeanne said.

At that moment, the door swung open, and a court officer told Jeanne it was time. Jeanne entered the courtroom and took her place on the witness stand. She stared out, then made herself lock eyes with Jack McCullough. Brother and sister scowled at each other. Like her sister Katheran before her, Jeanne had last seen him in 1993, at Thanksgiving. Then she shifted her gaze past the railing to the first row behind McCullough and found her brother Bob Tessier, giving her a toothy grin, nodding his head in encouragement, as if to say, *You can do this, sis. I've got you covered*. Next to Bob sat his wife, Kathy, his sweetheart from Sycamore High who he had married when he was 20. The rest of the row was filled with Jeanne's friends. There was Joetta Huelsmann, a nun from Indiana who had been her spiritual advisor when she became a chaplain. Next to Sister Joetta sat Coleen Powell, a friend from Louisville with whom Jeanne had created an exhibit for survivors of incest and child abuse. Also present was Pam Jackson, her friend from Sycamore High. Jeanne and Pam had lost touch with each other over the decades but reconnected when McCullough's arrest became front-page news in Sycamore. Now she was here for Jeanne in this time of crisis.

"Ma'am, could you please state your name?"

"My name is Jeanne Tessier."

Under state law, a woman claiming to be the victim of rape had the right to keep her name out of the public arena, but Jeanne had made the personal decision to permit the publication of her identity.

"Ma'am, where do you currently reside?"

"In Kentucky."

"How long have you resided in that location?"

"A year."

"How old are you?"

"Sixty-four."

"Are you currently employed?"

"I'm retired. I teach part-time at a university in Louisville."

"And prior to retirement how were you employed?"

Jeanne proceeded to list her impressive record of accomplishments. How after graduating Sycamore High School, she was accepted into Northwestern University and majored in speech. How she became a tenured faculty member at Indiana University and Purdue University in Fort Wayne, teaching in the communication department and coauthoring a college textbook, and leaving academia in 2003 to train for the chaplaincy. For seven years, she had been a chaplain in the intensive-care units at Kosair Children's Hospital, in Louisville.

Campbell asked, "Ma'am, could you briefly describe for the court what your duties were as a chaplain at that hospital?"

"I met families in the emergency room when their children were brought in in extreme distress. I cared for the most critically ill children and their parents, trying to meet their spiritual needs, and I was present at fifty to seventy-five deaths of children a year."

Sitting at the defense table, McCullough felt sick to his stomach. He later commented, "Oh, geez. She's a pastor. She passes out the bad news to the parents of dead children. She's a cum laude in every goddamned thing you can think of. She's an author. She's published books. She's a stellar citizen. I'm thinking, *Oh my God, I am so screwed.*"

Clay Campbell asked Jeanne about life in Sycamore in the 1950s and 1960s.

"Well, it was a charming small town," Jeanne testified. "My own life wasn't charming, but the town was charming. We walked to school. We walked to the swimming pool. Until I was nine years old, nobody worried about the danger." Jeanne was nine when Maria Ridulph was kidnapped.

The prosecutor brought Jeanne around to that day in 1962, when she was fourteen and her brother John was twenty-two.

"It was a warm day," Jeanne said. "I was sitting out on the front steps of our family home. John came by in a car that I had never seen before."

"What kind of car was it?"

"It was a convertible. And he stopped and said hello, and I had never had a ride in a convertible, and I asked him if I could have a ride in the car."

"Did you approach the car?"

"I did."

"Would you tell the court what happened next?"

"At first he said—he said no. I was eager to sit in a convertible, and I said, 'Please, just a ride around the block,' and he said OK."

"Did you get into the car?"

"I did."

"Did he take you for a ride?"

"He didn't take me for a ride around the block. He took me directly to a home."

"What happened next?"

"He told me to come in the house."

"Did you respond?"

"I followed him."

"Could you tell the court what happened next, ma'am?"

"He took me to a dark room toward the back of the house."

"Did you walk down a hallway?"

"Yes."

"And he took you to a room?"

"Yes."

"What happened next, ma'am?"

"He told me to get on the bed, and he took my lower clothes off of me, and he raped me."

"Ma'am, without being indelicate here, when you say that he raped you, could you specifically describe for the court what exactly your brother did?"

"He put his penis in my vagina with force."

"With force?"

"Yes." Jeanne dabbed at the tears that appeared at the corners of her eyes.

"Did you feel pain?"

"Yes."

"Was there anybody else in the room?"

"No."

"Did he say anything to you?"

"No."

"Not one word?"

"No."

"At some point did you discover that there were other individuals in the house?"

"Yes. I heard voices, and then the door to the room I was in was opened."

"At some point did anybody else come into the room?"

"When the door opened, John turned and spoke to them. They were other males. I couldn't see them clearly. He said, 'Hey,' something like, 'Hey, guys, this is my sister. You want a turn?'" Her voice cracked.

"So when he said—you're paraphrasing—'Hey, this is my sister. Do you want a turn,' are you laid down?"

"Mmm."

"On this cot?"

"Yes."

"And the bottom part of your body is naked?"

"Yes."

"Is he engaged in the same act that you described when he says this to them?"

"He was just finishing."

"What happened next, ma'am?"

"Two of those persons took turns with me."

"And when you say 'took turns with you,' could you be more specific?"

"They had intercourse with me."

"And ma'am, again, without being indelicate here, when you say 'intercourse,' did both of those gentlemen actually put their penis in your vagina?"

"Into my body, yes."

"You said it was dark in the room. Were you able to identify or see clear faces of any of these other two?"

"No."

"Do you remember what happened next?"

"A third man came into the room, but he did not rape me. He just sat there for a while and then he told me to put my clothes on."

Jeanne told the court she didn't remember how she got out of the house, but she recalled walking through Elmwood Cemetery and making her way home, where she put her clothes into the washing machine, took a shower in the basement shower stall, and then wrapped herself in a towel and climbed into her bed and fell asleep.

Campbell asked Judge Stuckert. "Judge, may I have a moment?"

"You may," the judge said.

Campbell consulted with his colleagues, Julie Trevarthen and Victor Escarcida, and asked them if he had covered everything. Meanwhile, Jeanne considered Robbin Stuckert. Jeanne was quite perplexed. The entire time she had been on the witness stand, it seemed to her that the judge had had her back to her, typing on a computer, as if transcribing her entire testimony. Jeanne didn't get it. Wasn't that why they had court reporters?

Now Campbell spoke up. "Judge, I have no further questions."

"Thank you," Stuckert said. She told Regina Harris, "You may cross."

Defense lawyers walk a fine line when cross-examining a woman who says she is the victim of rape. Generally, you don't want to come across as badgering, yet you still have a client to represent and are ethically bound to mount a vigorous defense. Harris realized she faced an exceedingly compelling witness. There was an intensity about Jeanne

Tessier that sucked you in. You wanted to hear what she was going to say next.

Harris began. "You indicated in your testimony that this occurred in the spring of 1962?"

"I didn't say spring," Jeanne huffed. "It was a beautiful day. It was a warm day."

"Were you out of school at the time?"

"I was out of school that day. I don't know if it was summertime or spring. I don't know."

The point was made. Fifty years later, the precise date of the alleged rape was impossible to determine. How can you convict a man of rape when you couldn't even fix the precise date the crime occurred?

"He pulled up, you said, in a convertible?"

"Yes."

"A red convertible, was it?"

"That is what I remember. Red and white is what I remember."

"You testified regarding three other men involved in the house that you were taken to."

"Yes."

"Do you recall anything about those men?"

"No. Only that they hurt me, two of them hurt me."

"Can you describe them physically at all?"

"They were young men. They were larger than me. One of them had dark hair. Two of them had light hair."

"Did you recognize one of them as the older brother of a girl in your class?"

"No. When I spoke about this incident with Brion Hanley and another officer of the Illinois state police . . . I told them that I thought that the last man who didn't harm me when he came into the room might have been an older brother of a classmate of mine."

"And what was the classmate's name? Do you recall her last name?"

"Yes, but is there a reason to have to make that public here? I only thought it might have been him."

"What was his last name?"

Jeanne turned to Judge Stuckert. "Do I have to answer that, Judge?"

"Yes, you do," Stuckert crisply replied.

Jeanne gave up the name. She had no choice.

Harris pondered what to do next. She really believed there was nothing to be gained by going after Jeanne. The quicker she got her off the stand, the better for Jack Mc-Cullough. Said Harris, "Judge, I don't have any other questions, thank you."

"Thank you very much, Miss Tessier. You may step down." As she did, Jack McCullough was thinking, *I am so fucked*.

The State called its next witness, Michelle Weinman.

Michelle had been sitting in the court hallway with McCullough's sisters Mary Hunt and Katheran Caulfield. When she got to Sycamore, she didn't know how the Tessiers would react to her presence as a prosecution witness; she was pleasantly surprised and grateful that they were being so supportive, considering the fact that she was testifying against their brother. Of course, she had no idea of the family dynamics, didn't know they were rooting for a guilty verdict, too.

Katheran held her by the hand.

"You are such a strong woman," she kept assuring Michelle. Speaking as a Tessier, Katheran apologized on the family's behalf for what Jack McCullough had done to her when she was a teenager.

Michelle took one more deep breath when the court officer came to get her and stepped into the courtroom. She was wearing stylish black pants with matching belt and boots and a gray sweater. As she swore to tell the truth, she could feel the presence of Jack McCullough directly behind her, his eyes blazing with a slow burn. It was intimidating and very scary. When Michelle took the stand, she took a quick look around, then settled on the defendant, sitting there with his lawyers. *Holy cow*, she thought. The John Tessier she had known was a buff forty-three-year-old cop with sandy-blond hair and a raffish *Magnum P.I.* mustache, but the Jack McCullough she was staring at was a man grown old, with snow-white hair—truly a senior citizen.

Victor Escarcida handled the direct examination. Escarcida had grown up in New Mexico and, like Regina Harris, had graduated Northern Illinois University school of law. He had a tightly wound intensity and a clipped way of firing off questions. And he was a true believer who saw McCullough as an evildoer who needed to be put away. Michelle felt completely comfortable with Escarcida. "I know he's on my side," she recalled thinking.

"Miss, what is your occupation?" he asked her.

"I'm a manager and server of a bar. It's in Tacoma, Washington."

Michelle laid out her biographical sketch: she was the

mother of three sons, and in her adolescence she had lived in Milton, Washington, with her adopted father and stepmother. She had run away from home when she was fifteen with her friend Dorothea, who introduced her to John Tessier.

"Why did you decide to stay with him?" Escarcida asked.

"He—he was a police officer, and he seemed like a nice man."

"Where was he living at the time?"

"I stayed with him at his girlfriend's house."

"When you moved in with him, how did he treat you?"

"Very good. We went to dinners. We'd go to movies. I had a chance to drive his police vehicle."

"Did you trust him during this time period?"

"Yes, absolutely."

Then things started "getting a little creepy," Michelle said. "He would lay me on the living room floor, and he would massage my back, and he would tell me I could be a masseuse and then he would pull my pants down to expose my butt and massage my butt and would describe to me that it's very important to pay attention to the muscles in the butt."

"Did anything else happen separate from the massages?"

"Yes."

"Can you tell the court, please."

"When—when I was sleeping on the couch and he had woken me up, he whispered in my ear and he then took my panties off and he was performing oral sex on me."

"And when you say he was performing oral sex on you, can you describe what he was doing with his body?"

"He was using his tongue on my vagina, and as he was putting his tongue on my genitals, he was taking his fingers and putting them in my vagina."

"Now, what was your reaction while he was sticking his tongue and fingers in your vagina?"

"Scared, extremely scared." Peering at the defense table, Michelle saw McCullough scribbling notes to his lawyer. He was not looking at her.

"At some point did he stop doing that?"

"Yes. He just stopped because he wanted me to get up and go into the bedroom with him."

"Did you do that or stay on the couch?"

"I stayed on the couch."

Michelle related how she'd told her friend Dorothea what had happened and went to school the next day. "I never went back to his apartment," she said. Introduced into evidence was a photo of Michelle as she looked when she was fifteen.

"Now, I just want to be clear, Miss Weinman. When this defendant sexually assaulted you, you would have been fifteen years old, correct?"

"Yes."

Escarcida told Stuckert, "I don't have any further questions, Your Honor."

"Cross?" the judge asked.

As Regina Harris rose, Michelle braced herself. She was very concerned that the defense lawyer was about to rip into her and try to tear her story apart. Michelle needn't have worried. Regina Harris had fought tooth and nail to keep Michelle from testifying, but the judge had allowed her to take the stand on grounds that it could establish McCullough's propensity to commit sex crimes. Once that ruling had been made, Harris had decided that she wasn't going to bash the witness because, in the lawyer's words, "I didn't feel there was anything to be gained by attacking her."

She threw out a few softballs. "There were two couches in the living room?"

"Yes."

"You were sleeping on one and Dorothea was sleeping on the other?"

"Yes."

"You indicated that you didn't wake her until after this occurred?"

"Yes."

"Did you try to wake her while it was happening?"

"I was so scared. I froze."

"The next day the school officials were told about this?"

"Yes."

"Did you go to the school or did your friend Dorothea go to the school?"

"They came to me. I believe that Dorothea must have told them."

"OK. So actually it was the school officials came to you to inquire about this. Is that correct?"

"Yes."

Harris turned to the judge. "I have no other questions."

Escarcida didn't have any redirect.

The judge told Michelle, "Thank you very much. You may step down."

The State had one more witness before they wrapped up for the day. James Gassaway was the army veteran who moved into 751 Carlson Street in 1962. He testified that three, sometimes four young men lived there: the Glen brothers, Richard Floyd Tucker, and, of course, Jack McCullough—then known as John Tessier. Gassaway testified about life at the Carlson Street address: an after-hours hangout where many guys came to drink after the main bars in Sycamore had closed for the night. He was called to establish that McCullough did in fact reside at 751 Carlson Street. When it was Regina Harris's turn to cross-examine Gassaway, there was this riveting exchange:

Harris: "Did you ever meet anyone that John introduced to you as his sister?"

Gassaway: "No, I didn't."

Harris: "Did you ever walk in on John engaged in any sort of sexual activity with a girl?"

Gassaway: "No."

Harris: "John ever say to you, 'This is my sister. Have a turn?'"

Gassaway: "No."

Court was adjourned. After McCullough got up to return to the county jail for the night, he was escorted right past Detective Ciesynski.

"Asshole," McCullough muttered.

Ciesynski just laughed. He had been around long enough not to take these things personally, and he responded with a cheerful, "Jack, come on!"

The next day, April 11, the State called its final witness: Special Agent Brion Hanley. His testimony must have been a shattering blow to McCullough's spirit because, for the first time, the defendant learned of the full extent of his five siblings' cooperation with the state police. Hanley gave the dates of where and when he had interviewed the Tessiers: Janet on October 17, 2008; Mary Hunt on May 4, 2009; Katheran Caulfield on August 13, 2009, at her home in Minnesota; Bob Tessier on November 13, 2009, at his home in Kentucky; and on the same day, his sister, Jeanne Tessier, who also lived in Kentucky. So all of the Tessiers, with the exception of the institutionalized youngest sister, Nancy, had pulled together to see McCullough put away. He couldn't believe it.

Hanley was asked to read into the record the agreement Jack McCullough had signed in 1983, when he had pled guilty to a charge of communication with Michelle Weinman for immoral purposes. Under cross-examination, Regina Harris asked Hanley about the first time he had initiated contact with Jeanne Tessier.

"She said nothing about any sexual assault of herself by her brother, is that correct?" Harris asked.

"That's correct," Hanley answered.

"It wasn't until November thirteenth of 2009 that there was any information provided by her to you regarding that kind of issue, is that correct?"

"That's correct."

"And you contacted her to interview her, is that correct?"

"That's correct."

"She did not contact you?"

"Correct."

When Hanley left the stand, Julie Trevarthen said, "The

State doesn't have any further witnesses. We would rest at this time." In all, the prosecution had presented five witnesses: Katheran Caulfield, Jeanne Tessier, Michelle Weinman, James Gassaway, and Brion Hanley. From Mike Ciesynski's perspective in the gallery, he thought the trial was going well for the prosecution. Jeanne Tessier and Michelle Weinman had made two strong witnesses. *Slam dunk*, he thought, confident that the judge would find McCullough guilty. He was already wondering why Regina Harris had gone for a bench trial. *What a blunder*, he thought.

Now it was the turn of the defense.

"Judge, we would call Floyd Tucker."

An old man shuffled in, and as he did, Chuck Ridulph, sitting in the second row with his sister Pat, shuddered. He knew Floyd Tucker from way back. When he was twenty-one, Chuck had tended bar one summer at a place called the Pastime, where Tucker had been a regular customer. *A bad guy then, bad news now*, Chuck thought. Even at age seventy-two and in poor health, Tucker was intimidating—"the one guy who scared me then and he still scared me today. I would be afraid to cross that guy."

After the retired ironworker was sworn in, Harris asked, "Are you known to your friends by another name as well?"

"Pardon?" Tucker was having trouble hearing. Old age was really catching up to him.

"Do your friends call you something other than Floyd?"

"Gator."

"Did you ever meet anyone that John Tessier introduced to you as his sister?"

"No, I did not."

"Did you ever walk into a room where John Tessier was located with a girl in the act of any sort of sexual encounter?"

"No."

"Did you ever have an encounter with John Tessier and any girl where he offered her to you sexually?"

"No."

Tucker testified to one other matter of consequence, that he could not recall Jack McCullough ever residing at 751 Carlson Street.

When it was the turn of the prosecution for cross-examination, Clay Campbell lunged out of his chair and really went after the witness. Tucker had been accidentally shot by John Tessier during target practice in October 1962 at Sportsmans Lake in Sycamore. A newspaper article introduced into evidence gave an account of the shooting and reported the home address for Tessier as 751 Carlson Street. James Gassaway had already testified that Tessier was his roommate. Did Gator Tucker really expect anyone to believe that Tessier had never lived there?

"You were friends with him, weren't you?" Campbell asked.

"Yes, I went to school with him."

"Same high school, Sycamore High School?"

"Yes, yes, sir."

"How long did you know Mr. Tessier?"

"I don't know."

"Fair to say years?"

"Yes."

"He had been to 751 Carlson Street, is that correct?"

"I don't know."

"You don't know?"

Campbell brought Tucker around to an interview he had given to Sycamore detectives Tiffany Ziegler and Dan Hoffman at his home in the city of DeKalb, in September 2011. According to the detectives, Tucker had told them that his roommate Terry Glen drove a red 1957 Chevy convertible. It was important evidence in that it established Jeanne Tessier's credibility when she had testified that her brother John had driven up in a red convertible borrowed from a buddy. Now Tucker was denying he had ever said such a thing.

"It's your testimony, sir, under oath, that you do not recall telling those detectives that Terry Glen drove a red 1957 Chevy convertible?"

"No."

Campbell sat down in disgust. Regina Harris rose to regain some lost ground.

"Are you here today to protect John Tessier/Jack McCullough, from consequences of something that he could have done?"

"No."

"Why are you here?"

The old geezer answered, "I have no idea."

The spectators howled in laughter.

Former Green Beret Terry Glen was next to be called. At age seventy-three, he was still residing at 751 Carlson Street. Now Glen took the stand and denied that he'd ever driven a red convertible. He was in the U.S. Army in 1962, when Jeanne says she was raped. When his testimony was completed and he got off the stand, Chuck Ridulph says he saw the witness give McCullough a thumbs-up.

With that, the defense rested. Regina Harris had decided not to call McCullough as a witness on his own behalf, and for good reason; he was such a loose cannon—on top of being an emotional wreck. The Tessiers, Harris had come to believe, were a screwed-up family; on some level, everyone was a mess, including her client. Besides, Harris believed she had the law on her side.

Victor Escarcida made the closing statement on behalf of the prosecution.

"The evidence has shown, Your Honor, that on the beautiful, warm day in 1962 that defendant over there violently raped his own sister Jeanne Tessier and on that day he took away her dignity and treated her like a piece of garbage. This case is not just about rape, but it's also about how the defendant put his own sister in a position to have to deal with this crime with the added horror that it had been committed by a person a sister should be able to trust, her older brother, an act of incest. Judge, a sister is supposed to be protected by her older brother and trust him, and the evidence shows, Your Honor, that this defendant violated that position of trust.

"The evidence shows, Your Honor, that once this defendant got Jeanne Tessier in that house, he had carnal knowledge of her . . . and then offered her up to two other men who also raped her.

"You also have the testimony of Michelle Weinman, and

with her testimony you know that this defendant twenty years after raping his sister took Michelle Weinman in when she was fifteen. She was a runaway and after that he sexually assaulted her. He again took advantage of a young teenage girl in order to satisfy his own deviant sexual desires and sexual gratification. He was a police officer at that time. She trusted him. She freezes out of fear and has to let that happen. What is she going to do? This police officer is sexually assaulting her. This is what he does. He uses his position of trust and authority to take advantage of these teenage girls. The sexual assault of Michelle Weinman also shows that this defendant has a propensity to commit sexual assault and more important a propensity to commit sexual intercourse with teenage girls under the age of fifteen and sixteen.

"What the evidence shows, Your Honor, is that Jeanne Tessier broke her silence because the police were inquiring about another matter. She kept this dirty little secret for all those years because of the circumstances, because it was done by a member of her own family. Jeanne Tessier, a chaplain, came in here and opened herself up to the exposure of telling this court what the defendant did, and you are able to see the damage that has been left in his wake of his sexually deviant behavior, the tears coming from Jeanne Tessier's eyes. He is guilty of rape and indecent liberties with a child."

There was silence in the courtroom. It was a compelling closing statement that laid out the evidence while reminding everyone of the personal consequences in the lives of Jeanne Tessier and Michelle Weinman.

"Thank you, Mr. Escarcida," Judge Stuckert said. "Miss Harris?"

Regina Harris rose. Rape cases always took a heavy toll on her. As a defense lawyer, she had to be mindful of every word spoken in closing arguments. Disparaging a rape victim could prove perilous.

"What are the kinds of things that a trier of fact considers in determining whether a sexual assault occurred? Well, first, prompt report. There is no report in this case of any kind for forty-seven years, not to a mother, not to a father, not to a sibling of which there are many, not to a friend, not to the police, to no one for forty-seven years.

"What is the second thing we look for? Well, some kind of physical evidence, even if it's minimal. In this case there is no physical evidence of any kind. There is no clothing. There is no rape kit. There is no physical examination by a doctor. There is absolutely nothing." Harris proceeded to express doubts about Jeanne Tessier's story. Hard to believe, she said, that three buddies walk in on Jack McCullough raping his sister "and no one says, 'Ooh, who did you say she is? Wait a minute. No, I don't want anything.' They don't even just walk away. It goes beyond the pale based on this description and there is no corroboration at all. This is broad daylight. This isn't late at night after the bars close down and people start flowing there. This is the middle of the day. Where do they come from?

"The State's argument, Judge, is that the 1982 events with Michelle Weinman corroborate Jeanne's testimony, but this trial isn't about what happened to Michelle Weinman in 1982. Michelle Weinman made a prompt outcry.

Michelle Weinman woke up her friend right after it happened. Michelle Weinman spoke to school administrators. Michelle Weinman spoke to the police. None of that evidence is available in this case.

"There is that old, old saying about the charge of rape, that it's easy to make but hard to defend, and that is why we require more than just someone's say-so. There just simply is not sufficient evidence in this case, Judge, to find this defendant guilty of the charges against him, and I would ask that you find him not guilty."

In Illinois, the last word always goes to the prosecution, and Clay Campbell had a lot to say in his rebuttal.

"Judge, I would be remiss if I didn't say the word that nobody has said yet, and it's that 800-pound gorilla in the room here." Perhaps everyone expected him to say Maria Ridulph, a name the judge had forbidden to be spoken at this trial. No, it wasn't Maria. It was *incest*.

"This case is about incest, so why would Jeanne Tessier not come forward and talk about this in 1962? Judge, the same reason today a young girl would not come forward and talk about this. Nobody wants to talk about incest. Her brother molested her. In 1962 is Miss Harris really suggesting that Miss Tessier should come home and say, 'Mom, Dad, guess what happened? This older brother of mine gang-raped me today.' People don't talk about that today, Judge. We can't blame Jeanne Tessier for not talking about that in 1962. Miss Harris talks about a lack of corroboration. There is no corroboration. Fifty years later we're supposed to be able to present corroboration? We're supposed to fault Miss Tessier or the police or the prosecution because Jeanne Tessier went home to her house that day and washed the semen inside of her out of her in the basement shower. We can't look at this through the lens of modern technology, Judge. It goes without saying that there is no scientific corroboration here, but take the testimony of Jeanne Tessier. That's all the corroboration you need.

"And, Judge, it certainly adds to Miss Tessier's credibility that she did not come forward with this. This isn't a lady with an ax to grind. Miss Tessier did not say to herself, 'I'm going to come up with a complete lie . . . I'm going to say my brother is the one that raped me and while he's raping me two other individuals come in the room and they rape me, too. Miss Harris would have us believe that that is a lie, a chaplain is going to make up that to come into court and commit perjury." He pointed to Jack McCullough. "And you know what? This defendant over here, he guessed right. You feel like raping somebody? Rape your sister, 'My sister will never come and tell anybody.' And, Judge, she didn't for fifty years until she walked into this court of law yesterday, a chaplain, a tenured professor. 'I know what I'm going to do. I'm going to completely derail my life. I'm going to come up to Sycamore, Illinois, a place I do not want to go back to because it has all this horrendous memory and I'm going to lie about my brother raping me.' Judge, he did rape her, and we're asking the court to hold him accountable for his actions and to say to people like Michelle Weinman and to say to people like Jeanne Tessier it doesn't matter how long time passes. It doesn't matter if it's fifty years."

Campbell was depleted. He had poured everything he had into the rebuttal. He sat down.

Judge Stuckert said, "The court is going to deliberate on this case. I'll have my verdict ready tomorrow morning at 10:30."

Court was adjourned for the night.

37

·········

THE VERDICT

Regina Harris got up the morning of April 12, 2012, thinking the verdict could go either way. It all depended on how Judge Stuckert was going to interpret the facts.

Striding into the courtroom shortly after 10:00 A.M., Harris found the front row taken up by three of her client's siblings: Bob Tessier, Mary Hunt, and Katheran Caulfield. Sitting next to them was Michelle Weinman. Witnesses are usually barred from the courtroom during testimony, but since the trial was over, they could sit in like any citizen and hear the judge's verdict.

Mary Hunt leaned over to tell Michelle something.

"That's Maria Ridulph's brother." She nodded in the direction of Chuck Ridulph, sitting on the other side of the courtroom. Michelle went over and shook his hand, and Chuck thanked her for testifying.

When court officers brought McCullough to the defense

table, he was wearing his usual black shirt, dark suit, and maroon tie. He was tense with worry. Harris tried to cheer him up, but the truth was, she just didn't know how it was going to turn out.

All rose when Judge Stuckert came in. Was her body language communicating anything that hinted at the verdict? It was like reading tea leaves, impossible to say.

"Good morning, everyone," Stuckert said. She began. "This matter comes before the court today for its verdict. The defendant, Jack McCullough, formerly known as John Tessier, is charged with one count of rape and four counts of indecent liberties with a child." After a broad review of the undisputed facts, Stuckert proceeded to punch holes in the prosecution's case. She noted that Jeanne Tessier had testified that she was in "danger" when she got a ride with her brother in the red convertible in 1962. But why?

"That question was not asked."

Nor did Jeanne testify that the rape had taken place at 751 Carlson Street. "She provided no evidence that would distinguish this house from any other house in Sycamore, or, for that matter, anywhere else," Stuckert said.

The only documentation the State introduced to place Jack McCullough at 751 Carlson Street was a newspaper article from the *Sycamore True Republican*, dated October 9, 1962, several months after the alleged rape occurred. That article, written by "author unknown," was an "unauthenticated document," Stuckert declared. Furthermore, Floyd "Gator" Tucker and Terry Glen had both testified that McCullough had never lived at 751 Carlson Street. Stuckert called their testimony "credible." She agreed that

Jack McCullough may have had unfettered access to the house because the door was always unlocked. "However, the State failed to ask any one of the residents of the house whether that was, in fact, the situation. They never asked their own witness or the defense witnesses."

Stuckert expressed bafflement over the 1957 red Chevy convertible testimony. "Gator" Tucker had told police that Terry Glen drove a red convertible. But Terry Glen said James Gassaway owned a red convertible. Gassaway said that wasn't true—he drove a metallic green Oldsmobile, and he was the only roommate who had a car. It was impossible to get to the truth of the matter, Stuckert said, because of the ages of these old-timers and the fog of memory after the passage of half a century.

The judge also pointed out that when Jeanne Tessier was interviewed by Special Agent Brion Hanley, in 2008, she never disclosed the alleged rape committed by her brother. She only revealed it to Hanley during her second interview, in 2009—"some forty-seven years after the occurrence." And she never disclosed to Hanley the name of the third man who refused to take part in the gang rape— this was the brother of Jeanne's classmate—thus denying Hanley the opportunity to locate and interview an important witness.

As for Michelle Weinman, Stuckert said the prosecution argued that both Michelle and Jeanne were about the same age, but "the State has produced no evidence to support their contention that the defendant held a position of trust with his half sister Miss Tessier. The evidence is strikingly void of any specifics regarding their relationship.

"Ms. Weinman was asked, 'Did you trust him?' Her response was yes and then she explained to this court why. Was Miss Tessier asked that question by the State? No. They simply did not ask."

In the gallery of the small courtroom, Michelle Weinman fought the impulse to stand and say, *This can't be happening.*

At the defense table, Jack McCullough was on the edge of his seat, but as he listened to the judge, he started thinking, *She's taking the prosecutor to the woodshed. I'm gonna get off. She's gonna say not guilty.*

Sitting directly behind him was his brother, Bob, who also was beginning to see where this verdict was headed. It startled him to hear the judge ream out Clay Campbell's office in such harsh language.

Stuckert continued. "In the same vein, this court is asked to set aside the fact that Miss Tessier waited forty-eight years to disclose the assault. The state argues that this is understandable for several reasons: first it was 1962, and the morals and times were different; and second, that this rape by her brother was incest, a subject that was taboo then and that even now people don't talk about. Generally a failure to speak when it is natural to do so under the circumstances discredits the credibility of the claimant and may amount, in effect, to an assertion of the nonexistence of the fact. And did the State ever ask Miss Tessier one simple question, 'Why did you fail to report this for forty-eight years?' We do understand that oftentimes because of sexual abuse that we handle it differently, and we do understand that there will be late reporting by individuals just because of the very nature of this . . . the shame, guilt, and embarrassment or perhaps fear from the perpetrator, but, once again, the State never asked Miss Tessier to explain her reasons for this report. The State does, however, ask this court to base its verdict on what occurred fifty years ago on the sole fact that Miss Tessier, a woman of faith, a chaplain, would not lie. I would suggest that this is an impermissible request of this court.

"With the passage of time, things change. The quiet, charming town of Sycamore has changed. In 1962 children walked to the park, pools, schools unattended. Today if parents allowed their children to roam the cities unattended, they would be considered neglectful. In 1962 doors were left unlocked. Today that practice would be considered quite foolish.

"With the passage of time, a fourteen-year-old girl who did not have a charmed childhood grew to be highly educated, accomplished, and a very caring woman. She compassionately assists parents during the most unimaginable time of loss in their lives, the death of a child. However, one thing has not changed since 1962. It has remained constant, as it should, that under the fundamental principles of law, all defendants are presumed innocent of the charges, and that presumption remains with him unless and until the State meets their burden proving the defendant guilty beyond a reasonable doubt. The State has failed to meet that burden. Therefore, the defendant is found not guilty of all charges."

There was an eruption in court. McCullough's sister Katheran Caulfield doubled over and sobbed.

"Why didn't she let me testify!" she said.

Chuck Ridulph just shook his head in disgust. Mc-Cullough himself let out a huge sigh of relief, and Regina Harris felt a great sense of satisfaction come over her. She thought her client was going to faint on the spot, but she heard him take another deep breath and collect himself. Over at the prosecution table, Clay Campbell was, quite simply, seething. In a few minutes, he would have to get to a phone and tell Jeanne Tessier that McCullough had been found not guilty. He dreaded making the call.

Judge Stuckert waited for things to settle down, and when they did, she got back to the business of setting the date for the murder trial, over which she would also preside.

"How are we proceeding on the other case?"

Regina Harris said any date after Memorial Day weekend was fine with her.

Court was adjourned, and everyone rose as Stuckert left the bench. That's when Jack McCullough turned to his brother and sisters sitting in the row behind him and shot them a look that can only be described as a self-satisfied smirk. Court officers escorted McCullough into a private room, where he hugged his lawyer and investigator Crystal Harrolle. Now that he was out of the public arena, he let go and broke down in sobs. He just fell apart. For the first time since his arrest for Maria Ridulph's murder, he saw light at the end of the tunnel. After this not-guilty verdict, he thought, with a few lucky breaks, acquittal on the murder charge was inevitable.

Outside the courthouse, there was more drama.

The Tessier clan had tears in their eyes, and Bob Tessier,

acting as family spokesman, told reporters, "We are very upset. This is a travesty of justice, is what we feel."

Michelle Weinman didn't want to talk, but her biker boyfriend, Jeff, made this plainspoken statement as they trotted down the courthouse steps: "The system sucks."

Clay Campbell was personally affronted by Judge Stuckert's verdict. She seemed to be questioning not just the facts of the case, but also the presentation and his lawyerly skills for failing to ask pertinent questions of Jeanne Tessier. It was humiliating, and he was taking it personally. "I think this was a miscarriage of justice," he said of the judge's verdict during an impromptu press conference. He also called it a "travesty" and said it sent a terrible message to victims of sexual assault.

"The court specifically chastised the state attorney's office for not asking questions of witnesses that we were barred by the court's ruling from asking." He said the judge, in a pretrial ruling, had forbidden him from questioning Jeanne Tessier about her claims that Jack McCullough had been violating her since the age of four and that other siblings of McCullough's had been molested at his hands.

"Had I asked that question, I would have been in direct violation of the court's order."

When a reporter asked Campbell whether he would request that Stuckert remove herself from presiding over the murder trial, the state's attorney said he'd consider all options.

Campbell's remarks sent shock waves through Sycamore's tightly knit legal community.

"It was appalling," Regina Harris said. "So inappropriate. You just don't do that." She said the prosecution could have found a way of introducing evidence without violating court orders. She says the prosecution lost the case in part due to its own "shitty lawyering."

The Ridulphs were also stressed out because Judge Stuckert seemed to have had it in for Clay Campbell, and she was going to preside over the murder trial.

When things settled down, Pat Ridulph Quinn walked up to Katheran Tessier Caulfield. They had known each other growing up in Sycamore.

"Kathy, I had the opinion that you and your sister Jeanne were very close." When Katheran said that was correct, Pat asked, "Is it true that you never ever heard the story of her rape before this trial?" Pat found it hard to believe, but Katheran said as firmly as she could, "No, we never knew." She said she only learned about Jeanne's allegations of incest and rape at the hands of their brother a few days before the start of the trial.

It was a low-key celebration at the public defender's office, beer for everyone, a little office chitchat, then back to work. Across the street, many of the key players from the prosecution found themselves commiserating over lunch and drinks at PJ's Courthouse Tavern. Julie Trevarthen was there, as were Victor Escarcida and Brion Hanley. Even Clay Campbell showed up. Michelle Weinman and her boyfriend were invited to sit at the table, and Michelle picked at the chicken salad. They were all very upset.

Michelle and Jeff flew back to Washington State the next

day. When she got home, she broke up with Jeff. The trial had had something to do with it—that, and her difficult life experiences.

"I never really liked living with anyone," she remarked.

Jeanne Tessier had left right after her testimony. She couldn't bear to stay for the verdict. She got in the rental car and drove back to Kentucky with her dog, Spirit. When the phone rang at her house and she heard the verdict, she wasn't surprised. "Before I got to Sycamore, I knew there wasn't going to be a conviction. I knew from the start it was futile. Here's a fiftysomething-year-old case, one person's word against another. You know rape victims historically don't fare well in court. Never have. I was just going to be another." What she found really offensive was Stuckert's questioning how a woman with so many accomplishments in her professional career could have sustained such terrible abuse at the hands of her own brother when she was a teenager.

Said Jeanne: "Would she have believed me more if I was a crack whore living up to the fate of many survivors of abuse?"

Jeanne was infuriated with everyone involved in this mess: Judge Stuckert; Regina Harris; her siblings, for pressuring her to testify. She had to agree that Michelle Weinman's boyfriend made a lot of sense. The system *did* suck. Most of all, she was irate with Clay Campbell. That night, she wrote a letter to the editor that ended up being published in its entirely as a guest column for the local Sycamore newspaper, the *Daily Chronicle*:

My name is Jeanne Tessier. In late 2009, I was called by Illinois State police officer Brion Hanley regarding the reopening of the Maria Ridulph case. Nearly a year later, Mr. Hanley and another officer arrived in Louisville, Ky., to interview myself and my brother Robert. I shared my knowledge of John Tessier, aka Jack McCullough.

A year later, in the summer of 2011, Jack McCullough was arrested for Maria Ridulph's kidnapping and murder and extradited from Washington to Illinois. On Sept. 8, 2011, at their request, DeKalb County State's Attorney Clay Campbell and Officer Hanley came to my home to talk with me about what Mr. Campbell in phone calls described as "this case." Naturally, I assumed "this case" meant the case for which Jack McCullough had been arrested.

What I learned after they arrived was that Mr. Hanley had been investigating the case that was tried this week in court. Mr. Campbell and Mr. Hanley made the trip to Kentucky to urge me to give my consent to the charging of Mr. McCullough despite the passing of fifty years.

It had never occurred to me that such a thing was possible after all these years.

During the visit, Mr. Campbell promised me several times that he wouldn't pursue these charges without my blessing. Mr. Hanley, on the other hand, insisted I had to agree to these charges because it was "the right thing to do." After they left I spent two days reeling from, considering and praying about their request.

Through years of therapy and the hard work of creating

a rewarding and meaningful life for myself in spite of the traumas of childhood, I had found ways to process and release—as much as that is possible—the harm that was done to me by my half brother and others.

With difficulty, and over many years, I had also released the malice I felt toward those who harmed me. I had no desire to reactivate these painful memories.

This request by Mr. Campbell and Mr. Hanley, using information I had shared in the context of another case, felt like re-victimization to me, and I believe it was. After all these years and all the healing work I'd done, it also felt like a regressive act to give my present life such an old and painful focus.

On September 10, 2011, I called Mr. Campbell and told him that my decision was, No. Mr. Campbell expressed his disappointment in my decision, but again affirmed that he would honor it because he promised he would.

Then, on Sept. 27, 2011, Mr. Campbell called again, this time to tell me that he was going to charge Jack McCullough with raping me when I was fourteen and that, in spite of my making clear that I wanted no part of this effort, he would be calling me as a witness.

From that day until yesterday, I—a survivor of a long-term long-ago trauma—was trapped in a nightmare from which I could not escape: these old wounds ripped open, plagued by nightmares of powerlessness and manipulation, my life for the last eight months held captive to the needs and demands of others in a situation I would never have chosen for myself.

Mr. Campbell is right when he says that the outcome of this case "sends a sad message to victims of sexual assault." I am so deeply sorry that the impact of my having to share a small piece of my life story in this context may discourage other victims and survivors from coming forward. In spite of this court case and its outcome, I have been healed by speaking my truth every time I've done so, and I urge all who are or have been victimized to do the same. To name truth is powerful; to speak our truth heals us and all those like us whose stories have been buried in secrecy, denial and lies.

I am grateful to the brave other victim/survivor who came forward to share her truth at this trial. I am grateful to all the family, friends and strangers who have held me in prayer and supported me through this ordeal. I hold Jack McCullough in prayer.

It was a huge embarrassment for Clay Campbell. The influential *Daily Chronicle* followed up with an editorial denouncing Campbell's decision to go forward with the rape trial with these brassy words:

When the accuser in the case recognizes the reality of the situation, you would hope the state's attorney would as well.

Instead, Campbell pressed charges against McCullough under the guise of keeping the public safe. We fail to see how charging someone already in custody of kidnapping and murder charges for something that may or may not have been fifty years ago is going to make our community

> *any more safe. McCullough posed no imminent threat to*
> *the community. Campbell should have considered the lack*
> *of evidence, the difficulty of burden of proof without phys-*
> *ical evidence and the accuser's wishes and determined to*
> *not press charges. Instead he subjected Tessier to a trial she*
> *didn't want to go through for a case he had little chance*
> *of winning.*

One veteran lawyer in Sycamore, Rick Turner, wondered in a letter to the editor whether Campbell pursued the prosecution against the wishes of Jeanne Tessier for "political gain," or perhaps to win "leverage" in the forthcoming murder trial.

Jack McCullough was returned to the county jail feeling pretty good about things, considering. He had gotten off the rape charge, and now, as he faced trial for the coldest case in American history ever to be brought before a court of law, he thought finally, finally he had the upper hand, represented as he was by a resourceful lawyer who truly believed in his innocence, and a fair-minded judge willing to buck public opinion. It was also gratifying to see the prosecutor on the ropes. Imagine his shock had he known that in a mere six weeks his lawyer would resign under pressure and the judge would have to remove herself from presiding over his murder trial.

BOOK V

38

....

DAY ONE

Chuck Ridulph, his sister Pat, and her husband, Bill Quinn, were sitting in the conference room at the state's attorney's office. They wanted to know how the rape trial had gone so badly. The unbridled hostility between Judge Stuckert and Clay Campbell had them very worried.

"Do we stand a chance with Judge Stuckert?" Chuck asked Campbell.

Pat also voiced her concern. "Everyone says how fair and impartial the judge is, but I don't see it."

Campbell told the Ridulphs that in all honesty he didn't know why Stuckert detested him. Maybe it had to do with the fact that early in their careers they'd been colleagues in the same law office. Hearing this, Chuck wondered whether petty politics were at play. "Was it really a good idea to publicly criticize the judge?" he asked.

Campbell conceded that it may have been a miscalculation but one that was made out of frustration. If it was any consolation, Campbell told the Ridulphs, the prosecution team had learned from its mistakes and would be better prepared for the murder case down the road.

It didn't take long for Campbell to get even with Judge Robbin Stuckert and Regina Harris. How this happened said a lot about revenge in a small town and the legal system.

Within hours of being upbraided by Judge Stuckert in open court, Campbell let it be known that he was suspending Drug Court, pending an "evaluation" of its effectiveness. Drug Court processed nonviolent substance abusers and emphasized treatment over jail. It was presided over by Judge Stuckert. Everyone in DeKalb County knew that it was her baby. Without Campbell's cooperation, Drug Court was dead.

Many speculated that Campbell was punishing Stuckert for questioning his competence during Jack McCullough's rape trial. In an editorial, the *Daily Chronicle* had this to say: "The best-case scenario for Campbell is that suspending Drug Court (is) an overreaction paired with really bad timing on his part. The worst-case scenario for Campbell is that this is a vindictive action in response to a verdict that didn't go his way."

Next to go was Regina Harris.

Campbell had gotten wind of the arrest of a woman in Chicago who was a client of Regina Harris. The woman had been pulled over during a routine traffic spot, and eleven bags of heroin were discovered in the car. When police ran a check on the vehicle, it turned out to be registered to none other than the public defender of DeKalb County, Regina Harris.

"Not to say it wasn't stupid on my part, but I thought the woman was clean for four years," Harris later said. "I believed in her attempts to rebuild her life. I believed her story that she was going to miss her kid's psychiatric appointment if she didn't have a car. When I loaned her the car, it was with the absolute belief that she was being honest about it." It was, Harris says, "an error in bad judgment on my part but one made in kindness. And it was blown into something a whole lot more."

To make matters even more embarrassing, the woman under arrest had recently graduated Drug Court, presided over by Stuckert.

Harris was forced to resign. Publicly, she tried to sound upbeat and said she was eager to go into private practice. "I've been doing this for twenty-four years," she told local reporters, "and sometimes there comes a point where you have to see what your other opportunities are." In point of fact, she was certain that she had been forced to resign because of Jack McCullough. "I think it was spiteful and vindictive. But for the result in the Jack McCullough case, I don't think Clay would have been so horribly outraged by me letting somebody borrow my car."

・・・・・・・・・

Four months after Jack McCullough's acquittal, Maria Ridulph's body was finally returned to the family for reburial.

The recommittal services were held on a Sunday at the Evangelical Lutheran Church of St. John, where Chuck Ridulph was now deacon. It was strictly private, only for immediate family and a few close friends. Every aspect of it was selected with care and symbolism. The little casket was a replica of the original and covered with plush white fabric and a spray of pink roses and carnations. The hymn "Jesus Loves Me," which Frances Ridulph had chosen for her daughter's funeral in 1958, was sung by Maria's great-niece, Rebekah McFarland, accompanied by Rebekah's sister, Hannah. The same photo that had stood on Maria's casket then was positioned there again. Four of Maria's nephews, all born long after her death, served as pallbearers. At the services in 1958, Reverend Going had spoken of Maria's having been the proud recipient of a pin for three years of perfect Sunday school attendance. That pin was now in Chuck's custody, and he gave it to his daughter, Maria Annette, as a keepsake.

On July 22, 2012, the Ridulphs gathered at Elmwood Cemetery. In 1958, Maria had been the first Ridulph to be interred in the family plot. Now, fifty-four years later, she was not alone. Her father, Mike, and mother, Frances, and her sister Kay, and Kay's husband, Larry Hickey, had joined her in everlasting peace. A very special mourner was also in attendance: Kathy Sigman Chapman.

That terrible day in 1958 when Maria was buried was still etched in Kathy's memory. Now, more than five decades later, she had to watch as Maria was buried once again.

....

On July 31, 2012, McCullough went before Judge Stuckert. She set the date, September 10, 2012, for his murder
trial to begin. Once again, McCullough waived his right
to a jury. He'd go with a bench trial, the strategy that had
worked so well for him in the rape case. He trusted this
judge to give him a fair shake.

Three days later, the other shoe dropped. Stuckert removed herself from presiding over the McCullough murder
trial, citing the rift between herself and Campbell. In an
editorial, the *Daily Chronicle* gave her a "thumbs-up" for
making the correct call.

"We doubt that a veteran judge such as Stuckert would
let personal feelings about the state's attorney cloud her
judgment, especially in such an important case. However,
her decision to remove herself was wise. No matter how
Stuckert eventually ruled in McCullough's murder trial,
either side could claim she was influenced by previous
events."

In a flash, Campbell had gotten rid of both Stuckert and
Harris.

Now McCullough had to break in a new lawyer. Robert Carlson was named acting public defender. He had
served as Harris's cocounsel during the rape trial and
had thirty-five years' experience as a trial lawyer, but the
rapport that McCullough had had with Harris just wasn't
there.

Then the new judge for McCullough's trial came on
board. Because of the tense political standoff in DeKalb

County between Campbell and Stuckert, Judge James Hal-lock was brought over from neighboring Kane County to insure impartiality.

When Jack McCullough stepped into court and had his first encounter with Hallock, he knew he was in trouble. "With Judge Stuckert, she would greet me. 'Good morn-ing, Mr. McCullough, how are you today?' Not him. He wouldn't even look at me."

Hallock's rulings started going against McCullough from the outset. A week before the start of the trial, the defense took a major hit when he ruled that FBI documents from 1957 that had cleared McCullough as a suspect could not be admitted into evidence. This included McCullough's so-called ironclad alibi—the record of the collect call made to his home at 6:57 P.M. that established he was in Rock-ford, Illinois. McCullough's lawyers had argued that the FBI documents were created when memories were fresh; with witnesses having died over the years, these files offered the only accurate account of events that had taken place fifty-five years before.

"It's the only way to cure the passage of fifty-five years," Robert Carlson argued. "The State can't be allowed to benefit from the late prosecution."

But Judge Hallock declared that the documents were laden with hearsay and in some cases double hearsay. As a matter of law, police reports are almost without exception inadmissible. It is the testimony of the cop, not his report, that is considered evidence. Unfortunately, all the FBI agents involved in the original investigation had died. Of course, if McCullough wanted to put forward an alibi at his trial, he had every right to take the stand in his own defense, but that would mean he would be subjected to cross-examination, and that, as the defense team knew, was a double-edged sword.

The trial would proceed as if the FBI reports did not exist.

McCullough, seated in court, turned to his lawyer and whispered, "I'm fucked."

Another blow came when Hallock ruled that Eileen Tessier's deathbed confession could be introduced into evidence under what was known as a "hearsay exception" because Eileen had essentially acknowledged taking part in a cover-up, "against her own interests." Some legal experts saw this as a stretch, and even Clay Campbell would later say he was "stunned" that the judge would allow Eileen's confession into the trial.

The defense had wanted McCullough's entire interrogation tape thrown out because he had not been provided a lawyer after asking for one. But the judge said McCullough's remarks—such as "We're done" and "I'm done talking to you"—were ambiguous. That, and the fact that McCullough, a former cop presumably well versed in his Miranda rights, continued talking. The judge agreed, however, that six hours and thirty-seven minutes into the interrogation, when McCullough said, "Now that I know you think I'm involved, I really do want a lawyer," left no room for ambiguity. Any comments that McCullough made from that point on would have to be discarded.

· · · · · · · · · ·

Courtroom 300 at the DeKalb County Courthouse is a grand space, a true architectural gem in the Illinois criminal-justice system. From the majestic height of the ceilings hung three chandeliers, and the benches, walls, and stained-glass windows had all been restored to their original 1904 beauty. Courtroom 300 is reserved for the big trials.

When Judge James Hallock took his seat on the bench, he shuddered slightly from the brisk chill in the courtroom. Somebody had decided to set the thermostat to 62 degrees. Figuring that's how they did things in DeKalb County, Hallock formally announced, "At this time we'll call *The People versus Jack McCullough*."

For the prosecution team, it was a replay of the rape trial: Clay Campbell, Julie Trevarthen, and Victor Escarcida.

For the defense, there was the assistant public defender, Robert Carlson, and a fresh face, the newly appointed chief public defender. He was so unknown in Sycamore, he had to introduce himself. "Judge, I'm Tom McCulloch."

Everyone in the packed courtroom was perplexed. What were the odds that Jack McCullough would have as his public defender a lawyer whose last name was almost indistinguishable from his own? McCulloch the lawyer was pronounced *Mic-cull-loch*; McCullough the defendant was *Muh-KULL-uh*.

Jack McCullough was waiting in the jury room when the judge told court officers to bring him in. He wore the same clothes he'd worn at the rape trial—a dark suit over a black shirt and a maroon tie, courtesy of the Goodwill wardrobe rack. His two greatest supporters—his wife, Sue

McCullough, and stepdaughter Janey O'Connor—could not afford the airfare and were not present in court.

"At this time I would invite the State to make its opening statement if you elect to do so," Hallock said.

Campbell would handle this. "Thank you, Judge." He started by taking the courtroom back to that terrible night.

"December 3, 1957, started out as a normal day for little Maria Ridulph in the town of Sycamore, Illinois. It was the holiday season, and the Christmas spirit was in the air. She lived at 616 Archie Place here in Sycamore, just blocks away from this courthouse. She lived there with her mother and father, her two sisters Pat and Kay, and her only brother, Chuck. Little Maria was the baby of the family. She was a little girl full of energy, outgoing, sweet, and trusting. One would expect her to be so, living in Sycamore, a close-knit town of neighborliness and charm. It was a safe place, cozy, secure. Little Maria attended West Elementary School right up the street from her house. She was in the second grade."

When Maria was kidnapped by the man calling himself Johnny, an atmosphere of panic fanned out across Sycamore, Campbell said.

"Word was out. Fear is spreading. Men of all ages have joined the search to find this little girl. Women and children in Sycamore are put on lockdown. Squad cars roamed the streets announcing the danger. Porch lights are all on. Basements are searched. Attics, eaves, septic tanks. Sirens are going off. It's bedlam. All males join the search. Friends of the defendant joined the search. All the men in Sycamore joined the search but not the defendant. He is gone, Maria is gone. No Maria, no Johnny.

"The defendant didn't join the search that night or the next day, and the reason he didn't is because the evidence will show that he was the one that gave Maria that piggyback ride on that fateful night. He was the reason she was gone. This man, he kidnapped her and then he killed her.

"The search for little Maria went on for days, for weeks, and for months. It ended in tragedy on April 26, 1958, five months later. Her badly decomposed body was found in a wooded area off of U.S. Route 20 in Jo Daviess County, Illinois. Animals had fed on her. She had nothing on but a pair of socks and an open shirt. No coat, no sweater, no pants, and no underwear. Rather than being at home for the Christmas holidays, she was found over a hundred miles from her home, her family, and her town, alone in the woods dead.

"Her killer would go unidentified for over fifty years. The family would wait over half a century to learn who visited this horror upon them. The defendant thought he got away with it, but what he didn't count on was the fact that Kathy Sigman could never forget his face. He didn't count on the Illinois state police reopening the investigation, when all signs pointed to him. Kathy Sigman picked him out of a photo lineup. She had waited more than fifty years to see that face again, and she finally did. The search began for John Tessier. The trail led police to Seattle, Washington, where they located Jack Daniel McCullough, this defendant, who confirmed that he was indeed John Tessier of Sycamore, Illinois. They finally found the man who fancied little girls and dollies and piggyback rides."

When it was the turn of the defense, the opening statement came from the practiced eloquence of assistant public defender Robert Carlson. The year 1957, Carlson said, was a time of cars with fins and telephone systems with human operators. People knew one another. Then he zeroed in on what he said were the defects in the State's case.

"There is no murder weapon that has been recovered. There are no fingerprints. There is no DNA linking our client, or anyone for that matter, to the little girl's death. There are no eyewitnesses to her exact time of disappearance, seeing her leaving. There is no direct evidence." Referring to the photo of Jack McCullough picked out by Kathy Sigman Chapman, the defense attorney said, "That photo lineup did not happen close in time to the occurrence of this matter. That photo lineup happened in 2010. We think there will be issues with that photo lineup as to the photographs that were used. Jack McCullough did not commit this murder. We, as the State, are sorry that the family has waited fifty years for a resolution to this case, but the reality is that it has not been solved by charging Jack McCullough."

Carlson was done. The state called its first witness.

"The People call Charles Ridulph," said prosecutor Victor Escarcida.

Even after all this time, it was still hard to talk about. Chuck broke down when he was asked to describe Maria.

"Take your time, Mr. Ridulph," Escarcida said gently.

Chuck collected himself. "She was a very smart girl, a

gifted child. She liked to sing. She liked to read. She was a very active child, friendly, outgoing, athletic. I often described her as a tomboy, but as I think about it, she really didn't do tomboy things. She spent her time on the girl things, playing with dolls, having tea parties and things that girls do. She was a very pretty young girl, tall, slender, dark-haired, always seemed to be smiling unless I was picking on her." Chuck was shown a photo of Maria. It was taken at her seventh birthday party in the front yard at 616 Archie Place. He knew that because there were seven candles on the cake.

Escarcida brought Chuck around to the night of December 3, when eight-year-old Kathy Sigman knocked on the Ridulph door to report that Maria was missing.

"What did you think about that?"

"I didn't think anything about it. I didn't really—didn't give it another thought until shortly after that. Kathy came back and said, 'I can't find Maria.' It was then that I went and told my parents."

Chuck remembered how he and his buddy Randy Strombom went looking for Maria, searching through backyards, calling out her name. Fifteen minutes later, he returned to Archie Place.

"There was already a commotion at the house. The police were called at that point." Soon, a hundred citizens were on the manhunt. Chaos reigned. "The next day I recall going with my father to the fire station, the old fire station, where the search parties were being organized and people were being assigned areas to search. People were even carrying guns."

At Sycamore High, classes were cancelled, and the male students joined the search with Boy Scout troops.

"Now, back in 1957, do you recall the family with the last name of Tessier?"

"Yes, I do."

"What do you remember about them?"

"I remember that it was a big family. The kids went to a different school system. They were in the parochial school, the Catholic school. We were in public school. I knew who they were."

Following a break for lunch, Chuck was back on the stand to face cross-examination by McCullough's defense lawyer Robert Carlson.

"Good afternoon, Mr. Ridulph. How are you, sir?"

"Fine, thank you."

"You did say you knew the Tessiers, is that correct?"

"That's correct."

"You knew them all?"

"No, I would not have known them all."

"Did you personally play with any of the Tessier family on any occasion?"

"Not that I recall."

"Sir, Center Cross Street is now Route 23. It was Route 23 at that time as well, was it not?"

"Yes."

"So that has always been a state highway. . . . Is that right?"

"Yes."

That was all. Carlson was laying the groundwork that

Center Cross Street wasn't a quiet country roadway but a section of a busy state highway system that drew lots of traffic and commercial trucks.

As a courtesy, Judge Hallock released Chuck from his subpoena and told him, "You may have a seat here in this courtroom." Chuck stepped off the witness stand and sat next to his sister Pat. They intended to be there for the duration.

The next witness called was Detective Irene Lau of the Seattle police department. Lau was the bantamweight polygraph examiner on duty the night of McCullough's arrest and interrogation.

Clay Campbell asked, "Could you describe his demeanor when you first started speaking to him?"

"Mr. McCullough I would say was—was not very happy to be interviewed by me. He alternated between rage and calm. He was pretty angry."

"Could you tell the judge what you recall Mr. McCullough saying on that day in regards to Maria Ridulph?"

"Well, when he described her to me, he described her as being very stunningly beautiful with big brown eyes, and he stated that she was 'lovely, lovely, lovely.'"

"Detective, when Mr. McCullough said those words to you in regards to Maria Ridulph, can you describe his demeanor as he was making those statements to you?"

"Well, he appeared to be discussing her as if he was talking about someone he had been deeply, deeply in love with. His entire face changed. It softened, and his body had been quite rigidly stiff during the interview, but he just totally relaxed at this point."

Her testimony seemed to paint a stinging profile of a pedophile.

When it was Carlson's turn for cross-examination, he had considerable damage to repair.

"When you were speaking with Jack McCullough, he vehemently denied any involvement with the crime of the abduction of Maria Ridulph, isn't that correct?"

"That's correct," said Detective Lau.

"So when he was being accused of having any involvement, he would become more upset, isn't that correct?"

"That's correct."

Pam Long, a sixty-eight-year-old widow, was the next witness. Like many women of her generation in Sycamore, Pam had married her high school sweetheart, Jerry Long. He had died fifteen years ago. Pam had reached out to the Sycamore police after she read that anyone with information on Jack McCullough should contact the authorities. She left this message with the cops: "I'm calling regarding your notice in the paper and wanted you to know my name is Pam Long. It was Pam Smith. I went for a piggyback ride with Johnny." Now she was on the witness stand. After taking the oath to tell the truth, Pam sat and glanced over at McCullough. He gave her the chills.

Pam told the court that she grew up on West Exchange and Sacramento Street in Sycamore with four brothers. Her father, Roy Smith, owned two Marathon gas stations in town. Her neighbor just to the north was a grouchy old-timer she knew as "Old Man Tessier." That would have been Johnny Tessier's grandfather, Eugene Tessier, who owned the house that abutted the Smith property.

Victor Escarcida brought Pam around to one summer in the early 1950s, when she was about eight years old. She couldn't be more precise about the year.

"During this time period were you familiar with a person named Johnny in your neighborhood?"

"Yes."

"Did you see him often?"

"Yes. He was thin and he had blondish-brown hair and strange teeth, something funny about his teeth."

"What, if anything, happened between you and Johnny during this time?"

"Well, he took me for piggyback rides."

"Can you tell the court whether or not he gave you more than one?"

"Yes, he gave me more than one. Most of them were just in front of our house."

Pam recalled the last time Johnny gave her a piggyback ride.

"Describe what your father did as you were riding on Johnny's back?"

"He jerked me off his back. I got the scolding of a life—"

Before she could complete the sentence, Judge Hallock told her to stop. Recalling what her father said to her was inadmissible hearsay.

Another woman from Pam Long's generation followed her to the stand. Cheryl Crain was now seventy and still lived in Sycamore. She was about to celebrate her fiftieth wedding anniversary. In 1957, she had been Cheryl Wiley, a sophomore at Sycamore High School. Her close friend was Jan Edwards. She still recalled the events of December 3, 1957. Around 6:00 P.M., she had dinner with her parents and two siblings.

Escarcida asked, "Now, after dinnertime, what were your plans that evening?"

"That evening Janice and I were going to go to her father's hobby shop and decorate the store for Christmas." The hobby shop was on State Street, next to the movie theater.

"To the best of your recollection who was Janice dating at that time?"

"John Tessier."

"Did you know who he was?"

"Yes, I knew who he was."

"During this time did you know the Tessiers?"

"I knew a couple of the sisters because they were in my 4-H group that my mother led."

"And when you arrived at the store, did you see (Jan Edwards) at the store?"

"Yes."

Cheryl testified that her curfew was 10:00 P.M. Escarcida asked, "Now, how are you going to get home that evening?"

"Her boyfriend was going to give us a ride home from the shop."

"And as you were decorating the shop with Janice what, if anything, unusual happened?"

"We heard the loudspeakers on the police cars going through town. We didn't know what had happened, but we knew something was going on—not long after that my father called."

Mr. Wiley said that a little girl had been kidnapped and the town was going crazy.

"After the phone call we locked the doors of the store and waited for him to come, my father." It didn't take long because her house was less than four blocks from the store.

"Where did you go after that?"

"Janice and I both went with my father. He took Janice home in the car and then he took me home. We were in a lockdown situation as far as being children. We stayed home."

Later that night, Cheryl said a band of volunteers came to her house on DeKalb Avenue and conducted a thorough search, from the attic to the basement; even the coal bin was inspected. The lockdown extended into many months. Cheryl said she was permitted to go to school, but she was under strict instructions to come right home, and she couldn't go out at night.

"Now, while you were at the shop with Janice do you recall whether or not John Tessier called the shop?"

"I only recall one phone call, and that was my father."

"Can you tell the court whether or not you recall seeing John Tessier at the shop?"

"No, I did not."

"Or stopping by the shop?"

"No, I did not."

"Did you see John Tessier that night?"

"No, I did not."

"Miss Crain, was John Tessier supposed to pick both you and Janice up that night?"

"Yes."

Escarcida turned to the judge. "I have nothing further, Your Honor."

Cross-examination was conducted by Regina Harris's replacement, Tom McCulloch, the new public defender. With everyone eager to assess his courtroom skills, comparisons to Regina Harris were inevitable. McCulloch's technique was cultured and well mannered but combative when it had to be, and he got right to the point. How could Cheryl Crain's memory of the events of December 3, 1957, remain so crystal clear?

"If I was to ask you what you had for breakfast or what classes you had that day, could you tell me?"

"I couldn't tell you that."

But Cheryl was unwavering in her testimony, and when Victor Escarcida got another turn during redirect, he asked a question that showed he grasped the special place that Maria's kidnapping held in Sycamore history.

"Miss Crain, defense counsel asked you some questions regarding your recollection of this night, December 3?"

"Mmm."

"And how you were able to recall that night. Why do you recall that day so vividly?"

"I can remember where I was, what I was doing the day that President Kennedy was shot. I can remember and recall where I was, who I was with, and what I was doing vividly the night Maria was kidnapped."

With that, Cheryl Crain wrapped up her compelling testimony.

Later that night, in a letter to his stepdaughter Janey O'Connor, Jack McCullough reflected on the opening day of his trial.

The first day was not damaging to me except for being blamed for the horrible kidnap and brutal murder of a beautiful child that was so full of life. I got a glimpse of the body remains and wish I never had. That picture is now forever etched in my mind.

This trial is perfectly designed to convict me. I can't even defend myself because all the FBI witnesses and agents are dead. All we can do is take apart their witnesses and hope for a not guilty. The trial will be over (perhaps) by the time this letter reaches you. No matter what the outcome, know that my love for you and the family is the forever kind and I will prevail—God willing. Love, Jack.

39

....

DAY TWO

Kathy and Mike Chapman left their house in St. Charles, Illinois, early Tuesday morning. Kathy was very nervous. She was going to be the first witness called to the stand, at 9:30 A.M.

They stopped by their favorite breakfast place, Gabby's Kitchen, for scrambled eggs, sausage, toast, and a fruit salad, then proceeded to make the twenty-five-mile drive to Sycamore. The courthouse was a hectic scene of TV satellite trucks and reporters, and a large crowd lined up to get into room 300 for day two of the McCullough trial. In the hallway, a burly fellow with a shaved head and prosthetic arm went up to Mike and introduced himself.

"I'm Bob Tessier," he said. "I'm the little brother."

Bob Tessier had come up from his home in Kentucky prepared to testify as a prosecution witness at his brother's murder trial, and he was eager for a conviction.

Mike Chapman found it extraordinary and thanked Bob for coming. "I think it's taking a tremendous amount of courage for you to be here."

Mike was introduced to the other Tessier siblings: Katheran was there with her husband, Joe, the psychologist, and even Jeanne was there. Mike was beginning to understand the family dynamics. It was, he says, "an uplifting experience because here was a family that really wanted to do right." They exchanged addresses and promised to stay in touch.

At 9:30, court was called into session. The thermostat setting in the courtroom had been elevated to a more comfortable 73.8 degrees. Judge Hallock told the prosecution team to call its next witness.

"The People would call Kathy Sigman," said Julie Trevarthen.

Kathy Sigman Chapman entered the courtroom wearing a black dress and conservative sweater. Special arrangements had been made for her husband to take a seat in the gallery where she could see him. Kathy was pleased that Julie Trevarthen would be conducting the direct examination. Over the course of the investigation, they'd formed a special bond. "She was like a daughter to me," Kathy would later say.

Kathy was sixty-two and still working, assembling parts for a small motor company. She had three grown children. When she was a little girl, she had lived at 646 ½ Archie Place in Sycamore, five houses from Maria Ridulph's.

"What did you and Maria like to play? What did you do together?" Trevarthen asked.

"Played with dolls. We played across the street on the

swing set at the school. We played hopscotch, kick the can. All those little games that kids do back in the fifties."

Trevarthen steered her to the events of December 3, 1957.

"It was a Tuesday," Kathy recalled. "It was a school day. I went to school and came home, and Maria and I played after we got home from school at her house."

"Did you at some point go home?"

"I went home for dinner at probably five o'clock, had dinner at five thirty."

"Did you see Maria again after you went home and ate dinner?"

"Yes. It was starting to snow outside, so I asked if I could go back to Maria's house and play in the snow. Maria and myself went out to play Duck the Cars."

"OK. Can you describe for the court exactly what the game of Duck the Cars entailed, how you played it?"

"Sure. It's a game where we would run around and hang onto the pole and wait for the cars coming up the street so we could run behind the tree and hide before those lights of the cars would hit our bodies and light us up."

"That evening of December 3, 1957, what, if anything, happened while you and Maria were playing Duck the Cars?"

"There was a person, a man that came down from the south walking by himself and approached us."

"And when this man approached you and Maria, what, if anything, happened?"

"He asked if we liked dolls and would we like a piggy-back ride."

Kathy shot a look at the defense table, establishing eye contact with Jack McCullough. "I wanted him to know what I thought of him," she said later.

"Can you please describe for the court what this man looked like?"

"This man had a slender face with hair that had a flip in the side—and he had large teeth. This man was wearing a sweater with lots of colors in it."

It was pitch-black outside, but Kathy said she got a good look at Johnny because they were standing directly under a streetlight.

"Did he introduce himself to you?"

"He introduced himself as Johnny."

"Did you know who this person Johnny was?"

"No, I had never seen Johnny before."

She described how Maria had hopped onto Johnny for a piggyback ride, and when she'd gotten back had run to her house to find a doll for him.

"As Maria went home to get her doll, what, if anything, did you and Johnny do?"

"I do not remember anything except for watching her go home and waiting for her to come back."

"And while you were standing at the corner watching Maria what, if anything did you observe?"

"I observed Johnny."

Maria was gone for "a minute or two," Kathy said, and when she returned she was holding a doll.

"What, if anything, happens next?"

"I did not have my mittens when I went out to play, and my hands were cold, and I went home to get my mittens."

Trevarthen asked Judge Hallock for permission to approach the witness box. She had a photograph she wanted to show Kathy, marked "People's Exhibit No. 78."

"My goodness!" Kathy exclaimed. The photo was of Kathy when she was a little girl, just a day or two after Maria's kidnapping, posing for a photographer from the *Chicago Sun-Times*. She was holding up her hands and showing off her mittens. Kathy had forgotten the photo existed.

"Thank you, ma'am. Now, after you went home to get your mittens, did you go back to the corner?"

"I went back to the corner looking for Maria. She should still be there."

"And was she there?"

"She was not there."

Kathy told how she'd knocked on Maria's side door and told Chuck Ridulph she couldn't find his sister. Then she'd gone up the block again calling out Maria's name, returned once more to the Ridulph house, then scurried home.

"I had to tell my mom about Johnny and Maria."

Kathy described how for the next three to four months the FBI and state and local police were with her every day, pretty much never leaving her side—even when she went to Sunday school.

"It was being taken to watch lineups of men, of men in books, of any suspects they could have me view." She said she was shown thousands of mug shots.

"Were you ever shown a photograph of the man named Johnny who stood under that light on the corner with you?"

"No, I had never seen his picture."

Flash forward to September 9, 2010, when Special Agent Brion Hanley of the Illinois state police showed Kathy a photo lineup from 1957 of six young men from Sycamore. Kathy said Hanley had laid them out one at a time on her coffee table.

"Where you able to identify one of those photographs as being the man named Johnny who was at that corner on December 3, 1957, with yourself and Maria?"

"Yes, I was."

"And can you please point to the photograph that you picked out as being Johnny?"

"This photo right there." The photo was marked "1D." It had Kathy's signature on the face where Hanley had asked her to sign it.

"Ma'am, when was the last time you have seen that face?"

"1957, December third."

"Thank you, ma'am. I don't have any further questions for this witness, Judge."

Kathy Sigman Chapman was the prosecution's star witness, and Tom McCulloch knew he had to knock some major holes in her story or the case could be lost. He began his cross-examination with the utmost civility.

"May I refer to you as Kathy?"

"Yes, you can."

He got Kathy to catalogue life in 1957 in her old neighborhood. The schoolyard of the elementary school she attended was just twenty-five yards from her house. The playground had a swing set and two slides, one for little kids, the other for the older ones. Slightly to the east was Center Cross Street, where the Tessiers had lived. All the neighborhood youngsters would shop for candy and treats at Ferguson's, a small grocery store. Kathy couldn't remember whether her family had had a TV set in 1957, but in those bygone days, girls and boys her age played outdoors more than today's youngsters.

"How much snow fell that day?"

"A trace. It had just started snowing—the first snowfall of the year."

Now Tom McCulloch got to the heart of the defense case—the timeline.

"In terms of clock time, what time was it when you got there?"

"Before six. Right before six, I would say." She said she was playing Duck the Cars for about "fifteen, twenty minutes, half an hour."

"And what time was it when you left to go get your mittens?"

"I do not know what time it was."

"Now, when you met the strange man on the street December 3, about what time was that?"

"Around six o'clock."

"And about what time do you recall it being when your parents called police that night?"

"Probably 7:30."

"Now, the next thing after you kids have been playing outside, you said you saw a man coming from the south?"

"Yes."

"And it was a man, not a boy?"

"It was an older person."

McCulloch stood corrected. "'An older person.' OK. And the man walked up to you and Maria and asked you do you like dolls and would you like a piggyback ride?"

"First of all, he told us his name was Johnny."

"OK. Nothing unusual about having a conversation with the person you didn't know?"

"No. This was a safe time in our lives."

"And we'll get back to that, but within a matter of hours you were speaking to some policemen about what it is you had seen, is that correct?"

"Yes."

"And those policemen were asking you to give descriptive information, is that correct?"

"That's correct."

"Would it be fair to say that there is a difference in your mind between twenty-four and twenty-five years old and seventeen?"

In Kathy's original description to authorities, she had put the kidnapper's age at around twenty-four or twenty-five. Jack McCullough had just turned eighteen. Kathy was smart enough to see where this was heading.

"Not as an eight-year-old child, no."

"How tall was he?"

"To a little kid he was a grown-up to me."

"How heavy was he?"

"Not very heavy. A slender person."

"In terms of pounds?"

Kathy was getting riled. "I'm a child of eight. I would say probably one-hundred fifty."

"What kind of pants did he have on?"

"In my recollection it would have been jeans."

"Anything unusual about his belt or belt buckle?"

Kathy rolled her eyes. "He had a sweater on."

Now it was the lawyer's turn to sound irritated. "That's hardly the answer to the question about belt buckle."

"I don't remember the belt buckle at this time. I do not remember a belt buckle."

"How about tattoos?"

"He had a sweater on."

"You yelled her name, you wandered around for a while, and then you went back to your mom's house, correct?"

"Yes."

"In the trace amounts of snow that had fallen, did you notice any footprints?"

"I went home—no, I didn't notice any footprints."

Next, Tom McCulloch asked Kathy if she could recall having observed a lineup in Madison, Wisconsin.

"And you were driven, I think, by FBI agents to Wisconsin to view a lineup, were you not?"

"To Madison, Wisconsin."

"And I assume that for a seven-year-old kid or eight in your case getting a drive with the FBI is a memorable experience?"

Kathy disagreed. "It was getting to be very old at this time. I was not happy to be having to do this all day every day."

"Did your parents go?"

"I think my father went."

Kathy said she could still recall eyeballing the suspects in Madison from behind a one-way mirror.

"And how many people were on the other side?"

"Six or seven."

"You told them that you recognized someone, is that correct?"

"No."

"Did you pick someone out?"

"I do not believe I picked anybody out."

Kathy said she had no memory of pointing to a farm-hand in the lineup and telling authorities in Madison, "That's him." The man was later cleared after his boss vouched for his whereabouts the night Maria was kidnapped.

The array of six vintage photos that Brion Hanley presented to Kathy in 2010 now came under scrutiny. McCulloch asked Kathy how it came to be that she picked out the defendant Jack McCullough.

"That picture was slightly different than other pictures, is it not—is that fair to say?"

"No," answered Kathy. "It was the picture of Johnny."

"But it's different than the other five pictures, correct?"

"No."

Tom McCulloch showed Kathy the six photos that Brion Hanley had laid out for her like a deck of cards. They were all clean shaven, young white men dressed formally in dark suits, white shirts, and ties, shot against a white background. Then he showed the witness the photo of Jack McCullough.

"Background is what?"

"Background is dark." She quickly added, "I wasn't looking at background."

"I'm just asking you what you saw at the time you make your pick. No suit, correct?"

Kathy had to agree. "No suit."

Had the state police formulated the photo lineup in such a way that it sign-posted the photo marked "1D" as Jack McCullough?

When it was Julie Trevarthen's turn for cross-examination, she asked, "Those photographs that you were shown, they were all black-and-white photographs, correct?"

"That's correct."

"And they were all of males?"

"They were all of males."

"Do they all appear to be about the same age?"

"Yes."

"All the individuals in those photographs were formally dressed, is that correct?"

"Correct."

"They all appear to be clean-cut. Would that be fair?"

"That would be a fair assumption."

Trevarthen proceeded to heap ridicule on the defense theory that the photo lineup had been engineered to finger Jack McCullough.

"Did the photograph that you picked out—did the photograph have a black eye?"

"No."

"Was there a tattoo on his face?"

"No."

Her work done, Julie Trevarthen called the next witness: Katheran Tessier Caulfield.

Katheran was sixty-seven years old and had gotten out of Sycamore nearly forty years before to live in Minnesota. She was now retired after working for many years as a secretary in an architectural firm. She had two daughters, the youngest aged forty-two and the oldest about to turn forty-five. Katheran's cry of anguish after her brother's acquittal of rape had shocked spectators in court six months earlier. Now she had returned to Sycamore to testify for the prosecution at her brother's murder trial.

Julie Trevarthen asked, "Is there a particular item of clothing that the defendant frequently wore back then in 1957?"

"Yes. It was a sweater my mother knit."

"Can you describe that sweater for us?"

"It had multicolors on it."

Katheran said that in December 1957, she was a seventh-grader at St. Mary's Catholic school and she knew and played with Maria Ridulph even though there was a big difference in their ages. Kick the can and games of hide-and-seek usually took place at the dead-end street on Roosevelt Court. "We all played together. I several times was in her house, played with she and Kathy and the other kids in the neighborhood. My sister Jeanne and I. I mean, we were a small neighborhood."

"Did Maria ever come over to your house to play?"

"No."

"Was Kathy Sigman ever in your house?" It was a pivotal question.

"No."

"To your knowledge did the defendant ever play with Maria Ridulph?"

"No. He's five-and-a-half years older than I am."

"So it would have been unusual?"

"Very unusual."

Katheran testified that the night of December 3, 1957, she'd skipped dinner to attend a 4-H meeting in the city of DeKalb, where she listened to rock-and-roll music and had a bite to eat. Her father, Ralph Tessier, had driven her over at around five that evening. The gathering had come to an end at seven or thereabouts.

"My dad picked me up and brought me home," she said. Driving down DeKalb Avenue into the city limits of Sycamore, Katheran said, "I noticed there were a lot of police cars, sheriff's cars with the lights flashing." Turning left on Center Cross Street, it was bedlam. "There were people outside everywhere, walking and looking, you know, in bushes. They were everywhere."

"Did you know why?"

"Well, I asked my dad. I said, 'What happened? Why are all these police cars here?'"

When Ralph pulled up to 227 Center Cross Street, Katheran says she darted into her house. Jeanne, her little brother, Bob, and her mother, Eileen Tessier, were all inside.

"So the defendant was not home?"

"No."

"What was going on in your house when you walked in?"

"My mother was very upset and so was my dad."

Katheran said her father wedged a piece of plywood against the side door to secure it from being opened from the outside and then he and Eileen joined the search for Maria. The front door was locked from the inside. Because Ralph couldn't find the key, the children were told to sit in the living room, never leave each other's sight, and wait for their parents to return. Ralph instructed everyone to stay in one place. When Katheran finally conked out at around 11:45 at night, her parents were still out there looking for Maria.

Trevarthen asked, "Now before you went to bed at 11:30 or 11:45 had the defendant come home?"

"No."

"When was the last time you had seen the defendant?"

"Probably a day or two before that, I think."

Next, Katheran recalled how two FBI agents had come to the Tessier house several days after Maria's disappearance, and Katheran listened as the agents asked Eileen and Ralph Tessier about their son John's whereabouts on the night of December 3.

"What did she say?" Trevarthen asked.

"She said he had been home."

"And it was your prior testimony that the defendant was not home, correct?"

"That's correct."

Katheran found it difficult to go on.

"Judge, could we get some Kleenex for the witness?" Trevarthen asked.

A box of tissues was quickly produced, and Katheran dabbed at the corner of her eyes, which were glistening with tears. It was almost unbearable to watch. With her testimony, Katheran was implicating her brother in the murder of a little girl and her parents in the cover-up of the crime. It was a searing experience for the witness. Trevarthen decided it might be best to move on to another serious topic—establishing Jack McCullough's connections to Jo Daviess County, where Maria's body had been dumped.

"Let's step away from December 3. As a family when you were growing up in Sycamore, during the summer was there anywhere that you as a family went as a type of vacation?"

"We'd make day trips."

"And were there typical places where you went?"

"I think it was called Apple River Valley. We went to Starved Rock State Park. Every summer there was a day trip to somewhere. My aunt Mary mostly would take us, and my mother." Apple River is a state park in Jo Daviess County celebrated in northern Illinois for its hiking, fishing, and scenic river bluffs. The Tessiers would always leave on a Saturday and come back the same day. Sometimes Aunt Mary drove, and sometimes Ralph did the driving. All the Tessiers would climb in the car, and off they'd go.

"Did the defendant attend those trips as well?"

"Yes."

"I just have one last question for you. The multicolor

sweater that you referred to that your mom knit that the defendant wore—"

"Yes."

"Did you ever see that sweater again after December 3, 1957?"

"No, I did not."

Tom McCulloch sprang to his feet. He got right into it with Katheran and asked her about the time Ralph and Eileen lied to the FBI about their son's whereabouts on December 3.

"And it's your recollection now that both your mother and father said that your brother was home?"

"That's correct."

"Now, did you step forward and say, 'Mr. Policeman, I have some information for you' or anything like that?"

Katheran shook her head. "I was twelve years old. I didn't do that to my father."

"I didn't ask that question."

"No, I didn't."

"You didn't step up and speak up?"

"No. I would never do that."

With that, Katheran left the stand. She was back after lunch break, this time as a spectator. Julie Trevarthen asked the judge's permission for Katheran to observe the rest of the trial. When the defense raised no objection, the judge released her from her subpoena.

"Thank you, sir, very much," Katheran said. She took a seat.

Now it was Jeanne Tessier's turn to take the stand. Her memories of the ill-fated rape trial would never go away, but this time, Jeanne was a fully cooperating witness at her brother's murder trial. When Julie Trevarthen asked her about the night of Maria's kidnapping, she bolstered Katheran's story.

It was after supper, she said. "Some men came to the side door of the house off the driveway and knocked and asked for my dad and asked him to go open up the hardware store where he worked in town so that some of the men could get flashlights and lanterns to go look for Maria Ridulph." Old Man Hagen may have owned the hardware store, but just the same, Ralph put on his heavy coat and followed the men downtown, where he handed out the entire inventory of flashlights and lanterns. To do otherwise would have risked inciting the wrath of the citizens' army that was being formed to look for Maria. Eileen also got dressed and went to the armory, where the women of Sycamore were gathering to make coffee and sandwiches for the search parties.

Jeanne testified that she had dozed off on the couch when her mother, Eileen, finally returned. "I was sound asleep. When my mother knocked on the door, it was the middle of the night, and I let her in."

Like Katheran, Jeanne testified that she was home when two FBI agents had come calling several days later and asked Eileen about her son, John.

"She was asked if he came home that night."

"And you recall what your mom told the officers?"

"She said he did, yes."

"And it's your testimony that he did not, correct?"

"It is my testimony that he did not."

Assistant public defender Robert Carlson took on the task of cross-examining Jeanne. They knew each other from the rape trial, when Carlson served alongside Regina Harris, and he was well aware of what a compelling witness she made in court.

"Miss Tessier, how are you this afternoon, ma'am?"

"I'll be better when this is done."

"I'm sure."

Carlson had questions about December 3, 1957. Jeanne testified that after her mother had come home from the armory, she had gone up to her bedroom and tried to fall asleep.

"And your father had not come home when you went to bed?"

Jeanne answered, "No, but I heard him come home sometime later."

Carlson pounced. "You heard someone come home later in the night?" Evidently, he was attempting to validate Jack McCullough's story that he had climbed into the house through an open window when everyone was sleeping.

Jeanne dismissively shot it down. "I heard my dad come home sometime later and my mom and dad speaking downstairs."

Jeanne acknowledged that she might have seen her brother on December 4.

"So you might have seen him. You're not sure?"

"I'm not sure."

"So I take it then you're not sure what time you might have seen him, either. Is that correct?"

"Sir, I did not see my brother the night Maria was

missing, and I did not see him in the morning when I woke up."

"But you might have seen him the next day and you don't recall?"

"I might have."

That was all, but the defense signaled it might consider calling Jeanne back as a witness. Judge Hallock told her that she could leave the stand but added, "You'll be called again, sounds like."

Julie Trevarthen stood. "The People would call Janet Tessier."

The time had come for the third Tessier sister to take the stand.

Janet Tessier had started it all. Without her e-mail to the state police in 2008, this murder trial would not be happening. At age fifty-five, Janet was earning a living driving a taxi. Sitting in the spectator's gallery was her daughter, Mary.

"Ma'am, your parents are deceased, correct?"

"That's right."

"When did your mother die?"

"In January of 1994. She had cancer."

Janet said her mother was being cared for at home but then had to be taken to Kishwaukee Community Hospital, in the city of DeKalb, because she'd kept pulling out her IV and catheter and required professional nursing care.

"Something unusual occurred when yourself and your sister Mary were in the hospital room with your mother?"

"Yes."

"What did your mother say?"

"She said, 'Janet?'"

"And where were you sitting when this happened?"

"At the foot of the bed. I was sitting in a chair."

"And you said that your sister Mary was present as well, correct?"

"Yes."

"And when your mom called out 'Janet,' what, if anything, did you do?"

"I jumped out of the chair and went to her bedside and leaned down so I could—she could focus in on my face."

"OK. Were your mother's eyes open?"

"Yes."

"Once you get up to the head of the bed what, if anything, did your mother say or do you say next?"

"She grabbed my wrist with her hand and she said, 'Those two little girls and the one that disappeared, John did it. John did it and you have to tell someone. You have to tell someone.'"

"Now, after your mom said this to you, did you at any point contact law enforcement?"

"The Sycamore police department. I spoke to a detective."

After zero follow-up from the local police, Janet said she notified the FBI field office in Chicago a year or two later.

"What happened when you contacted the FBI?"

"Nothing."

"After that did you ever contact law enforcement?"

"Yes, in 2008." This was the e-mail she sent to the Illinois state police.

"Did you receive any response from them?"

"Yes. Very quickly received a phone call."

"Did you then after that have an opportunity to speak with them?"

"Yes. I met with them in Elgin, Illinois."

"And did you provide them with information?"

"Yes."

Defense attorney Tom McCulloch knew he had to go after Janet on the issue of credibility and Eileen Tessier's deathbed confession. He asked, "Near the end, you were present with your mother in the hospital?"

"That's right."

"Is it fair to say that your mother never told you how she knew or claimed to know whatever it was she was saying?"

"That's true."

"So we're simply repeating words for which we have no context. Is that fair?"

Janet looked puzzled. "I'm not sure I understand how I can answer that question."

"You have answered it, I guess. You don't know how she knew whatever it was she knew?"

"I do know."

It was turning into a verbal tug-of-war.

"You don't know—she never told you how she knew?"

Janet had to concede the point. "No, sir. I didn't ask."

"You didn't ask. She didn't tell?"

"I'm not a cop. I was the daughter."

"Who did you contact in the Sycamore police department first?"

"Don't remember the name, sir."

"What time or what day did you call them?"

"I can't remember that, either, sir."

"And did you contact them by phone or in person?"

"By phone."

"Did the person on the other end of the line identify himself or herself?"

"I don't remember, sir. I know that a detective came to my apartment."

There was further lack of specifics regarding her call to the FBI.

Tom McCulloch asked, "Can you tell me who you talked to?"

"I don't remember. It was a man. I did remember that."

Now the defense lawyer zeroed in on Eileen's deathbed confession.

"You had said that part of the reason why she had been readmitted to the hospital was an inability, if you will, to care for herself or keep the IVs inside of her, is that right?"

"That's right."

McCulloch asked, "Would it be fair to say that your mother at the time when she was in Kishwaukee and speaking to you was disturbed emotionally?"

"That's a fair assessment."

"Thank you." He had no further questions.

Julie Trevarthen had to do some damage control. "Counsel just asked you if your mom was disturbed when she was in the hospital and you said yes."

"Yes."

Trevarthen asked, "Can you explain to us what you mean by that?"

"Initially, when she was preparing to die, she accepted that and she was very calm, but the closer to actual death that she approached, she was very agitated, emotional, and expressed a great deal of guilt."

"When your mom made the statement to you about Maria?"

"Yes."

"And about the defendant?"

"Yes."

"Was your mother coherent when she made the statement?"

"Yep." Janet looked at the judge. "May I explain why I know this?"

Bench trials are traditionally less formal than trials by jury, so Hallock said, "Sure." He sounded curious to know the answer himself.

"She would sometimes be very lucid and very clear, and there were other times when she was disoriented and would sleep, and at this particular moment I could tell by her face and her eyes and how she was focusing on me and how she was speaking that she was lucid at this point. That's in my own opinion."

This Tessier sister was done for the day.

There was one other witness of note on day two of the trial.

Sitting at the defendant's table, Jack McCullough did a double take when he saw an elderly gent approaching the witness stand. It was his high school buddy from bygone days, Dennis Twadell. Hard to believe this was the same scrawny kid he knew growing up in Sycamore. The fellow taking the stand was seventy-three years old and weighed way more than 300 pounds. Judge Hallock warned the hulking Twadell about the two steps he had to climb to reach the witness chair. The bailiff brought Twadell a glass of water. Everyone tried to be as accommodating as possible. Over at the defense table, McCullough gave his friend from long ago a wink to say hello.

Twadell testified how he had had two best friends before dropping out of high school. There was Jack Manis, who was his hunting and fishing pal, and there was John Tessier, who was the buddy he did everything else with.

Victor Escarcida handled direct examination.

"Now, in the year 1957, can you tell the court among whom in your circle of friends had a car back then?"

"Not a whole lot of us. I didn't. John had a '48 Plymouth." It was a two-door, battleship-gray coupe with a flashy set of '55 Buick hubcaps on the tires.

"To the best of your recollection, did John Tessier let anyone drive his car?"

"No. I don't recall him ever letting anyone drive his car. I think it was an insurance issue."

"Do you recall what John Tessier would wear in the wintertime?"

"Most of the time he did have some flannel shirts, but a lot of the time when it was cold it would be sweaters, sometimes a solid color or a multicolored sweater." The sweaters were for the most part crewneck. Green was John's favorite color because of his Irish heritage. The night of December 3, 1957, Twadell said, he was home on North Main Street when a pal, Dave Fredericks, called and told him that Maria Ridulph was missing. Twadell didn't know the Ridulphs very well, but they went to the same church, St. John. Dave Fredericks told him that search parties were in the process of being organized.

"Now, when you found out that Maria went missing, what, if anything, did you do that night?"

"Well, I called—called John."

"Tessier?"

"And—yes. And he was not at home."

40

....

DAY THREE

On the third day of the trial, the methodical but circumstantial case being constructed by the prosecution took a surprising turn when a prisoner named Christopher Diaz was called to the stand.

Diaz was brought into the courtroom wearing belly chains and encircled by court officers. The judge was taking no chances with this fellow. A detective positioned himself next to Diaz, even as he took the witness stand, in the event he made any sudden moves.

"Sir, you're currently in the custody of the DeKalb County sheriff, correct?" asked prosecutor Julie Trevarthen.

"Yes."

Diaz was a twenty-one-year-old menace with stringy black hair down to his shoulders and tattoos across his neck and arms. Based on his criminal record, it seemed that he was one of those offenders who couldn't stay out of trouble. When he was seventeen, he'd been arrested for "mob action" for his role in chasing and stabbing an acquaintance twenty-two times at a party fueled by out-of-control drinking. He'd pled to a misdemeanor. He also had a conviction for possession of a phony ID card. Two months before McCullough's murder trial, Diaz's criminal history had taken a sharp turn into serious felony when a DeKalb city police officer saw him on the street late at night with a thirteen-year-old girl. A curfew in force in DeKalb made it illegal for anyone under seventeen to be outdoors after midnight without a parent or responsible adult. When the girl was questioned, she told cops she'd met Diaz on the Internet three months earlier, and they'd had consensual sex at least three times. Diaz was charged with aggravated criminal sexual abuse of a minor.

From his perch at the defense table, Jack McCullough sneered at the prisoner he'd first gotten to know during his incarceration at the county jail in Sycamore. The six inmates in Cellblock G shared a common room where they ate and watched TV. "Mexican gang-banger" is how McCullough contemptuously described the witness. Diaz had written a large letter A on his prison jumpsuit and was questioned about being a suspected member of the notorious Almighty Ambrose street gang. He denied any association with it.

On September 4, 2012—six days before the start of McCullough's murder trial—Diaz had written a letter to Clay Campbell concerning a conversation he claimed to have overheard on September 1 between McCullough and another inmate, identified in court only as John Doe to protect his identity.

"Where were you when you overheard this conversation?" Trevarthen asked Diaz.

Diaz said he was in his cell on the lower bunk wearing a set of headphones and listening to music when Jack McCullough stepped in to say hello to John Doe. Diaz said he lowered the volume on his headset so he could eavesdrop on the conversation.

"He started talking about his case to John Doe."

"OK. And what did he say?"

"He was saying about how he was giving the little girl, the victim, a piggyback ride and he—he ran with her down this alley [when] the other girl that was there went inside the house to grab the mittens."

"What did you hear the defendant say to John Doe at that point?"

"That he had the victim in his house for quite a while and that his mom knew about it."

The next day, September 2, Diaz continued, the prisoners of Cellblock G ate dinner at the usual time, 4:30, and then, at 6:00 at night, as he lay on his bunk listening to music, Jack McCullough stepped in to chew the fat with John Doe again. Diaz says he lowered the volume on his headset to listen to the conversation.

"He starts describing about his case, they start saying that he strangled [Maria] with the wire and he did the motion of like kind of holding a wire." The belly cuffs were removed so that Diaz could demonstrate McCullough supposedly showing John Doe how he'd held a ligature in each hand and yanked it around Maria's throat.

It was testimony at odds with the results of the 2011 autopsy, which revealed that Maria had been killed with a knife that had been plunged into her three times, in the throat and chest. There was no medical evidence that she had been strangled, unless the original autopsy in 1958 had missed it. Was Diaz lying? Or was Jack McCullough muddying the waters?

On September 3, McCullough appeared one more time, right after dinner. This time, Diaz says, he was in his cell drawing on a sketch pad when McCullough came in and started telling John Doe about the first car he'd ever owned, the one with the flames that looked like wings painted on the side. McCullough couldn't stop talking about that car. According to Diaz, McCullough said he had told investigators that he had sold the car when he hadn't, "just to throw people off."

"What, if anything, did the defendant say next?"

"Well, they were talking about legal stuff . . . just talking about like how mad he was at the state's attorney Mr. Clay Campbell, that he wanted to kill him. Like you can tell he was mad because his face goes red and he put his hands in two fists like he was really angry at him."

September 4 found Diaz killing time in the common room in Cellblock G when he saw McCullough wandering into John Doe's cell around two in the afternoon. Diaz casually returned to the cell and reached into a bin where he stored tea bags to make a cup.

"Jack said that the state's attorney offered him a deal. He didn't say what kind of deal. He specifically said, 'Fuck that.'" Diaz claimed McCullough was boasting that "the State has no evidence whatsoever, only his mom who passed away and his sister who he referred to as a 'dumb bitch.'"

Trevarthen asked Diaz, "Sir, has the state's attorney's office offered you anything in return for your testimony here today?"

"No, they have not."

"Have any promises of any kind been made to you?"

"No."

Diaz maintained he'd written the letter to Clay Campbell because it was "the right thing to do."

Defense attorney Tom McCulloch was itching to get a crack at this guy.

"Mr. Diaz, let me start in the year 2009, if that's OK. Do remember that year?"

"Excuse me?"

"Do you remember that year?"

"Who?"

"The year 2009?"

"Yes."

"Do you remember being charged with a crime of stabbing a person?"

"I was charged with mob action and battery."

"And you were charged with mob action because you were with other people at the time, is that right?"

"Yes."

"Those other people, were they gang members?"

"That I know of, yeah."

Tom McCulloch had to scratch his head at the response. "You what?"

"Yes."

It turned out that Diaz's immigration status in the United States was shaky at best, and he admitted he was worried that, because of the criminal charges pending against him, he could face deportation.

McCulloch followed up. "You believe that your assistance in this case might help you with the immigration people?"

"No."

"Now, in 2010, when you had your fraudulent identification card, you pled guilty to that, too, is that right?"

"Yes."

"It wasn't the only thing that you pled guilty to in 2010, though, was it?"

"Excuse me?"

"Right. How about the unlawful contact with street gang members?"

"Yeah, that too."

"That too?"

"Yeah."

The inmate known as "John Doe" was up next. He'd been so apprehensive that word of his testifying would leak to the prison grapevine, he insisted that, in return for his cooperation, the prosecution obtain a court order requiring all parties to refer to him only as "John Doe." Like Diaz, he was escorted to the witness stand under heavy guard and in belly cuffs. Judge Hallock conveyed a tinge of pity when he told John Doe to raise his restricted right hand and be sworn in—"to the best of your ability."

John Doe was another loser with a violent criminal past. He said that on August 30, 2012, Jack McCullough had gone over to him where he was sitting at a table in the common room.

"He introduced himself to me. Didn't say much, you know, asked me if I had seen anything on TV or heard of him, and I told him no."

Making friendly conversation, McCullough asked John Doe why he was in jail. Doe answered that he was serving a life sentence in state prison following his 1986 conviction for a home invasion and murdering a woman with a screwdriver. He'd been temporarily transferred to the DeKalb County Jail in Sycamore to attend a court hearing in which he was seeking a reduced sentence. McCullough's curiosity was aroused. A few days later, as John Doe lay on the top bunk, McCullough ambled into his cell. He was eager to hear more about the dystopian hell that convicted child molesters faced in the state penitentiary system, which is where he'd end up if he was convicted of murdering Maria Ridulph.

"He asked me what it would be like for him in there, was there any way that I could protect him to make sure nothing happened to him there. I informed him, you know, probably not." John Doe had the correct credentials for such personal services. Twice, in state prison, he'd been convicted of possession of a homemade shank. Within the

Illinois Department of Corrections he was designated STG, for Security Threat Group.

John Doe claimed that McCullough started blabbing about what had really happened on December 3, 1957.

"He said at first that he met with the little girl along with another little girl and one of the girls had to go inside to get her gloves or her mitts. And at that time, he either had the little girl on his back or he carried her and ran down the side of an alley behind a building."

"OK," said Julie Trevarthen, encouraging John Doe to go on with his story.

"And he slipped and fell, and he said that the little girl hit her head and started crying or yelling, so I asked—he said it was an accident. I said, 'Well, why didn't you tell anybody?' He said because they wouldn't believe him. And then he got quiet. He didn't say much, and then he said that he went to the back of his house, crawled on top of the garbage can or something and pulled the little girl inside of the window and had her inside the bedroom." John Doe said he found the story hard to swallow. He says he told McCullough, "If you're going to talk to me, don't try to blow smoke up my ass."

"What, if anything, did he tell you about who was home when he dragged this little girl through the window?"

"He never said, never said whether anybody was in the home at the time. However, he did say that his mother knew that he had the child in the home, but he didn't get into whether . . . she knew the child was there when the child was there or learned about it later and that his mother despised him."

"Sir, what, if anything else, did the defendant say to you?"

"He told me that he choked her. Then he later changed it up and told me that he strangled her with a wire."

John Doe testified that McCullough also opened up about how he'd managed to sneak Maria's body out of Sycamore.

"He said that he had a 1948 Ford Coupe, I believe it was, with fire striping on it that he painted there hisself. He said that he lied by saying that the car was sold, I guess on December 3 or something, that he didn't sell it until he went to the military. I believe he said his father sold it to somebody in Genoa or something like that. He said that he put the little girl in the back of the car. He didn't get into specifics whether it was in the trunk or in the backseat or any of that, and he said he went to Jo Daviess County."

"What, if anything else, did the defendant say to you at that time?"

"He said that he got rid of the body, that he placed her by some trees, some fallen trees or something."

McCullough, said John Doe, would talk nonstop. "It's like he couldn't stop himself. He would just keep going and going."

Defense attorney Tom McCulloch wanted to know why John Doe would risk his life by testifying in open court. Could he be seeking relief or special consideration?

"You asked for some promises from the State, did you not?"

"No, sir. State didn't promise me nothing."

"How come we're calling you John Doe? Were you born to Mr. and Mrs. Doe?"

Even the witness had to smirk at that zinger.

"No, sir."

When the defense was finished with him, John Doe was dismissed, but before he left the witness stand, he turned to Judge Hallock.

"Is there any way I can say something?"

The judge told him, "No, not unless there's a question pending. It's one of the rules. You may step down."

A forlorn John Doe shuffled off the witness stand, surely invoking a prayer that word he was a jailhouse stool pigeon would not leak out.

One more inmate who had had a memorable encounter with Jack McCullough at the DeKalb County Jail was called to testify.

Kirk Swaggerty stood just five feet six, but he had a husky physique and a fearsome tattoo on his left bicep of a wolf clawing its way out of his skin. Back in 2009, he'd been named the most-wanted criminal in Illinois as the mastermind behind the home invasion of a drug dealer from Genoa that had left one man blown away. After four years on the run, he was arrested on Valentine's Day 2009 in Mexico, where he was living under the name Adan Castellanos-Smith. In 2011, Swaggerty had been in the county jail awaiting his own murder trial when he'd recognized Jack McCullough from TV reports.

"We asked him if he was the guy they were talking about, the whole jail was talking about," Swaggerty said. "He just said yes, that was him, and we just started talking."

They became not just cellmates but also soul mates in Cellblock G. For some reason, McCullough really opened up to Swaggerty and said he was thinking about taking a plea and getting off on probation. A skeptical Swaggerty asked him how that would be possible on a murder rap?

"He said because it was an accident. He said he was giving the girl a piggyback ride on his shoulders and when she fell that she wouldn't stop screaming and he was trying to keep her quiet and she suffocated."

Julie Trevarthen asked, "What, if anything, did he say to you about evidence?"

"Oh, he said that you had no evidence whatsoever. The only evidence you had is whatever you had fifty years ago."

"What, if anything, did he say to you about DNA?"

"He said that you would not find any, and if you did, then he would talk plea bargains."

The prisoner claimed he was testifying because, "I really just want to do something right. I'm going to die in prison, and I just feel like I should do it."

The People rested after having called, in total, twenty witnesses over three days.

Now it was the turn of the defense.

"Defense would call Mary Hunt, Your Honor."

Mary Tessier Hunt was the fourth Tessier sister to be called to the stand. Jeanne, Janet, and Katheran had all testified for the prosecution, and now Mary, who worked as a nurse, was coming forward as a defense witness—but a hostile one. She didn't want to be there. She'd been evading the defense subpoena for quite some time, but she'd gotten nailed by a process server one morning when she'd stepped outside to feed her dog. On the stand, she immediately made her feelings about Jack McCullough known.

"He's your half brother," stated assistant public defender Robert Carlson.

"He was," Mary responded tartly.

Mary Hunt had been present with Janet when their mother, Eileen Tessier, blurted out her deathbed confession. Janet was certain that the episode had taken place at Kishwaukee Community Hospital, in DeKalb, but all Mary could remember was that it "was at a bedside," so perhaps it had been at home. The inconsistency in their memories was something that the defense was keen to exploit.

"Could you tell us what you remember specifically your mother saying?"

"She said, 'He did it.'"

"And she did not say who 'he' was, is that correct?"

"No, sir."

"And she did not say what 'did it' was, is that correct?"

"Not that I recall."

"So you don't recall your mother telling you anything more specific than what you've just told us here today?"

"No."

"Not even as to who the person was that had done it?"

"I knew who that was."

"But she didn't tell you?"

"No, she did not."

"You had to imply who did it?"

"Yes, sir."

"And, in fact, you remember telling Detective Hanley that she talked cryptic and you had to read into what she said?"

"No, I don't remember saying that."

How credible was Eileen Tessier's deathbed confession? Could anything she blurted out as she lay dying be taken as evidence in a murder trial? The issue was hammered home when the defense called as its next witness a surgeon who had examined Eileen back in 1994. Dr. John Prabhakar didn't really recall Eileen Tessier. It was so long ago, eighteen years, and he had only been a consulting physician. To refresh his memory, Dr. Prabhakar was shown Eileen's medical records from when she was a patient being treated for metastatic cancer at Kishwaukee Community Hospital. She was on pain medication, a "continuous morphine infusion" being administered to her by an IV in her neck because the nurses couldn't find a good enough vein in her arm. She was also on the antipsychotic drug Haldol, which is usually administrated to patients who are agitated, uncooperative, or in a state of confusion.

Carlson asked, "What are some of the potential side effects for morphine as a medication?"

"It could be anything from nausea, constipation, sleepiness, confusion," Dr. Prabhakar said.

"So morphine can cause confusion?"

"Yes."

According to the old medical files presented to Dr. Prabhakar, he had written that Eileen appeared to be "pleasantly confused."

"You said that she was 'pleasantly confused,' is that correct?"

"Yes, that's correct."

"And do you remember making any other comments as to her orientation of the time?"

"I think I said 'disoriented.'"

Eileen's medical records also showed that she was diagnosed in those final days with "unspecified psychosis."

Under cross-examination, Dr. Prabhakar agreed that the only time he had examined Eileen was on January 10, 1994, and at most he was with her for a half hour because her regular doctor wasn't available. Eileen died thirteen days later.

That was all. After three witnesses, the defense rested.

Judge Hallock spoke the following words directly to the defendant, Jack McCullough.

"Sir, at this time I'll ask you, or advise you, you have the right to testify. You're not required to testify. You're not required to testify. You don't have to testify, and there's no presumption of guilt . . . should you elect not to testify. It's up to you. The only one who can make that decision is you and you alone. Do you understand that?"

"Yes, Your Honor," McCullough said. Up to this moment, he had not spoken a word in open court.

"All right. Your attorneys cannot force you to get up here and say anything, nor can they force you to sit there in your chair. You understand?"

"Yes, Your Honor."

"All right. At this time is it your election to testify or not testify?"

"Not to testify."

Behind the scenes, McCullough and his lawyers had been squabbling. "I could have taken the stand," McCullough said later, "but they didn't want me to because they didn't want stuff that was brought up from the first trial. I told them, 'I want to take the stand.'" McCullough says it was frustrating for him because the alibi that had gotten him off the hook in 1957 had not even been introduced at this trial—most important, records of the 6:57 P.M. collect call made from Rockford to his parents' house in Sycamore.

"I said somebody has got to say that I was in Rockford," McCullough told me. "Somebody has got to say it. Nobody at the trial has said that I was in Rockford. Nobody has said it. And I begged them. They said, no don't worry about it, we've got things under control, don't worry about it."

Kathy and Mike Chapman were also a little rattled when they went home that night but for different reasons.

"The prosecution case was somewhat weak," Mike had to admit. "We had been told they had a really strong case, so we were surprised by the lack of physical evidence." Having said that, Chapman added, "I had absolutely no doubt in my mind that Jack McCullough is Maria's killer." McCullough's interrogation tape from Seattle was never played in court. Nor did the prosecution introduce the so-called smoking gun—the unpunched government-issued train ticket that had been turned over to the state police by McCullough's former high school girlfriend, Jan Edwards. Since McCullough had not taken the stand, there was no need to impeach his testimony or his alibi, because he had offered none.

41

....

THE VERDICT COMES IN

The next day in court, it was standing-room only. Among the spectators were Detectives Cloyd Steiger and Mike Ciesynski, both in from Seattle. They could not stay away from this epic trial.

The prosecution laid out its evidence in closing arguments by Victor Escarcida. He was hardly out of his seat when he started denouncing the defendant.

"Judge, you know now that just a few feet away from you sits the man who murdered Maria Ridulph. Let me introduce you, Judge, to Johnny, and he now goes by the name Jack Daniel McCullough."

Escarcida depicted McCullough as a textbook pedophile who enticed Maria with a piggyback ride and who fifty-five years after her murder still got "almost giddy" when he spoke about her, calling her "stunningly beautiful with big brown eyes . . . lovely, lovely, lovely . . . a little Barbie doll."

"This seventy-two-year-old man still thinks about this little girl in that way. He desired Maria. The way he talked about Maria shows you what his intent was on December 3, 1957."

The proof all pointed to McCullough's guilt, Escarcida argued. McCullough matched the description of Johnny. Before he legally changed his name to Jack, he called himself Johnny. He lived in the neighborhood. It was the "uniqueness" of his face—his do-up, the flip—that made Kathy Sigman's identification after five decades so plausible. And the multicolored sweater he was known to wear, a sweater that seems to have vanished from sight after December 3, 1957.

There was more. Jan Edwards and Cheryl Crain waiting for McCullough to pick them up that night, but he never showed up. The testimony of his sisters Katheran and Jeanne that he didn't come home on December 3. His links to Jo Daviess County, where he'd gone on day trips with his family and where he'd dumped Maria's body because he was familiar with the lay of the land.

Then there was the testimony of the three informants, Diaz, Swaggerty, and John Doe. Through these scoundrels, Escarcida said, "You heard what it was like to be in the midst of a man who loved to talk and reminisce about the little girl he killed." The jailhouse snitches had put forward details of the murder—for instance, how McCullough had put his hands over Maria's mouth to suffocate her—that only the killer would know.

"Because of what this defendant did to her, she never got to put those eight candles on her cake. She never learned to drive a car. She never got to go to prom, walk down the aisle, to enjoy a full life. She was supposed to feel safe on that corner. She didn't deserve to die the way she did. She couldn't protect herself from this man who fancies dolls and piggyback rides. Now, the defense may get up here and argue that because this case is over fifty-five years old you can't trust the witnesses' recollection, that you can't convict on evidence from fifty-five years ago. Well, Judge, it is never too late for justice, and justice requires, Judge, a verdict of guilty on all charges."

Everyone agreed that the tightly wound Victor Escarcida had done well.

It was time for public defender Tom McCulloch to have his moment. He had put forward only three witnesses, versus the prosecution's twenty. With almost every pretrial ruling regarding evidence having gone against him, the outcome of the case could hinge on his closing argument.

"Where do we start? Let's start at the beginning," McCulloch said, with Maria Ridulph's cause of death. The original autopsy, conducted in 1957, declared that Maria had been killed by "manner unknown." But the new autopsy, conducted in 2011, had determined that Maria had been stabbed three times in the throat and chest. Now come the three jailhouse informants. One snitch claimed Maria was killed by accident, another by suffocation, yet another by strangulation with a wire. Which was it? "We have a choice," McCulloch said, his voice laced with mockery. He compared it to a sick "buffet."

"What do I mean?" he asked. "The State has failed to prove or produce a weapon. The State has failed to produce any DNA. There were no footprints found. There was no hair to examine." Tom McCulloch pointed to the passage of time and the unreliability of testimony about events from fifty-five years earlier. He also took note of Jack McCullough's extradition back to Illinois. At no point during this daylong "cheap and cheesy" return to Sycamore in the company of Seattle Detectives Steiger and Ciesynski did McCullough make any admissions. "They had all day with a guy," and Jack McCullough didn't crack. He kept insisting he had been in Rockford when the kidnapping occurred. The timeline was the key to his case, and he quoted McCullough as telling the detectives, "I wasn't in Sycamore. I didn't do it." Don't pay attention to Jack McCullough calling Maria a Barbie doll or saying she had big, beautiful brown eyes, said the public defender. That was just the prosecutor trying mightily to add an "element of creepiness" to Jack McCullough's memory of Maria.

"You know, that's what she was," said the public defender. "She was cute. She was lovely. So, is it significant? Well, no, I don't think so. It's descriptive and that's about it."

Regarding prosecution witness Kathy Sigman Chapman, he had this to say:

"Everyone wants to protect little kids. Everyone wants them to be well treated. That doesn't mean they're accurate. She said the guy she saw, and she said it was a stranger, was twenty-four, twenty-five. We know that the evidence is such that Jack was seventeen at the time. We know that she said, 'I didn't know him. I had never seen him before,' and to me that's significant because these are kids in that neighborhood. We're not talking about great distances away.

"Would it have not made sense for her, if that was true, to say, 'He's the boy from the next street over. He's the brother of the girls I play with.' You know, they lived there for years and yet she said, 'I don't know him. I've never seen him before.' That's what she said in 1957."

When the state police showed Kathy the photo lineup in 2010, the public defender said, "We know that she picked a photo, and we know that that photo was more than fifty years after the fact. We know that the police were there talking to her for an hour and a half the week before." He said he had major problems with the manner in which the lineup was handled because five of the young men wore high school graduation suits and ties and had starched white shirts and scrubbed haircuts.

"And then the other photo, the one where the kid is not in the high school yearbook setting. He's got the black background, a shiny white shirt, no coat, no tie. But really, I mean, that's a bad procedure. If they were going to show her photos, why not show her photos of guys who were twenty-four or twenty-five? That's who she said she had seen on December 3, 1957. It's troublesome, too, knowing that the Sigmans knew the Ridulphs, the Ridulphs knew the Sigmans, they both knew the Tessiers."

He dismissed the other prosecution witnesses as irrelevant. Pam Long testified that Jack McCullough had given her a piggyback ride. Big deal, Tom McCulloch was saying. That ride, if it occurred at all, took place several years before Maria's kidnapping. "Different house, different place. Does that prove anything? There was nothing unusual about piggyback rides and nothing unusual to be offered a ride." Cheryl Crain testified that Jack McCullough failed to pick her up the night of December 3, 1957, when she was putting up Christmas window decorations at the hobby shop. Proof of nothing, Tom McCulloch said.

"If she was to be picked up, who's to say she wasn't already picked up by her dad or her friend's dad, and taken back to her home and locked behind the door."

Dennis Twadell testified that he couldn't reach Jack McCullough when he telephoned the Tessiers' household on the night in question. "Well, this wasn't 2012," said the defense lawyer. "We didn't all have our pocket cell phones. We weren't texting, and he called a house and got no answer. That's all that proved, and so is that proof that Jack did anything? It isn't."

Tom McCulloch pointed to "Exhibit 9," a photo of the Tessiers' home, at 227 Center Cross Street. Nine people lived in the house, he said. The house was so small that friends as a rule didn't come to the Tessier home to play because there was no room. "Now, this is the scene where, according to the informants, a dead body was snuck through a back window and kept in that house? Are you telling me that they wouldn't know about that? Didn't happen. It's a stupid story that some informants got together and decided to present.

"Similarly, we have the statement coming from Mom. And again, Mom's statement makes no sense. Was Mom referring to the prior sexual abuse allegations in the family? When she said the phrase, 'He did it,' who is he? What's 'did it' mean? We know that she was elderly. She was terribly ill. She was described by one of her own daughters as emotionally disturbed. We know she was diagnosed with an unspecified psychosis. And yet we treat this like some lucid statement of a perfectly healthy twenty-four-year-old on the courthouse steps? It just makes no sense."

McCulloch oozed sarcasm when he uttered the names of the three jailhouse informants, Diaz, Swaggerty, and, in his brittle words, Mr. and Mrs. Doe's son, John. No official deal may have been reached with the state's attorney, but this trio had other motives, namely making their lives in prison less oppressive.

Diaz was "so damned stupid," McCulloch said. "He sits there and tries to tell you that he's not a gang member when, in fact, the records of the jail would indicate otherwise and his prior convictions would indicate otherwise. And on top of everything else, does he need a little help with the Immigration Department and does he think maybe that this might help him? He's got every reason to make up a story.

"Mr. Swaggerty. The State says, well, we never made a deal and in his court file is his very own petition saying, 'I helped the State; I want a deal. I want favorite treatment on my sentence.' Well, good Lord.

"Mr. Doe same deal. Maybe worse. Who knows? As much as he wants to say he didn't broker a deal, he started by saying, 'I'll testify but you can't use my name.' He's telling you the terms and conditions under which he'll testify.

"They made up this story based on information on the

news channel or gossip that they got from the visitors at the jail and no one told them, 'Oh, by the way, this girl was stabbed in the neck and throat.' So when they come in here and they tell these stupid stories about the kid being hit in the head or choked, well, that's physically not what the evidence is, but the State threw them up here and I would suggest to you that shows a level of desperation." He called the case "totally circumstantial," comparing it to a chain link where if one link fails, "the whole thing falls apart."

"So there's any number of missing, broken, and weak links, Judge, and on that basis a circumstantial evidence case cannot exist, Judge. We're asking that you find Jack McCullough not guilty of all charges. Thank you."

When he sat down, there was no question that Tom McCulloch had mustered a compelling closing argument. It was left to Julie Trevarthen to deliver the rebuttal, and she honed in on the key issue of Kathy Sigman Chapman's identification.

"Defense counsel wants you to believe that Kathy Sigman is mistaken, that she was mistaken when she picked the defendant out of the lineup as being the man named Johnny who took Maria. This was the face she had been looking for every day since Maria was kidnapped and murdered on December third of 1957. This face was burned into her mind fifty-five years ago when she stood on that street corner at Archie Place and Center Cross as Maria went home to get her doll. Little kids remember really good things that happened and really bad things that happened. It's all the other stuff in between that little kids can't remember. They remember Disney World, ice-cream cones, birthday parties, Duck the Cars, and they remember the face of the man who took their little friend. Kathy will never forget the face of Johnny. The evidence, the overwhelming amount of circumstantial evidence, all pointed to the defendant and that's what led law enforcement to include the defendant's photo in the lineup that was shown to Kathy Sigman. And what do you know, Kathy Sigman says that this photo is the Johnny who took her friend. This photo is the Johnny who stole Maria from her family and from this community, and this photo is John Tessier and John Tessier turned himself into Jack Daniel McCullough but underneath it all, he's still Johnny."

What Jack McCullough told Diaz, Swaggerty, and John Doe were variations on fundamentally the same story, Trevarthen argued, divergences that were "nothing more than the shifting sands of a guilty mind." The jailhouse informants may be bad people, but "crimes conceived in hell don't have angels as witnesses." She assured the judge, "None of them received any promises, consideration, or favors in return for their testimony.

"Just because he admits to strangling her with his hands or strangling her with a wire doesn't mean that he didn't also stab her. Human beings minimize their own culpability every day." She pointed her finger directly at Jack McCullough. "Cowards prey on little girls, and that's why he stops short of describing those three plunging stabs into Maria's throat and down into her seven-year-old tiny little chest."

Even after fifty-five years, Trevarthen said, Jack Mc-Cullough remained obsessed with Maria. As for Mc-Cullough's character, Trevarthen had this biting appraisal: "The defendant isn't stupid, but he also isn't half as smart as he thinks he is. Believing that you're smarter than everyone else doesn't make you smarter than everyone else. A smart person would stop talking about their crime after their first confidante sends a letter to the state's attorney's office ratting him out, but the defendant, he just keeps on talking because he just can't help himself."

When Eileen Tessier lied to the FBI about her son's whereabouts, it was because "she knew what he did."

"She didn't want to die with that on her conscience. Mom was lucid. We know that she was lucid because Janet told us that she looked at her mom's eyes and she said, 'Those two little girls, one was missing, he did it. He did it. You have to tell someone. You have to tell someone.' And Janet did tell someone. Mom was able to put into motion what she wished she put into motion fifty-five years ago, and it's poetic justice that the same woman who gave him life and provided him with an alibi is also the catalyst for this ultimate demise, and because of her courage before she died, for the first time in seventy-two years, today isn't about the defendant. Today is about Maria. Find him guilty, Judge."

It was 10:35 in the morning. Judge Hallock said he wanted to take a short recess, ponder all the evidence, and review his notes from three days of testimony and today's closing arguments. In just twenty-five minutes, he said, he'd be back with the verdict.

Even so, the wait was agonizing. At the defendant's table, Jack McCullough boiled with indignation. There he sat with his two lawyers and Crystal Harrolle of the public defender's office who in her nearly ten years as chief investigator never once had been asked to sit with a defendant, but there she was now, affirmation of the special relationship she shared with McCullough. With Crystal Harrolle, McCullough could vent. He couldn't get over the fact that Julie Trevarthen had called him a coward. It offended his manhood.

"The last thing on earth I am is a coward. I have faced down men with guns. I have risked my life for other people. The last thing I am is a coward."

In the hallway outside court, Detective Ciesynski took Chuck Ridulph aside. He told Chuck to brace himself for a not-guilty verdict because the odds of winning a conviction in a fifty-five-year-old murder case were "slim at best." Ciesynski praised the work of Clay Campbell and his people. Should the judge return a guilty verdict, Ciesynski told Chuck, it was all due to Campbell. Not many prosecutors would have the boldness to pursue a cold case this old.

Promptly at eleven, Judge Hallock returned to the bench. Everyone rose.

"We're back in session," the judge said. "The evidence has been completed. The closing arguments have been completed. All the attorneys are present. The defendant is present."

Public defender Tom McCulloch was confident of victory, certain in his own mind that Judge Hallock was about to utter the words *not guilty*. How could he not? From the defense attorney's point of view, it was just an incredibly thin case.

Crystal Harrolle wasn't so certain. Way back, when the judge had ruled the FBI documents inadmissible, she'd thought the case had been dealt a serious blow.

Just down State Street, at her law office, where she was now in private practice, Regina Harris, Jack McCullough's former lawyer, was pacing the floor. Everyone at her firm gave her space because she was really on edge waiting for news from the courthouse, which she knew to be imminent. *Good God*, she thought. How much she had wanted to try this case.

Judge Hallock started by declaring that a defendant must be found guilty beyond a reasonable doubt, but that didn't mean beyond any doubt. Regarding the three jailhouse informants, Diaz, Swaggerty, and John Doe, they were all bad men who belonged in prison, but the judge said he was convinced that no underhanded deal had been offered for their testimony, although they all hoped to benefit one way or another.

"A defendant who is under indictment for these types of charges is not going to meet good guys in jail," the judge said.

On balance, the judge said, they knew information that they could only have obtained from Jack McCullough—"and in that regard the court finds the testimony credible."

Hallock said he found the testimony of Kathy Sigman Chapman to be "most convincing." There was no defect in the photo lineup procedure, he determined. As to the other witnesses, their memories may have been "clouded by the passage of time to some degree or another depending on the witness, but that's to be expected after these many years.

"Based on the totality of the evidence the court has heard over this week, the court finds that the defendant has been proven guilty—"

A roar came from the gallery. Spectators shot to their feet and applauded. Clay Campbell had never seen anything like it in a court of law: raw jubilation. People were in tears.

"Yes!" someone shouted.

Jack McCullough's flushed face was the color of blood. He was in a state of shock, and he couldn't believe the eruption of joy at his conviction, with his siblings in the front row cheering, raising their arms triumphantly. It reminded him of the home team scoring a winning touchdown at a high school football game. *My own brother and sisters.*

Judge Hallock was beside himself. Repeatedly pounding his gavel, he said, "You'll all be cleared out of here! I'm not finished. You'll all be cleared out of here if there's one more outbreak."

He glared at the spectators, and, so scolded, they returned to their seats. In the front row, Chuck Ridulph refused to take part in the demonstration. At his side was his sister Pat, who also exercised self-restraint. No shouts of joy rose from the Ridulphs. They saw no win, only a hole in their hearts for the life stolen so long ago.

When things had settled down, Hallock directed his

next comments to the crestfallen defendant, reminding Jack McCullough that he had the right to file for an appeal within thirty days. He also revoked the defendant's $3 million bond. Sentencing would be handed down in eight weeks.

McCullough was taken away in handcuffs. Crystal Harrolle kept it together, but once she got back to the privacy of her office, she burst into tears. A young law school intern from Northern Illinois University who was assisting with the defense went over to comfort her. It had been a long, hard week. The hostility the spectators in the courtroom had displayed had been incredibly stressful. It seemed that everyone had been rooting for a guilty verdict. Harrolle had gone beyond the call of duty on this case, spending time with McCullough because she knew his family in Seattle couldn't afford to visit, listening to his nonstop rants, and serving as shrink. She may have been expecting the verdict, and yet when it came down, it was still a shock.

She had one more duty to perform, and that was to call McCullough's wife, Sue, and inform her of the verdict. Sue was devastated because she had been told that the rape trial that ended in his acquittal four months earlier had been the stronger case. She had wanted to attend the murder trial, but Jack had told her not to. "You wouldn't be able to do anything for me," he had said. Now this.

Crystal Harrolle went home early.

Clay Campbell and his team were joyous. They hugged Chuck Ridulph and Pat. Speaking on behalf of his family at a press conference, Chuck said, "I was one who, from the very beginning, never doubted the guilt of John Tessier, also known as Jack McCullough. We're happy. We're relieved that this part of the story is now behind us." He thought that Campbell had done an amazing job. Chuck was emotionally spent. Two photo boards with images of Maria had been on display in the courtroom for closing arguments. It was like reliving the horror of those days from 1957 all over again.

"Some things I wish I did not know. I feel like I've been run over by a truck."

Campbell beamed, but he had the good sense not to gloat. He took the time to pay tribute to the unsung hero of the case, Janet Tessier, whose tip to the state police in 2008 had launched the investigation. Without her, he said, "We would not be here."

The Tessiers were out in force: Katheran, Jeanne, Janet, Mary, and Bob were all present and elated by the outcome.

Jeanne said she was thankful that her brother Jack McCullough was in jail and could no longer hurt anyone else. Bob Tessier expressed gratitude to the people of Sycamore for welcoming the Tessiers back and offering comfort and understanding. He said he didn't want the name John Tessier used anymore, and that henceforth he hoped people would always refer to his big brother as Jack McCullough. He said he was ashamed. And he left no doubt about where he stood on the question of his brother's culpability.

"He is guilty. He really did do it." The verdict came as "a great relief to us."

Janet Tessier stood on the sidelines listening to Chuck's

press conference, then asked if she could step up to the microphones because she wanted to speak directly to the citizens of Sycamore. Her eyes suffused with tears, she asked the Ridulph family for forgiveness for this half-century delay in justice.

"I'm so sorry. I'm so sorry it took so long. And I apologize on behalf of my mother."

Kathy Chapman, with her husband, Mike, standing next to her, said she was very pleased with the outcome. Lest anyone doubt her, she repeated the essence of her testimony, telling reporters, "You never forget a face." She and Mike went from the courthouse steps to Elmwood Cemetery. At Maria's grave, Kathy placed seven pennies on the gravestone, one for every year of her friend's fleeting life.

Michelle Weinman was at work in Washington State when her cell phone rang. It was prosecutor Victor Escarcida.

"Michelle, he was found guilty."

Michelle sobbed in relief. "You did it this time, Victor."

Home in South Carolina, Mark Lemberger read about the verdict on the Internet. Janet Tessier had been working as a part-time caregiver for his elderly mother, Alma, in 2008, when he'd challenged her to contact the police with her story. He sent Janet this e-mail:

Well done, Janet. It took courage and determination to make this happen.

Good luck and you can take a lot of pride in it.

Mark

Janet sent this in response:

Thank you, Mark. If it hadn't been for your encouragement, none of this would've happened. Back in 1957, although Jack/Johnny had an alibi, he was a prime suspect. They couldn't break his alibi because my parents lied. My mother gave up that lie on her deathbed, and here we are. I will never forget this experience. Thank you again for getting me to move on it.

Jan

42

·········

THE BOGEYMAN

Just seven weeks after State's Attorney Clay Campbell had exulted in his victory on the steps of the county courthouse, earning national praise for successfully prosecuting the oldest criminal case in U.S. history, he was defeated in his bid for reelection. The race had been tight—he'd lost by 739 votes out of 39,051 cast in DeKalb County.

Campbell was beaten by a local Sycamore lawyer, Richard Schmack, who hadn't even contemplated running for office until April 20, 2012, when he was approached by Democratic Party power brokers who urged him to throw his hat in the ring. It wasn't lost on anybody that Schmack had been recruited just eight days after Campbell's extraordinary public attack on Judge Robbin Stuckert.

Chuck Ridulph went to bat for Campbell during the campaign, publicly endorsing Campbell and writing in a letter to the editor of the *Daily Chronicle*, "We need men and women in public office who have the courage to do the right thing. I urge you all to ask yourself why would you wish to make a change in something that has proven to be so right."

Schmack campaigned on a platform that DeKalb County needed to take traffic court more seriously and pursue drunk drivers, the implication being a fifty-five-year-old murder case was not a major threat to public safety. At least that's how many voters interpreted it.

On election night, Schmack watched the returns trickling in at Joker's Bar and Grill in Sycamore. At his side, cheering the results, was former public defender Regina Harris, forced out of office by Campbell. How sweet her revenge must have been when Schmack was declared the victor.

In Seattle, Detective Mike Ciesynski called Cloyd Steiger at home. Steiger thought the detective was calling about Barack Obama winning a second term as president.

"I've got worse news for you," Ciesynski said. "Clay Campbell lost."

Steiger couldn't believe it. "I thought he was gold."

Campbell's two years in office were coming to an end.

On his final day as top prosecutor, he was asked about his proudest achievement. That had to be obtaining the conviction of Jack McCullough for the murder of Maria Ridulph.

"It was amazing to have achieved some measure of justice for the family and to hold Mr. McCullough finally accountable after half a century of being free." He spoke about coming to know the Ridulphs and Tessiers. "I'll never forget how gracious they were to me. That will leave an indelible print on the rest of my life."

Two weeks after the election, Campbell's successor, Richard Schmack, informed Julie Trevarthen and Victor Escarcida that they were out. It was a clean sweep of every prosecutor involved in the McCullough case.

Campbell bristled. He called Trevarthen and Escarcida "superstar lawyers" and blamed their dismissals on professional jealousy.

Sue McCullough now had to live with the difficult reality that people were looking at her as the wife of a convicted child killer. She had taken over Jack's job as night watchman at the Four Freedoms retirement tower. The slights she experienced may have been unintentional, but they still stung. Late one night, a pizza deliveryman buzzed to be let in.

"How do I know you're the pizza guy?" Sue asked.

He showed her the flat box he was holding. "Well, I've got a pizza."

When she opened the door, he said he couldn't blame her. "I can tell why you're being careful—after that killer was arrested."

Another time, paramedics rushed over after an elderly resident called 911. Sue got into a discussion with one of the medical technicians, and the subject of Jack McCullough came up. Sue defended him without letting on who she was.

"So, you're friends with a killer?"

She stiffened her back. "You mean my husband? And no, he's not a killer."

Living so far away from the court battle had added to Sue's stress. She says she e-mailed her husband's defense lawyer several times about her concerns, but he'd never responded. Same with the phone—not one call back, she says.

Two weeks after the verdict, McCullough made an extraordinary appeal to the people of his hometown. He sent a letter to the *Daily Chronicle* in which he clung to his assertion that the FBI files had cleared him of any role in Maria's murder. "I could not have been 'Johnny' because at the exact time of the kidnapping, I was in Rockford, forty miles away," he wrote.

"People of Sycamore: these documents are in the courthouse at 133 State Street. They are public records. Go there, demand to see them, and set me free."

McCullough's call for a storming of the gates never came to pass. Only 14 pages in the FBI files actually deal directly with his role in the Maria Ridulph investigation. Of the 4,000 pages amassed by the FBI, the defense team had access to every one, though only about 200 have been released to the public. The rest remain sealed.

"The truth is that the FBI reports did not and could not clear the defendant," Clay Campbell insisted.

Chuck Ridulph disdains the armchair detectives who dispute McCullough's guilt. He points out that since his arrest, McCullough has told so many variations of his story he can't keep them straight.

"Here are the facts. If Jack wanted that information to be considered at trial, he needed to get on the stand and say it. He chose not to. He chose not to present an alibi at trial, but the evidence was there to disprove his alibi, had he presented one."

Even if McCullough made the collect call at 6:57 P.M., Maria's abduction had in all probability taken place forty-five minutes or so earlier, giving McCullough enough time to drive to Rockford, make the call, and establish his alibi.

"Maria was kidnapped closer to 6:00 than 7:00 P.M. as the defense would like you to think," Chuck Ridulph maintains. "At 7:00, Maria would have been home getting ready for bed. When you put all the pieces of the puzzle together, it leaves no room for doubt."

After McCullough's conviction, Sue finally got the money together to fly out to Sycamore and visit with her husband. It depressed her to see how frail he'd become in jail.

"He told me I could divorce him if I wanted to, or go back to my maiden name if I wanted to. But I'm not going to do either one," she said. "I'm a loyal wife."

She is convinced that an innocent man has been railroaded. "I know Jack. People don't change that much. You don't kill a kid and say, 'Oh that was fun, but I'm never going to do that again.'" As for the Ridulphs, "I'm sorry for their loss, even though it was many years ago. But Jack didn't do this. There is no closure if they've got the wrong guy."

Sentencing day for Jack McCullough took place on December 10, 2012. Chuck Ridulph was there pushing for a life sentence; his sister Pat thought a symbolic sentence of fifty-five years was appropriate—a year for every year of Maria's life that had been taken from her. Of the Tessier siblings, Mary Hunt was present, representing the family. Kathy and Mike Chapman sat in the first row in room 300. In attendance were many of the detectives who had been involved in the investigation, including Brion Hanley. Clay Campbell also showed up. His last day in office had been December 3, 2012; as fate would have it, the fifty-fifth anniversary of Maria's kidnapping. Julie Trevarthen took time off from her job search to bear witness to the sentencing.

Once again, McCullough was shown into court in handcuffs from a side entrance.

Chuck Ridulph asked that his victim's impact statement be read into the court record.

"Jack McCullough kidnapped, raped, and murdered my sister Maria. The fact is Jack McCullough took this innocent little girl and stole away her life, all but seven short years. The fact is Jack McCullough has left the hole where there should be none. He has left questions: Would she have excelled at music? How would I have scrutinized her first boyfriend? Where would she have gone to college? Would she have married? How many children would she have had?

"As you now consider the sentencing of Jack McCullough for this most vile of crimes, I ask that the verdict which you pronounce make a bold statement to all that we as a society will not tolerate such evil crimes against children."

McCullough's stepdaughter Janey O'Connor had flown

in the week before intending to speak out at his sentencing but, just her luck, the court session that had been scheduled for that week had been cancelled and rescheduled for the tenth. Unfortunately, Janey couldn't financially swing another trip back to Illinois, but she did visit McCullough at the DeKalb County Jail. When he saw her, a big grin had crossed his face, and he'd said, "Oh, honey, you're so beautiful."

When McCullough's sentencing hearing took place, Janey, back in Seattle, had asked public defender Tom McCulloch to read a statement on her behalf to Judge Hallock.

"My name is Janey O'Connor. I am Jack Daniel Mc-Cullough's stepdaughter. He is the man I call Dad. He is the man my children call Grandpa. Jack came into my life and started dating my mother when I was twelve years old. When I was fourteen, Jack and my mother decided to get married. In all my experience with Jack, all the time we were doing activities together, shooting, time around the house, walking the dogs, discussions on literature and politics, Jack never—and I emphasize never—touched me inappropriately or gave any inkling he would ever do anything sexually to me.

"When Jack was arrested, I did not know if he had committed the crime or not. The crime took place twenty years to the day before I was born." It was true. Yet another odd occurrence: Janey O'Connor was born on December 3, 1977.

"My heart told me he was innocent, but logically I knew it was possible for someone to portray one version of himself and keep another one hidden." Janey said she spent the weeks and months following McCullough's arrest reading about the case and studying the documents.

"My faith in the judicial system is completely altered. Whether or not the FBI records are admissible in a court of law or not, no adult could read those records and still believe Jack, my dad, committed this crime. Our legal system is corrupted and manipulated by the egos, desires, and wants of the men and women who comprise it. Until Clay Campbell got involved in this case, the abduction happened at 7:00 P.M. At 7:00 P.M. my dad made a collect call from Rockford, as verified by the FBI. He could not have committed this crime. Perhaps they think sacrificing one innocent old man is worth giving an entire community a false sense of closure and a legal team notoriety. I hope the pain caused my family is worth the five minutes of fame you all have received. This case is unprecedented, and in the future I am positive it will be overturned on appeal. Those involved and the decisions made in this case will be scrutinized, and I can only hope the people involved will be held accountable for their actions.

"Again, my name is Janey O'Connor. Jack McCullough is my dad. Jack McCullough is innocent."

Sue McCullough also gave a stinging statement to the public defender, to be read in court. In it she leveled vitriol at the judge who had found her husband guilty, insulting him as a "judge from DUI court" who had been promoted to a higher court somehow as a reward after convicting McCullough.

"Do the words 'beyond a shadow of a doubt' sound

familiar to anyone? There is no evidence to convict him except a woman in her sixties trying to remember someone she saw when she was eight years old and hadn't seen in fifty-five years. Can any of you identify someone you haven't seen in fifty-five years? I think not.

"Judge, you may be able to send him to prison for however many years he has left on this earth, but I won't be silenced. Everyone will know about the corruption in DeKalb County. My husband, Jack, was convicted just to close the oldest case in U.S. history. You should all be ashamed of yourself."

When he was finished reading the declarations from Sue and Janey, the public defender asked Judge Hallock to consider McCullough's age—he was seventy-three—and his medical issues, which included taking nine medications for high blood pressure, diabetes, and prostate problems. The statutory minimum of fourteen years imprisonment seemed like a fair sentence, the lawyer argued.

Victor Escarcida spoke on behalf of the prosecution. Although he was out of a job, the new state's attorney had asked him to stay on until the sentencing because of his familiarity with the case.

"Nothing about this trial was a sham. There was no conspiracy. This case is not about Clay Campbell. This was about one person, Jack McCullough, and his sick behavior, the crimes that he committed back in 1957, pure and simple." Escarcida read from a presentencing report in which McCullough was asked in an interview what caused him the most anxiety. He listed the many ways: "Corruption, Democrats, socialism, rude people, noisy people, black people, and Muslims." Once again that mouth of his was getting him into trouble.

Said Escarcida, "Jack McCullough left a lifetime of emotional wreckage in his wake, and this poor family had to wait all these years for the killer to face the justice system. Because of what he did, Jack McCullough made Sycamore a scary place. It made people less safe. Now there was a true bogeyman living among them.

"Maria was a happy little girl who loved to play with friends and family. She deserved, Judge, to live a long and happy life, and she was taken from a mother and a father and her siblings by that horrible, sick human being. He is the definition of evil, Judge, and that is the only way to think of this child killer and that is why he deserves natural life in prison."

Judge Hallock turned his attention to Jack McCullough.

"At this time do you wish to make a statement or do you wish to stand silent?"

"I wish to make a statement, Your Honor."

The old man held a speech in his hand. He had a lot to get off his chest. He had spent weeks crafting it. A first draft that he'd shown to Crystal Harrolle was teeming with bile.

"You're not going to be heard," she warned him. It was way over the top. She advised him to tone it down.

"Ladies and gentlemen, I'm Jack Daniel McCullough. I did not, *did not* kill Maria Ridulph, did not." Before him was a large cardboard box containing the 4,000 pages of FBI documents that he claimed would have proved his innocence had they been introduced into evidence.

"I was cleared by these people. The truth is in this box. This box that was not allowed at my trial. The truth is in this box.

"This is the oldest active cold case in American history. The kidnap occurred on December 3, 1957, at about 7:00 P.M.—7:00 P.M. Remember that time."

Suddenly, an electrifying moment: McCullough turned to face the gallery and aimed his remarks directly at Kathy Sigman Chapman sitting in the front row.

"I was well known in the town of Sycamore and in the local neighborhood, and interestingly enough, Kathy Chapman's father struck me with his car on April 1, 1947, as I was walking home from school. I was in a coma for a week. I was seven years old."

Kathy truly felt physically threatened. Her husband, Mike, wanted to shout back, "That's not an eight-year-old kid you're talking to; that's my wife."

"Sir," Judge Hallock warned McCullough, "turn and face the court."

"Yes, Your Honor."

"Continue."

When it came to Kathy Sigman Chapman, you couldn't hold McCullough back.

The defendant presented his interpretation of the timeline: Frances Ridulph had told the FBI that Maria had gone home to retrieve her doll at 6:40 P.M. When Kathy Sigman ran home for a pair of mittens because her hands were cold, she asked Johnny what time it was. He answered 7:00 P.M. Yet McCullough had placed a collect call from Rockford at 6:57.

"The FBI reports that you would not allow into trial show that I could not have been in both Sycamore and Rockford at the same time. That time is 7:00 P.M. when it is documented that Maria was kidnapped. You ruled to keep the FBI reports out because of hearsay, but you failed to recognize those reports should have been allowed in because they are both reliable and out of necessity. I have shown you the error of your judgment. Your Honor, in the name of justice and fairness, open the box and view the truth."

Nothing Jack McCullough said helped his case.

He got the max—life in prison.

Outside, a light snow was falling, much like it had on December 3, 1957. Tiny flakes wafting over a small town that very few Americans outside its boundaries even knew existed.

Epilogue

....

The Menard Correctional Center is the state of Illinois's largest maximum-security facility, a harrowing solid-brick structure constructed in 1878. The prison is so old, there are no automatic locking mechanisms on the cell doors, which even now require old-fashioned steel keys to open, keys made to last a life sentence. During his time at Menard, Jack McCullough was twenty cells away from Drew Peterson, the former police sergeant serving a thirty-eight-year sentence for the murder of his third wife. Violence is ever present at Menard. Four inmates were found murdered in their cells in the year 2013, all by manual strangulation with a bedsheet.

Following his sentencing, this is where Jack McCullough began serving his life-prison term. In a letter to his step-daughter, McCullough wrote, "Few would believe that our society could produce such an inconsiderate noisy ignorant and dangerous culture of criminals."

McCullough lived on a diet of ramen noodles bought from the commissary. He was losing about a pound a day. His first cellmate was an ex-marine also serving life for murder. Then he was transferred to another cell, and, lo and behold, his new cellmate turned out to be a Muslim. Considering the rude things McCullough had had to say about Muslims in his presentencing report, somebody in the penal system must have had a sense of humor. Or maybe it was just the luck of the draw.

As a convicted child killer who had once worn a badge, McCullough figured he had two strikes against him, and he applied for protective custody.

Weeks passed, and by some higher power, McCullough was transferred to the Pontiac Correctional Center, about two hours southwest of Chicago. Pontiac is 150 years old, the eighth oldest prison in the United States, a maximum-security, Level 1 facility but better suited to deal with inmates in protective custody who have medical issues. Half the prison population at Pontiac are serving life sentences.

"This is a piece of cake here compared to Menard," McCullough told me.

He looked in good health. He plays handball and basketball in the prison yard, lifts weights three days a week, has access to a library, and eats chow with the other inmates in protective custody. Not paradise by any means, not hell on earth either.

This saga of crime and family in America is not over.

McCullough says he is confident an appeals court will overturn the guilty verdict and grant him a new trial and that one day he will be free. He hopes to see China. He's learning Mandarin to prepare for the trip. We shall see.

McCullough says he may have sinned, but he is no murderer. He believes he is a victim of embittered siblings out to get him because he was his mother's favorite.

"This is vendetta. This is get Jack."

"For what?" I asked him.

"For whatever animosity they have."

In Jack McCullough's mind, they are all lying, Jeanne, Janet, Katheran, Mary, and Bob. He calls Jeanne his "nutty sister."

"She has the whole family convinced I'm a murdering rapist. This is a nightmare."

I asked about Jeanne's story of incest at the hands of her father, Ralph Tessier.

"That's a lie."

"That's a lie, too?"

"That's a lie. Ralph was a solid guy. That didn't happen."

His sister Janet told me that he once threatened her with a gun when she briefly lived with him in Washington State.

"That's a fucking lie, too."

And the testimony of Pam Long, who said McCullough gave her a piggyback ride when she was a child?

"It was a lie. It didn't happen. It's all made up. Somebody wanting to be famous."

What about Michelle Weinman? And Kathy Chapman?

They are all liars, McCullough says. Everybody's lying. That's his story. It's quite a conspiracy to contemplate.

McCullough did make one significant adjustment in his chronicle of what had happened on December 3, 1957. Eileen and Ralph Tessier, he is now acknowledging, lied when they told the FBI that Ralph picked him up in Rockford after he made the collect call at 6:57 P.M. Ralph never drove the forty miles to Rockford that night, McCullough now admits. Ralph and Eileen fabricated the account.

"He didn't pick me up; he and Mom lied for me. They thought that I was in some kind of trouble. They were very afraid, this is the FBI, so they just covered for me. I wish they hadn't because that confused the story and made Mom an untrustworthy witness."

In this new narrative, McCullough says he hitched a ride in Rockford, was dropped off on State Street in Sycamore, and then walked a couple of blocks to his house on Center Cross Street.

"I got home and I noticed that the front door was locked, and the back door was blocked by a two-by-four, and I thought, well, this is strange. My bedroom window is right by the side door, and I stood up on the garbage can and climbed in and went to bed. And I did so quietly because I didn't want to wake anybody up. And the next morning when I got up to go to the bathroom, my mom says, 'How did you get in?' Well, I got in through the bedroom window."

So that's his story and he is sticking with it.

There was something that I had been wondering about. The state police had begun investigating McCullough in 2008 and had interviewed all his siblings. You would think that somebody in his family might have wanted to let him know that he was the subject of a murder probe. McCullough saw where I was headed with these questions.

"And nobody told me," he said, shaking his head.

"No one tells you?" I asked.

"Nobody told me. Even my son didn't tell me."

Sean Tessier is a musician living in Seattle. He learned about the investigation during a Tessier family reunion in Kentucky. They were good people, Sean would say, from "good stock." He had deep affection for the Tessiers and was enjoying the company of his aunts and cousins when his uncle Bob Tessier pulled him aside and said, "I don't know if I should be telling you this, but I'm going to anyway." And he did. And yet, not even his son took it upon himself to inform Jack McCullough that he was suspected in the 1957 murder of Maria Ridulph.

I asked McCullough about his troubled daughter Christine, who had once made a living as a striptease dancer. Christine was last seen in 2005, leaving a motel in San Antonio, Texas, with her boyfriend. A nationwide missing-person report described her as thirty-four years old with strawberry blonde hair, hazel eyes, and piercings on her ears, nipples, and navel, and a ball-piercing through her lip. A body had been discovered a month later next to a drainage ditch near the thirteenth hole of a San Antonio golf course, but it was so badly putrefied it wasn't identified as Christine until June 2013. She left behind two young daughters. Their father is a deep-sea diver.

"I don't know the guy," McCullough told me. "He's Mexican. I don't even know his name."

McCullough says he has no relationship with his two

biological granddaughters. "I don't know where they are now."

His slain daughter's full name was Christine *Marie* Tessier. She was born in 1970, thirteen years after Maria's murder. I had to ask, did he name her after Maria Ridulph? Was this some twisted tribute?

"No, no, no, no. The name just sounded cool."

Life at the Pontiac Correctional Center didn't turn out to be the piece of cake McCullough had anticipated. On October 4, 2013, I received an e-mail from Sue McCullough.

"Jack wanted me to let you know that he was stabbed in the eye with a toothbrush while he slept. He had an operation and the doctor said he thinks he'll be able to see again. His cellmate did it."

I asked Sue what the fight was over.

"There was no fight. Jack was sleeping. The toothbrush wasn't sharp, but it still did the job. His cellmate has a lot of mental problems, and he tried to stab Jack's other eye and his ears."

McCullough was learning that the most horrific thing about prison was living with other prisoners.

In her log cabin in Kentucky, Jeanne Tessier told me, "I don't believe in a vengeful God. I don't think that my brother's justice is going to be hellfire, although I could be wrong. But I think that when we die, we come face-to-face with everything we've done, for better or for worse, and that's when John will meet his justice, when he finally sees what he has never been able to see in his life, which is all the terrible harm he's done. You know, I don't care about justice on earth. I really don't. Not that I don't wish it exists; I do wish it exists. I don't think the courts deliver it—most of the time. I don't think Chuck and Pat got justice. I don't know what they got. I don't believe in closure either. Nothing ever closes. It just goes on the back burner. But nothing brings Maria back. Nothing restores that terrible loss to that family. Nothing."

When Maria Ridulph was on this earth, Americans drove Oldsmobiles, and Eisenhower was president. Girls went steady. Young men married their high school sweethearts. Then the bogeyman came along, and Maria had her life taken away, a life that vanished like a trail of footsteps in the snow.

The story of one of the most bizarre mass murders ever recorded—and the girl who escaped with her life.

From national bestselling author

ROBERT SCOTT

with Sarah Maynard and Larry Maynard

The GIRL in the LEAVES

In the fall of 2010, in the all-American town of Apple Valley, Ohio, four people disappeared without a trace: Stephanie Sprang; her friend Tina Maynard; and Tina's two children, thirteen-year-old Sarah and eleven-year-old Kody. Investigators began scouring the area, yet despite an extensive search, no signs of the missing people were discovered.

On the fourth day of the search, evidence trickled in about neighborhood "weirdo" Matthew Hoffman. A police SWAT team raided his home and found an extremely disturbing sight: every square inch of the place was filled with leaves, and a terrified Sarah Maynard was bound up in the middle of it like some sort of perverted autumn tableau. But there was no trace of the others…

INCLUDES PHOTOGRAPHS

Praise for Robert Scott and his books:

"Compelling and shocking…[A] ground-breaking book."
—Robert K. Tanenbaum

"Fascinating and fresh…[A] fast-paced informative read."
—Sue Russell

RobertScottTrueCrime.com | penguin.com

M1129T0613

The shocking continuation of the
national bestseller *Zodiac* by

ROBERT GRAYSMITH

ZODIAC
UNMASKED

The Identiy of America's Most Elusive
Serial Killer Revealed

"[GRAYSMITH'S] ACCESS IS AS GOOD AS IT GETS.
A meticulous reconstruction of the way the case
evolved. By far the best book on the subject of the
Zodiac murders." —*New York Press*

After painstaking investigation, and more than 30 years of
research, Robert Graysmith finally exposes the infamous
Zodiac killer's true identity. With overwhelming evidence he
reveals the twisted private life that led to the crimes, and
provides startling theories as to why they stopped. America's
greatest unsolved mystery has finally been solved.

**INCLUDES PHOTOS AND A COMPLETE
REPRODUCTION OF THE ZODIAC'S LETTERS.**

penguin.com

M112T0907